IMAGES
of America
PUERTO RICAN

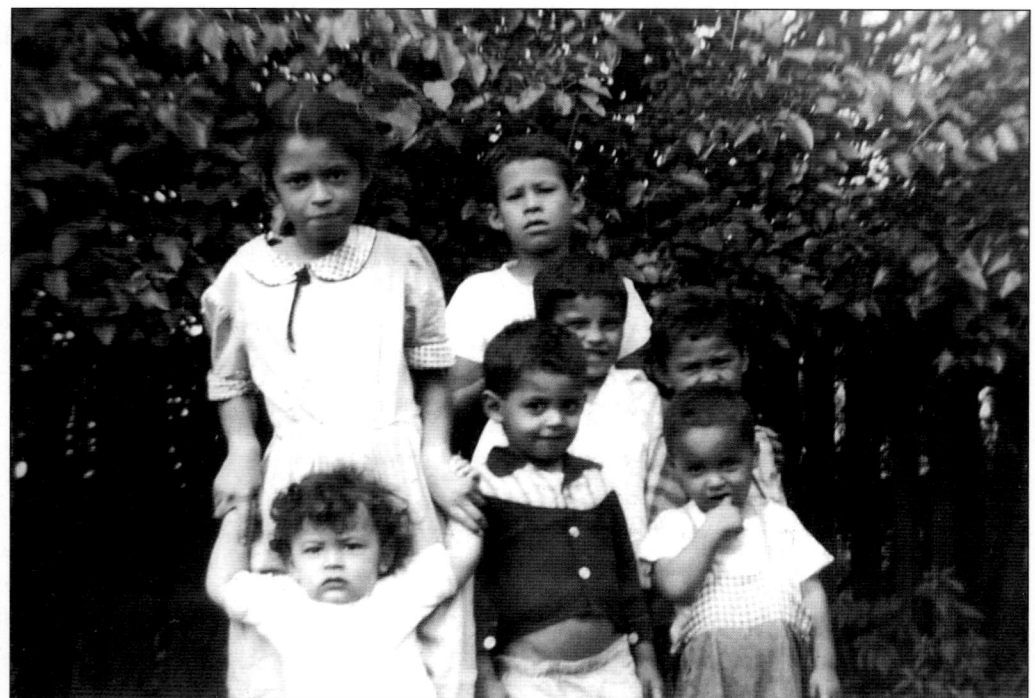

The author (center) is pictured with his brothers and sister during an outing in Calumet Park on Chicago's far South Side in 1957. Pictured are, from left to right: (bottom) Eduardo, Wilfredo, and Alberto; (middle) Olga, Hector, and George; and (top) John. (Cruz Photograph Collection.)

IMAGES
of America
PUERTO RICAN CHICAGO

Wilfredo Cruz

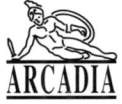

ARCADIA

Published by Arcadia Publishing
Charleston SC, Chicago, IL, Portsmouth NH, San Francisco, CA

Printed in Great Britain

Library of Congress Catalog Card Number: 2004115832

For all general information contact Arcadia Publishing at:
Telephone 843-853-2070
Fax 843-853-0044
E-mail sales@arcadiapublishing.com
For customer service and orders:
Toll-Free 1-888-313-2665

Visit us on the internet at http://www.arcadiapublishing.com

*This book is dedicated to my wife, Irma,
and to my children, Wilfredo Jr., Daniel, and Alexandra.
I appreciate the assistance and motivation you provided
during the time I worked on this project.*

CONTENTS

ACKNOWLEDGMENTS

I wish to thank Columbia College Chicago for granting me release time from teaching. The time was most valuable in helping me to research and write a major portion of this book.

I am most grateful to the many community institutions that permitted me to use their photographs. Special thanks to the Puerto Rican Parade Committee, Association House of Chicago, Casa Central, Segundo Ruiz Belvis Cultural Center, *La Raza* newspaper, Aspira Inc. of Illinois, the Puerto Rican Cultural Center, the Southeast Historical Society, San Lucas United Church of Christ, Hispanic Housing Development Corporation, Roberto Clemente High School, and Los Caballeros de San Juan Credit Union.

Many individuals kindly offered insightful photographs from their institutional or personal family collections. They trusted me with their important photographs. These individuals are too numerous to name, but I extend a most heartfelt thank you to all of them. Special gratitude is extended to Julio Cruz, Anna Rivera, Antonio Villalobos, Cesaro and Luz Maria Rivera, Efrain López, and Alexandra Cruz.

I especially want to thank certain individuals who have done a wonderful job of photographing the Puerto Rican community over many years. They made their extensive, impressive photographic collections readily available to me. A special thank you to Tomas V. Sanabria, Jaime Rivera, Delma Serrano, Carlos Flores, and Marixsa Alicea.

Mike Ogata and Ken Nomura from Triangle Camera did an outstanding job of restoring, cleaning, and enhancing many of the photographs. They work magic making old, dull photographs look new again.

INTRODUCTION

Puerto Ricans have had a long-standing presence in Chicago. Around the 1920s, a handful of middle-class Puerto Rican families from Puerto Rico sent their daughters and sons to study at prestigious universities like the University of Chicago. After completing their educational studies, most of these early Puerto Ricans returned to Puerto Rico.

However, in the early 1950s and 60s, Puerto Rican migration to Chicago peaked. Thousands of poor and working-class Puerto Ricans migrated to Chicago. They came with hopes and dreams of making a better life. Like previous waves of European and Latino immigrants, Puerto Ricans came to Chicago searching for good-paying jobs, economic opportunities, and a brighter tomorrow. Some came with dreams of making money in Chicago, and then returning to Puerto Rico to buy a small business or home. But most came with intentions of staying and carving out a new life in the windy city.

In 1950, there were only 255 Puerto Ricans in Chicago. By 1960, the number of Puerto Ricans in Chicago had jumped to 32,371. Thirty years later, in 1990, Chicago's Puerto Rican population had more than tripled to 119, 800. Today, after Mexicans, Puerto Ricans are the second largest Latino group in Chicago. According to the 2000 U.S. census, the Puerto Rican population in Illinois stands at 157, 851. Over 70%, or 113, 055, of these Puerto Ricans reside in Chicago. Chicago's Puerto Rican population is second in size to New York. Nationally, the Puerto Rican population increased 25% from 1990 to 2000. There are now over 3.4 million Puerto Ricans in the continental United States.

Puerto Ricans are the first ethnic group to have come to the United States predominantly by airplane. Their migration is dubbed the "airborne migration." Unlike other immigrants, Puerto Ricans come as American citizens. The United States acquired Puerto Rico after the Spanish-American War of 1898. Puerto Rico is a Commonwealth of the United States, and, in 1917, an act of Congress made Puerto Ricans American citizens. Because they are American citizens, some view Puerto Ricans more as migrants than immigrants.

As American citizens, it was assumed that Puerto Ricans would have a much easier time adjusting and making a better life for themselves in Chicago. Yet American citizenship conferred few privileges to Puerto Ricans. Instead, Puerto Ricans faced many of the same struggles and hardships most immigrant groups encounter when coming to a new city. Many early Puerto Rican migrants to Chicago came as unskilled laborers escaping unemployment and poverty in their homeland. One major disadvantage was that early Puerto Rican arrivals in Chicago were usually uneducated and did not speak English.

Another disadvantage was that Puerto Ricans arrived in Chicago at the wrong time. For decades, Chicago's image as a blue-collar town with plenty of manufacturing jobs was unquestioned. Successive waves of immigrants to the city found good-paying manufacturing jobs. However, by the early 1950s, Chicago, like most older American cities, was losing hundreds of thousands of manufacturing jobs. Manufacturing companies were leaving the city for greener pastures in the suburbs and in third world countries. Chicago's economy was shifting from manufacturing to service. A strong back and strong arms were no longer sufficient to land a good factory job. Many of the more highly skilled, highly paid jobs required college education.

Some early Puerto Rican arrivals found decent-paying jobs as laborers in the dangerous steel mills. But many others, instead of finding steady, well-paid manufacturing jobs, found mainly low-paying, menial service jobs. They worked on the assembly lines of small factories; they performed janitorial work, and hotel and restaurant work. Puerto Ricans toiled in the hot foundries of the city. They worked in suburban factories in light industry, making things like pipelines. Puerto Rican women worked as assemblers, laundry and dry cleaning operatives, and packers and wrappers. Some unemployed families were forced to go on public aid.

Puerto Ricans also faced covert and overt discrimination in Chicago. They were often relegated to low-paying, dead-end laborer jobs in which they became trapped. Some white ethnic groups did not welcome Puerto Ricans into their neighborhoods. Some Catholics and Protestants refused to allow Puerto Rican to worship in their parishes.

Despite the hardships and difficulties they faced, Puerto Ricans persevered. Second and third generation Puerto Ricans are increasingly college-educated. They are the new leaders of their community. They are steadily climbing the economic ladder into middle-class respectability. Meanwhile other Puerto Rican families still face major problems, with high rates of poverty. But despite the problems they encounter, many Puerto Ricans do not express a defeatist attitude. Instead, they are optimistic that through their hard work, things will only improve in Chicago. Today, Puerto Ricans continue to make important contributions to the political, educational, social, and cultural institutions of Chicago. They are making significant strives. They continue to push ahead.

One

THE EARLY YEARS

The first Puerto Rican workers in Chicago came as unskilled, contract laborers. Castle, Barton and Associates, a Chicago employment agency, set up an office in Puerto Rico to recruit workers to Chicago. In 1946 the agency brought 329 Puerto Rican women and 67 men to Chicago as contracted domestic and foundry workers. The employment agency offered a full year of work, and paid the workers' airplane costs which they later deducted from their wages. The contracted Puerto Rican women were between the ages of 16 and 35 years of age, and most were unmarried. The domestics lived in the Chicago homes that employed them. The women were probably light-skinned, as Castle, Barton, and Associates had a Florida office that hired dark-skinned Puerto Rican women to work as domestics in the southern United States. The Puerto Rican domestic women often worked 15 hours a day, six days a week. Some became dissatisfied with their employment conditions and returned to Puerto Rico.

The contracted Puerto Rican men worked in unskilled jobs in the Chicago Hardware Foundry company in North Chicago. Few of the men knew English. The men lived in reconverted railroad cars belonging to the North Chicago foundry. They too became dissatisfied with the low wages and hard work. They were promised $35 a week. Yet their paychecks, after deductions, seldom amounted to over a dollar a day. Some returned to Puerto Rico. Others decided to stay in Chicago to search for better-paying work.

Other large companies in the Midwest began to bring in Puerto Ricans as contract laborers. In 1947 the United States Steel company brought several hundred Puerto Ricans to Lorain, Ohio for the National Tube Company, one of its subsidiaries. In 1948 U.S. Steel brought in over 500 Puerto Rican contract workers for its Gary, Indiana plant. An agency of the Department of Labor of Puerto Rican was established in Chicago in 1949 to help recruit Puerto Ricans for work in the city.

A major factor that pushed Puerto Ricans to migrate from Puerto Rico to American cities was Operation Bootstrap, a 1950s effort to industrialize Puerto Rico. Through Operation Bootstrap, Puerto Rico's government gave generous tax breaks, free land, and low-interest loans to American companies if they relocated their plants to Puerto Rico. Puerto Rico's government promised these companies a large pool of supposedly docile and cheap workers. Many companies took up the offer. But the much-heralded Operation Bootstrap did not create enough jobs for the growing Puerto Rican population. Therefore, thousands of Puerto Ricans voluntarily moved to large cities like New York and Chicago. They came fleeing unemployment in their homeland, with dreams of landing good-paying jobs in the steel mills, factories, and other manufacturing plants.

Some of the first Puerto Ricans in Chicago settled in the city's north side, in neighborhoods like Lincoln Park. A distinct Puerto Rican community took shape in Lincoln Park during the 1950s. Families saved their hard-earned money and bought small homes. Often, two families pooled their money and bought a two-story brownstone or greystone building. Some Puerto Rican families owned small mom-and-pop stores and restaurants in Lincoln Park.

However, by the late 1960s, gentrification had taken place in Lincoln Park. The attractive neighborhood near Chicago's lakefront soon became desirable to developers and young, white middle-class professionals. Rising property taxes and expensive new homes forced thousands of Puerto Ricans to move from the up-scale Lincoln Park to more affordable, working-class neighborhoods. Most of the small businesses and homes were later torn down and replaced by expensive homes, condominiums, and trendy stores. Very few Puerto Ricans live in the neighborhood today.

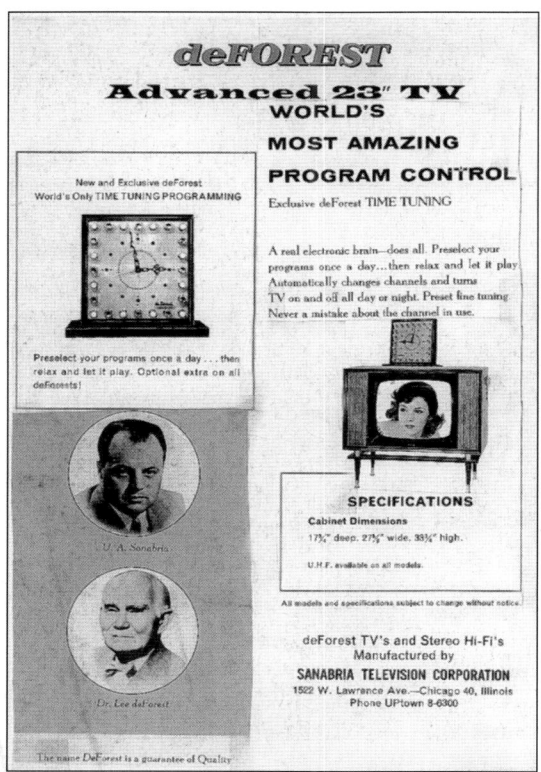

One early Puerto Rican to settle in Chicago was Ulises Marcial Sanabria, who came to study medicine at Rush Medical College in Chicago in 1901. He was a renowned concert pianist. He married in Chicago and had four children. Sanabria died of a heart attack at age 46. His son, Ulises Armand, shown here c. early 1950s, became a famous inventor in the field of television. His numerous inventions helped perfect the modern television. In 1931, he founded the Sanabria Television Corporation in Chicago. (Courtesy Antonio Irizarry.)

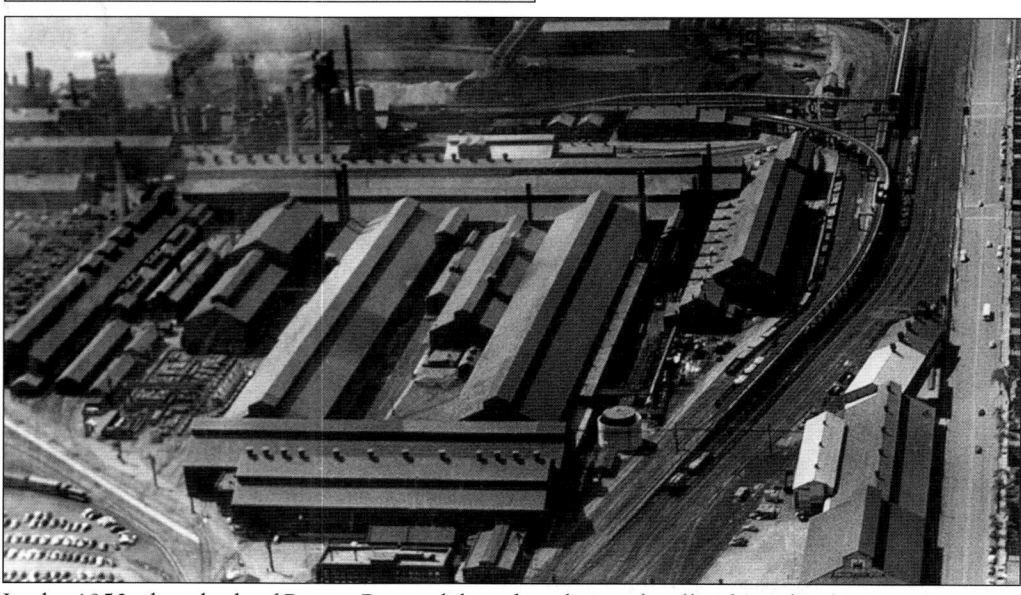

In the 1950s, hundreds of Puerto Ricans labored in the steel mills of South Chicago, Gary, and East Chicago, Indiana. Puerto Ricans worked largely as unskilled laborers in the blast furnaces, where the work was unbearably hot and dangerous. Pictured here is Wisconsin Steel in 1948 in the South Deering neighborhood. In the 1980s and 90s, most of the mills in the area, including Wisconsin Steel, shut down. (Courtesy Southeast Historical Society.)

Ricardo López came to Chicago in 1944 from Mayaguez, Puerto Rico. He worked in the steels mills of Gary, Indiana for over 15 years. He is shown here in 1949 in Chicago's Garfield Park neighborhood. Four of Ricardo López's sons became police officers in the Chicago Police Department. See pages 76 and 77. (Courtesy Efrain López.)

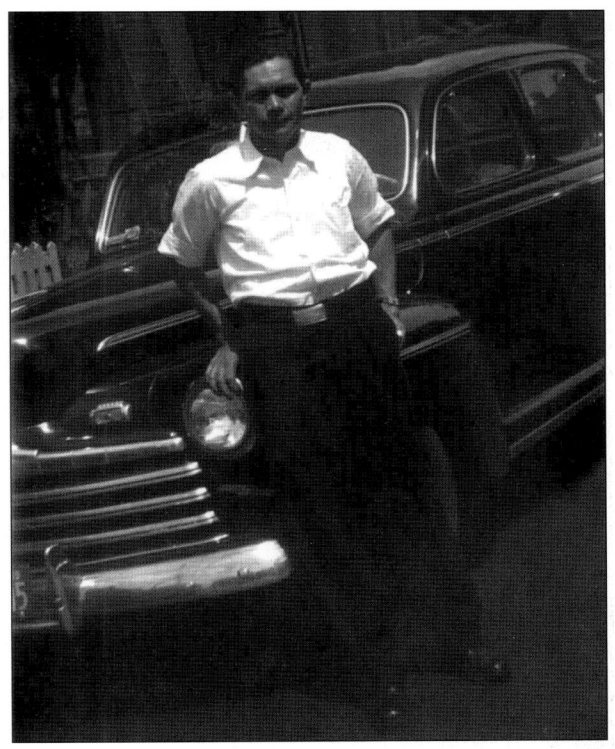

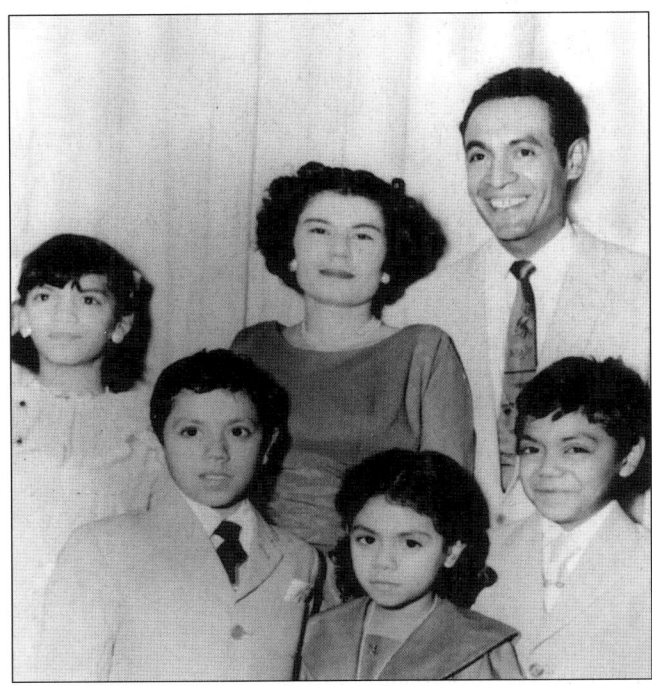

Eduardo Ortiz migrated to Chicago in 1953 from Puerto Rico. He worked for over 30 years in the steel mills of South Chicago. He is pictured here with his family in 1958. Pictured, from left to right, are: (bottom) Pablo, Providencia, and Wilfredo; (top) Elisa, wife Maria, and Eduardo. Eduardo's son, Wilfredo, became a high school principal with the Chicago Public Schools. (Courtesy Wilfredo Ortiz.)

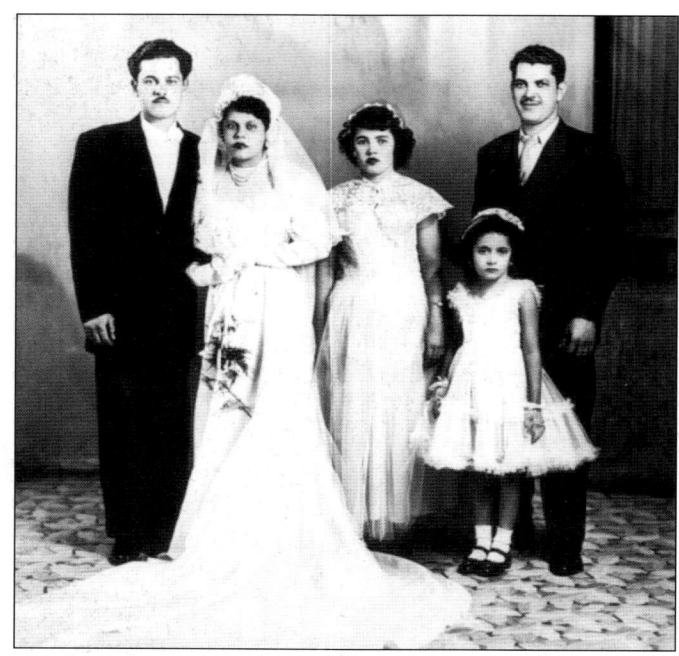

Manuel and Ana Alicea are pictured here on their wedding day in 1953 in Hammond, Indiana. The other relatives are unidentified. Manuel worked in the steel mills of Indiana. He came to Chicago and worked for over 30 years as a janitor. Ana worked in small factories in Chicago. They have one son and two daughters. In 2003, they celebrated their 50th wedding anniversary. (Courtesy Marixsa Alicea.)

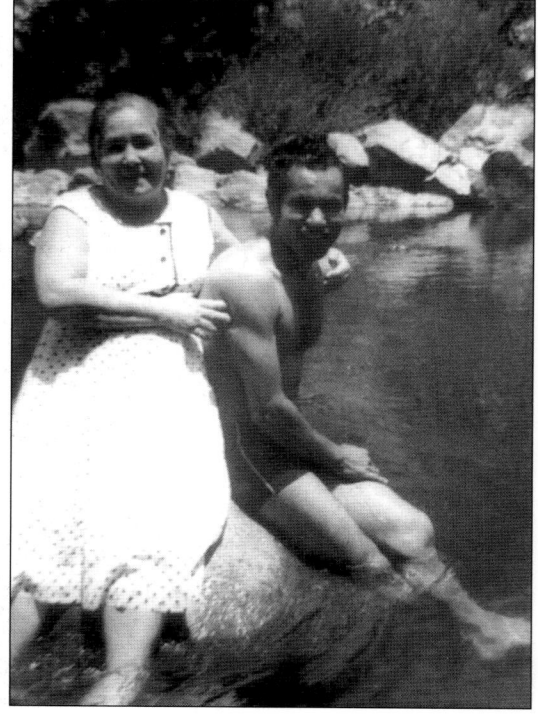

Eligio Quiñones and his mother, Fundadora, in California in 1960. Quiñones and thousands of other Puerto Ricans came to the United States from Puerto Rico during the 1940s and 50s as contracted farm workers. Quiñones worked in New York and California. Puerto Ricans eventually left farm work for better-paying work in the city. Quiñones came to Chicago in 1967, and worked for many years cleaning kitchens and preparing food for American Airlines. (Courtesy Eligio Quiñones.)

Leonor and wife Blanca Diaz are pictured in 1966. Leonor came from Puerto Rico as a contracted farm worker to pick crops in Florida in 1949. He came to Chicago in 1950 and worked butchering livestock in the Union Stock Yard in the Back Of The Yards neighborhood. He also worked as a janitor for many years. Blanca worked washing dishes and clothes in hotels. They raised three sons and a daughter. All three sons joined the U.S military. See pages 47 and 48. (Courtesy Hilda Frontany.)

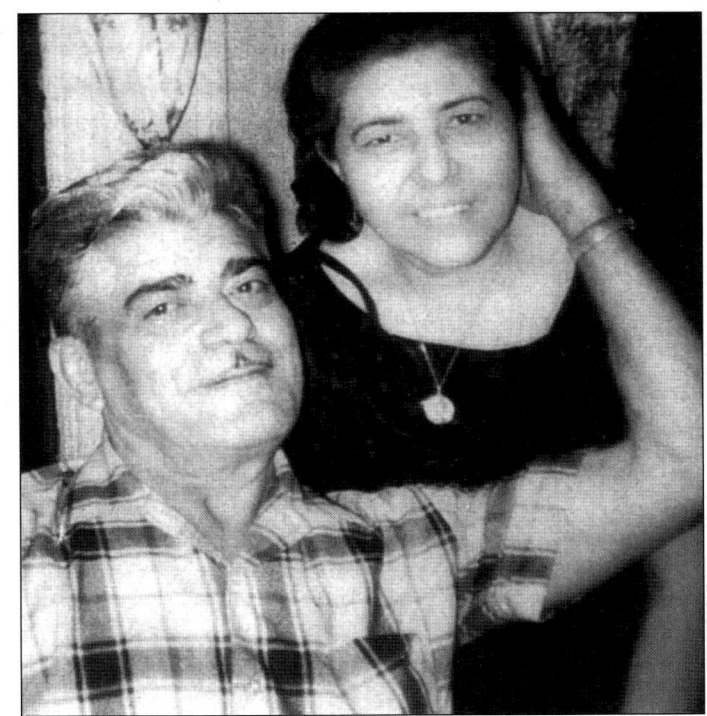

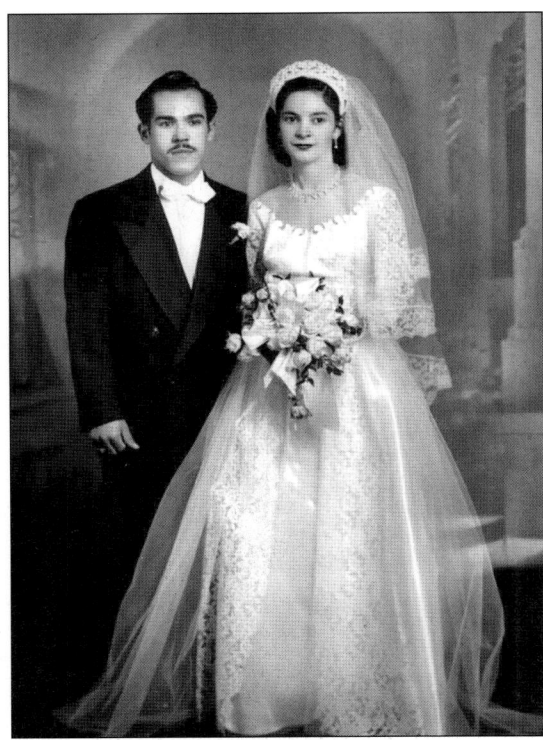

The wedding of Cesareo and Luz Maria Rivera in Chicago in 1952 at Our Lady of Guadalupe Church in South Chicago is seen here. Cesario came to Chicago in 1951 from Caguas, Puerto Rico. He worked in the steel mills of Indiana, and later in Chicago factories. The Riveras settled in the Lincoln Park neighborhood, but because of gentrification they moved to the Englewood neighborhood where they currently live. (Courtesy Cesareo and Luz Maria Rivera.)

13

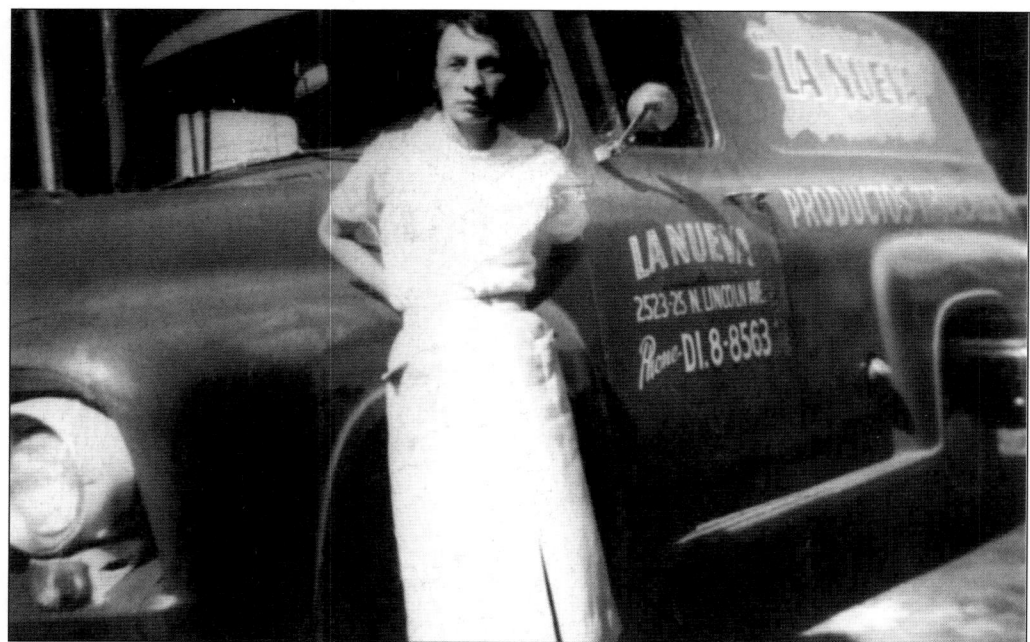

In the early 1950s, large food chains did not carry Puerto Rican food products. A Puerto Rican family owned "La Nueva" a small grocery store in Lincoln Park. The small store offered credit to struggling families. The store owner delivered its Puerto Rican food products to customers. The unidentified woman is the wife of the owner. (Courtesy Tomas V. Sanabria.)

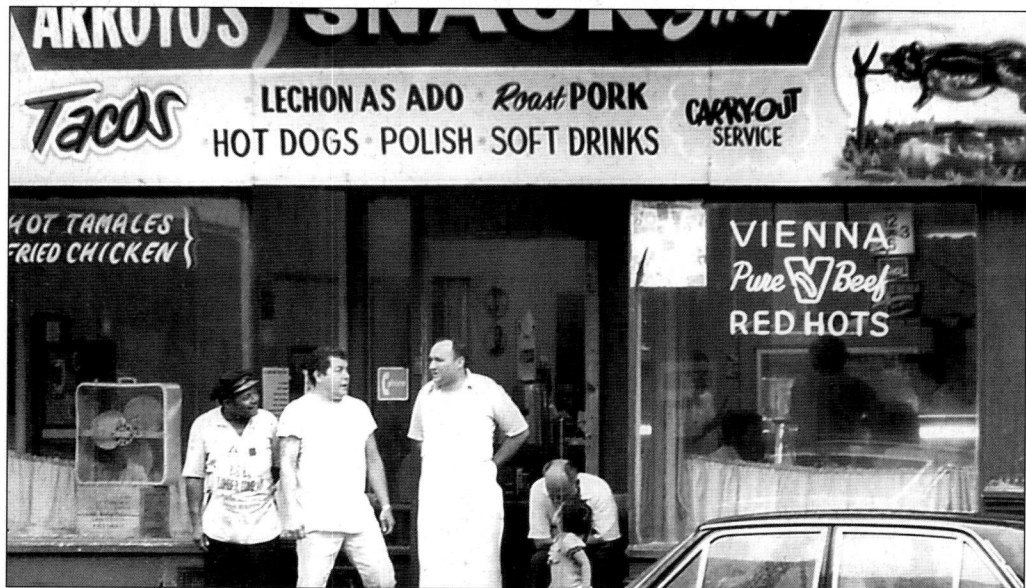

Arroyo's was a small Puerto Rican owned restaurant on Armitage Street in the Lincoln Park neighborhood. The restaurant carried American, Mexican, and Puerto Rican food. The restaurant's sign shows a pig being roasted on a spit in the outdoors, as was often done in Puerto Rico. Unidentified customers enjoyed hanging out at Arroyo's. This photo was taken in 1970. (Courtesy Carlos Flores.)

Some Puerto Ricans made a living as street vendors. Cabo "Cabito" Cruz was a piraguero on Armitage Street in the Lincoln Park neighborhood in 1970. Piragueros are Puerto Rican pushcart vendors who sell piraguas, or snow cones, flavored with sweet syrup. (Courtesy Carlos Flores.)

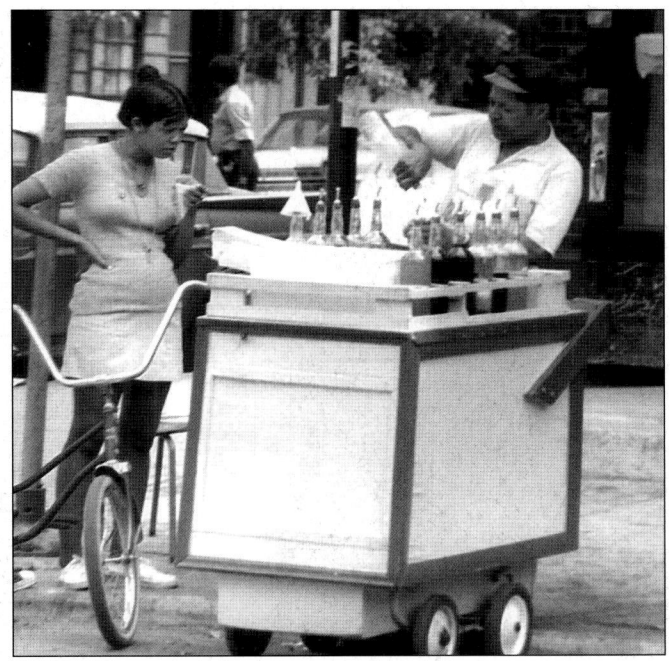

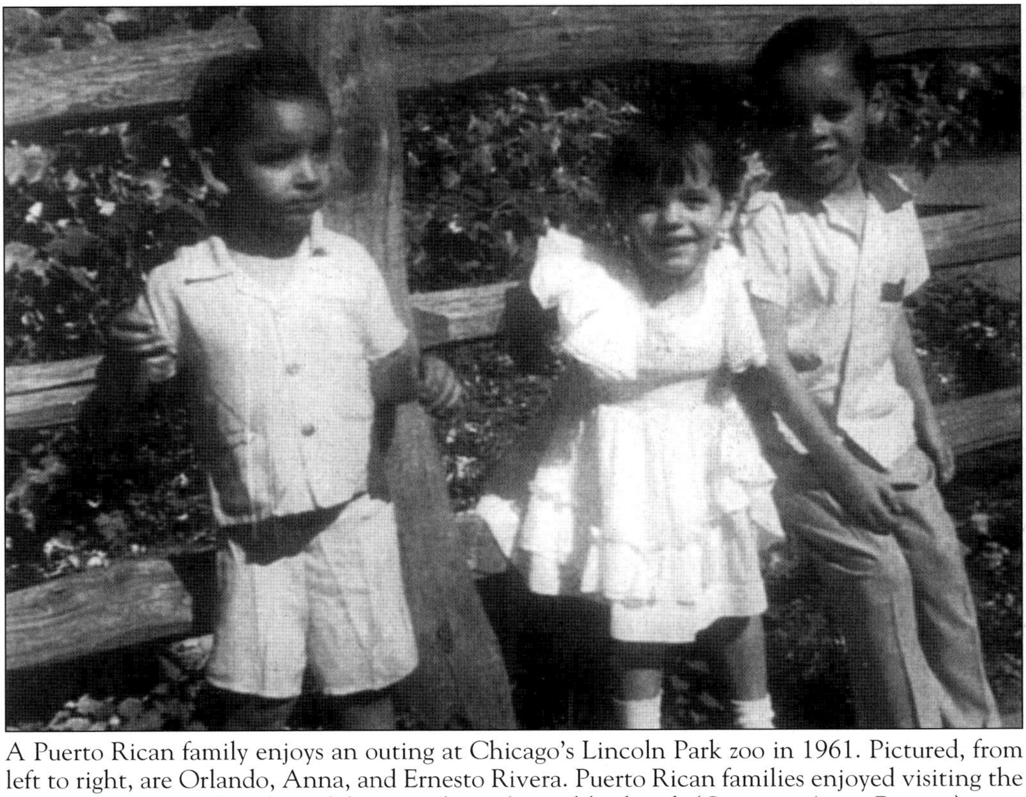

A Puerto Rican family enjoys an outing at Chicago's Lincoln Park zoo in 1961. Pictured, from left to right, are Orlando, Anna, and Ernesto Rivera. Puerto Rican families enjoyed visiting the zoo and the nearby beaches of the Lincoln Park neighborhood. (Courtesy Anna Rivera.)

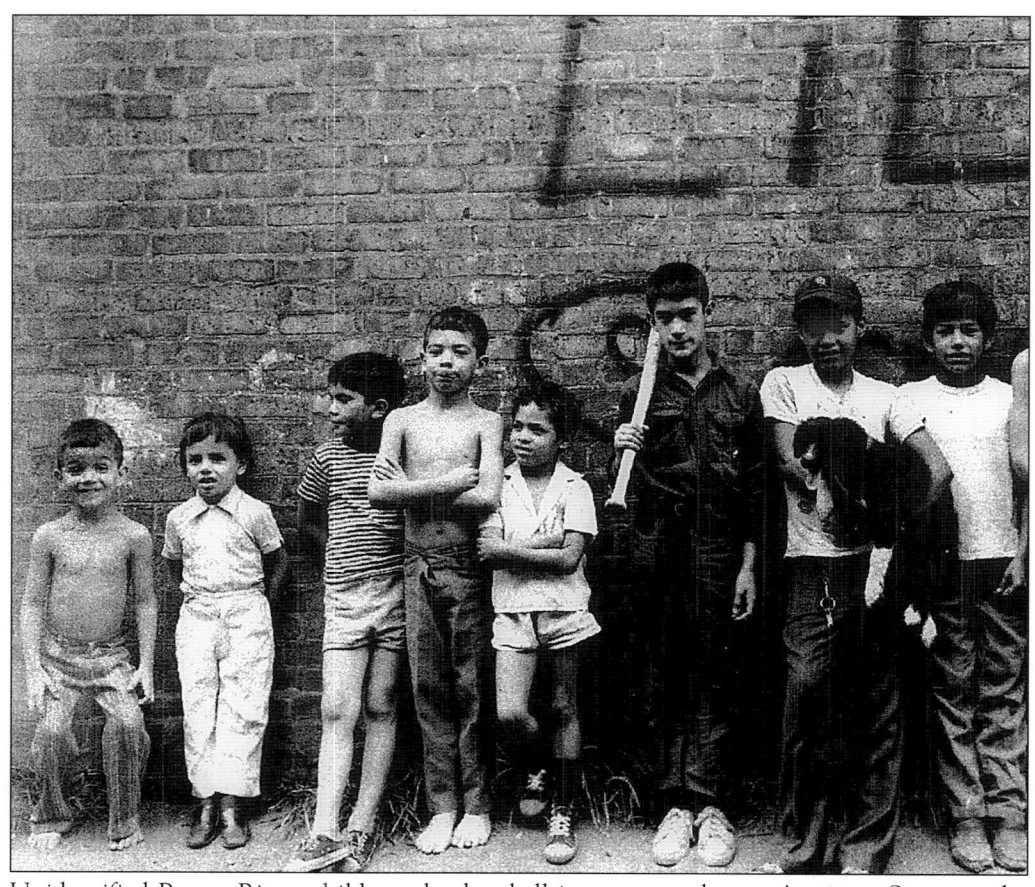

Unidentified Puerto Rican children play baseball in an empty lot on Armitage Street in the Lincoln Park neighborhood in 1970. It appears the parents of the kids were having a hard time making ends meet, as some of the kids are not wearing shirts or shoes. (Courtesy Carlos Flores.)

Two

FAMILY

Why did Puerto Ricans take the bold step of moving from familiar surroundings in Puerto Rico to a strange, cold city called Chicago? Surely, like waves of previous immigrants, they came looking for steady, good-paying jobs. But they were not merely concerned with making things better for themselves. They came with the expectation that life would be much better for their children.

Puerto Rican parents often lamented the fact that they came to Chicago knowing little English, with few skills, and with very little formal education. Some parents could not even help their children with their school homework, as they did not understand the English language. In parent and teacher conferences at school, children often had to translate what the teacher was saying for their parents. Certainly, parents often wished they had more skills to pass on to their children.

But what the first generation of Puerto Ricans lacked in skills, they made up through their hard work, determination, and perseverance. They worked hard at whatever jobs they found. They were willing to deny themselves the good things in life. They were willing to sacrifice and save their hard-earned money. Many purchased small homes and buildings. This was all done with the hope that life would not be as hard for their children. Parents wanted a good education for their children. They did not want their sons and daughters to work in factories and dead-end jobs. They hoped their families and future generations would acquire the education, skills, and motivation to lead rewarding, productive lives.

Today, many first-generation Puerto Ricans speak proudly of their families. The living rooms of Puerto Rican families are often filled with framed photographs celebrating the accomplishments of their children. The older generations are proud when their children acquire college education. They are proud when their children enter white-collar professions. They are proud that their children were raised with respect and dignity.

Cesario Rivera, an early Puerto Rican migrant to Chicago, is hopeful about the future of the Puerto Rican community. "The community is growing," says Cesario. "A lot more people are getting educated. They are preparing themselves. We have more politicians, doctors, and lawyers. There's a growing middle-class."

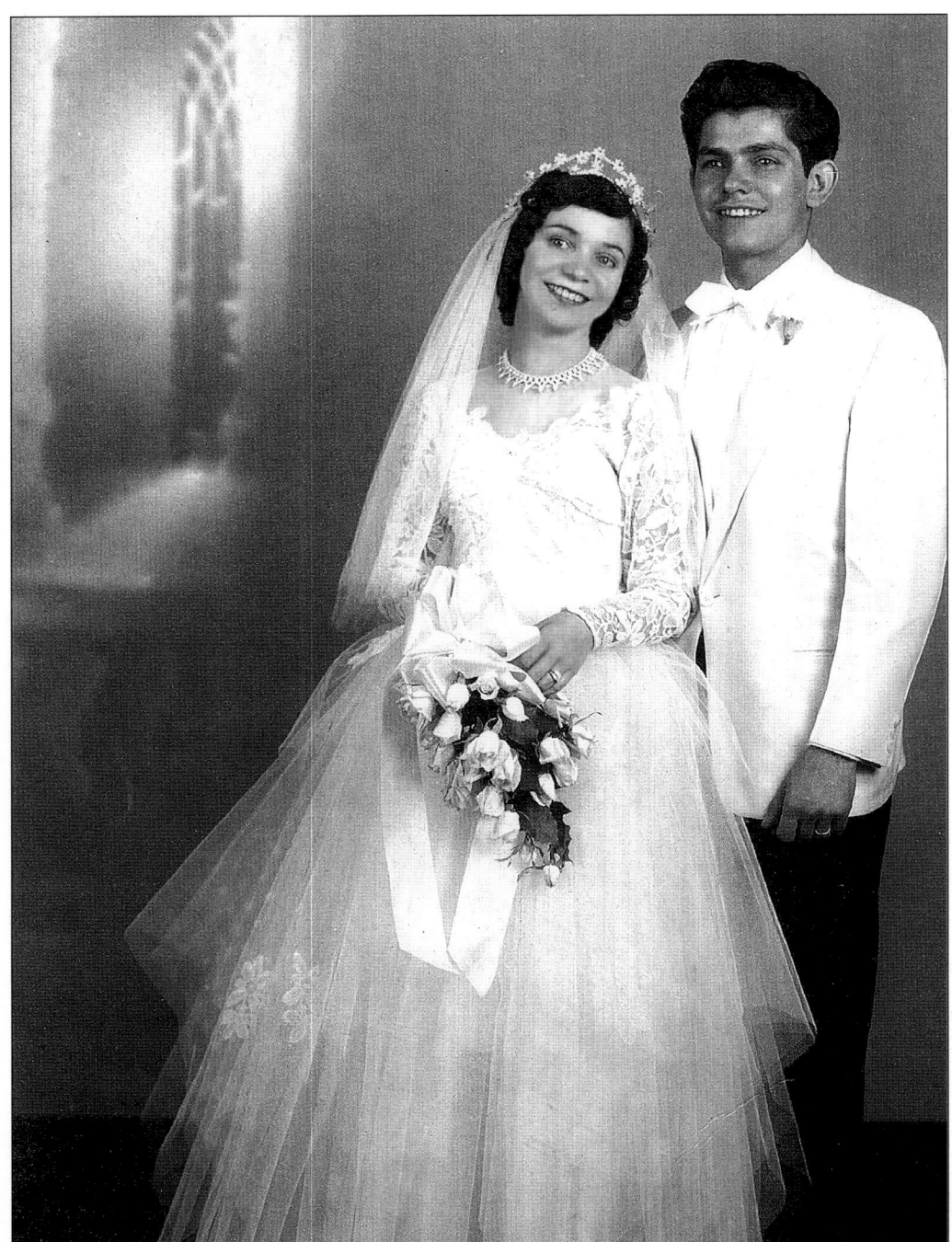

Gilberto and Martha Hernandez both came from Puerto Rico to Chicago in 1952. They met in Chicago, and married in 1954 at St. Francisco of Assisi Church, 813 West Roosevelt Road. Gilberto worked for the steel mills in Indiana, and later drove his own taxi in Chicago. Martha worked in factories. The couple had two sons and five daughters. Gilberto passed away in 1981. (Courtesy Martha Hernandez.)

Nictor and Carmen Cardenas married in 1967 at St. Francisco of Assisi Church. Nictor is Mexican and Carmen is Puerto Rican. Marriages between Puerto Ricans and Mexicans are common in Chicago. Nictor and Carmen both worked in small factories in Chicago and the suburbs. One of their three sons is a police officer with the Milwaukee Police Department. The couple retired in 1995 to their large new home in Florida. (Courtesy Nictor and Carmen Cardenas.)

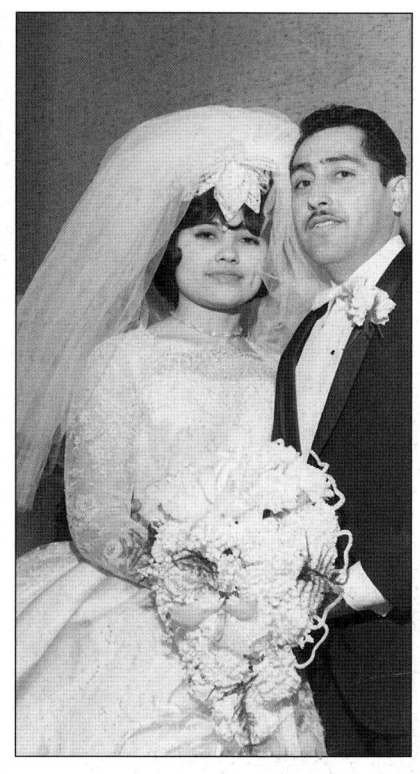

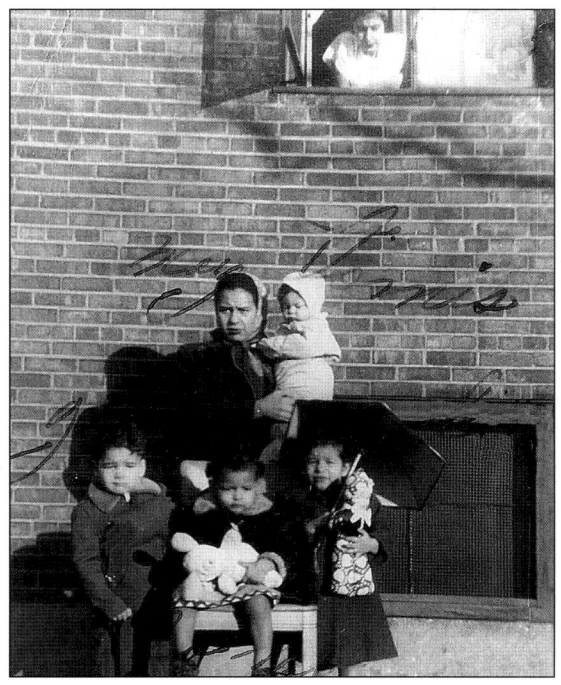

Margarita Sanabria and her three children are seen here in front of Chicago's Alba Public Housing Project in 1954. The child on the chair is a family friend. An aunt, above, looks on. In the 1950s and 60s, some struggling Puerto Ricans families were forced to go on public aid, and lived in public housing. Mrs. Sanabria's son, Tomas, in her arms, later became a photographer and Pentecostal reverend. See page 62. (Courtesy Tomas V. Sanabria.)

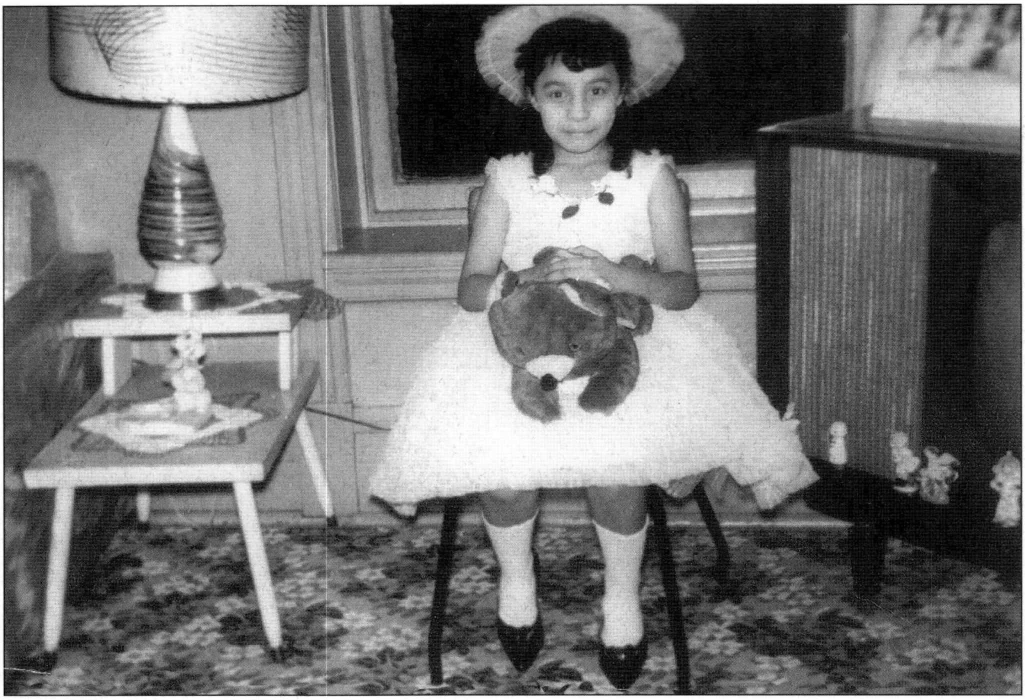

A young unidentified Puerto Rican girl is pictured at a birthday party in the early 1950s in Humboldt Park. At the time, working-class Puerto Rican apartments often had miniature ceramic figurines, colorful linoleum-covered floors, homemade embroidered table coverings, and a sofa wrapped in plastic, so as to last longer. (Courtesy Tomas V. Sanabria.)

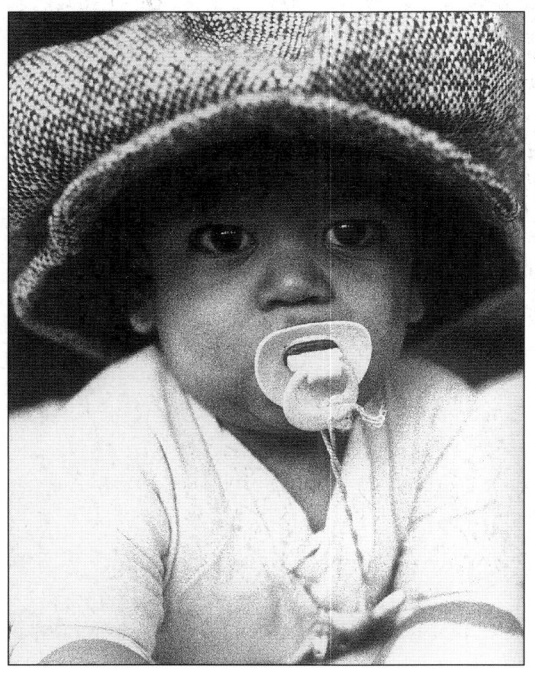

"Don Alberto Jeremi Garcia," a Puerto Rican baby sporting a large hat and pacifier, is seen here in the Humboldt Park neighborhood in 1978. (Courtesy Tomas V. Sanabria.)

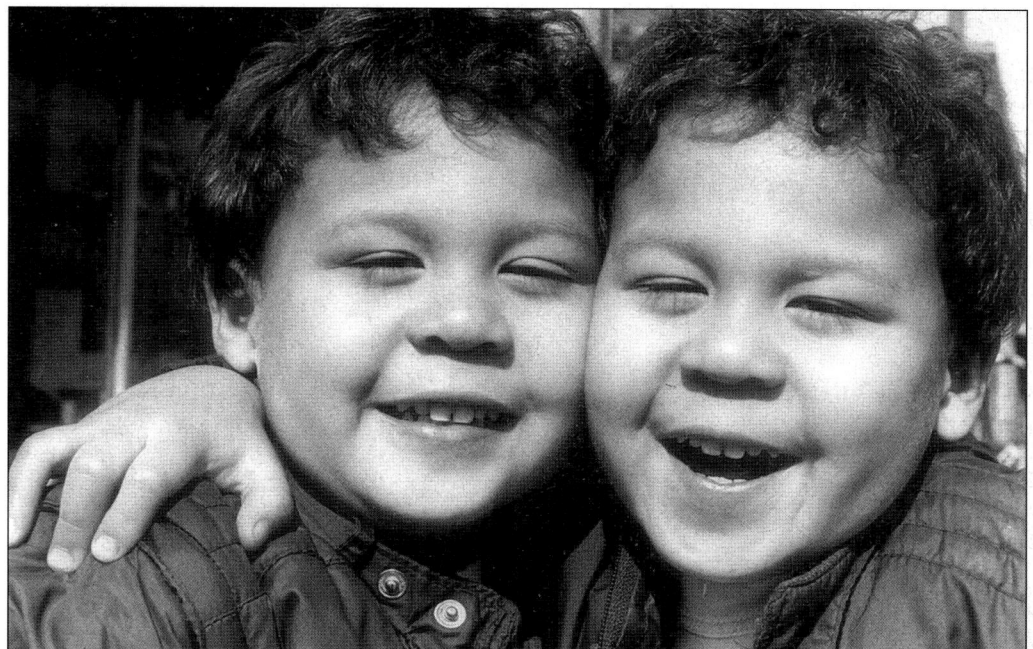

Two unidentified Puerto Rican identical twins are pictured in the Logan Square neighborhood in the early 1980s. The brothers are playing in front of their house. (Courtesy Delma Serrano.)

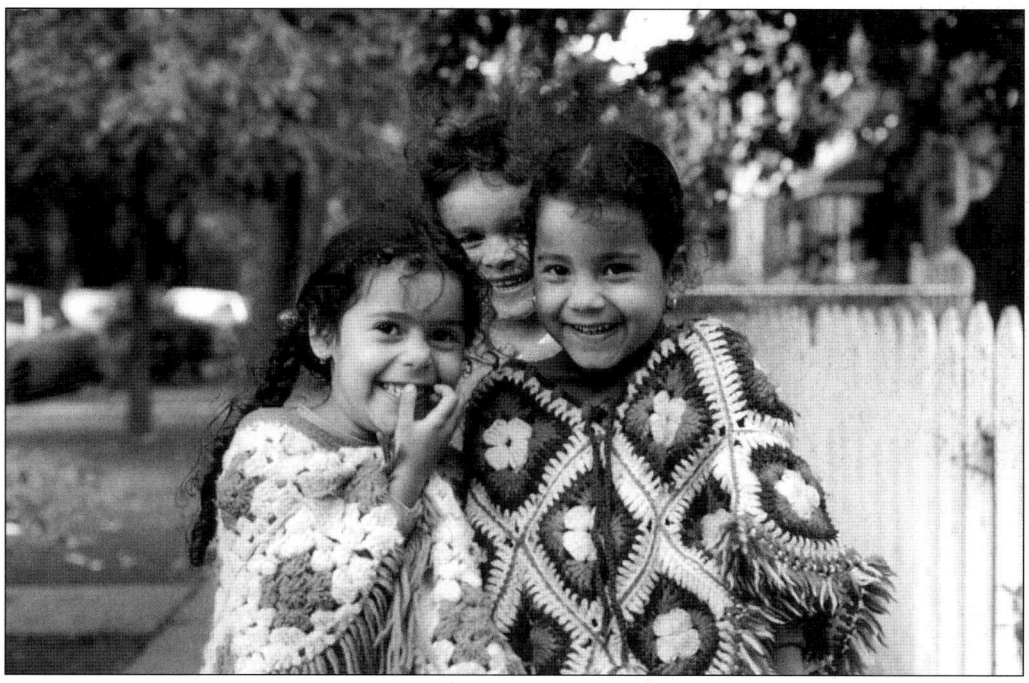

Three unidentified Puerto Rican sisters playing in front of their Humboldt Park home on a cool September day in 1972. The sisters are wearing colorful, homemade crotcheted ponchos. (Courtesy Jaime Rivera.)

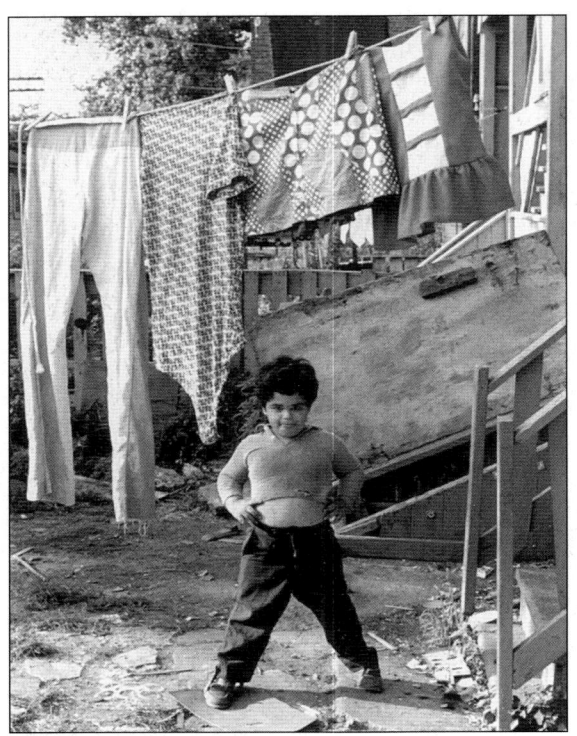

An unidentified Puerto Rican boy plays in his back yard in the summer of 1972. He lived on Claremont Street in the Humboldt Park neighborhood. The family clothes dries on a clothesline. (Courtesy Jaime Rivera.)

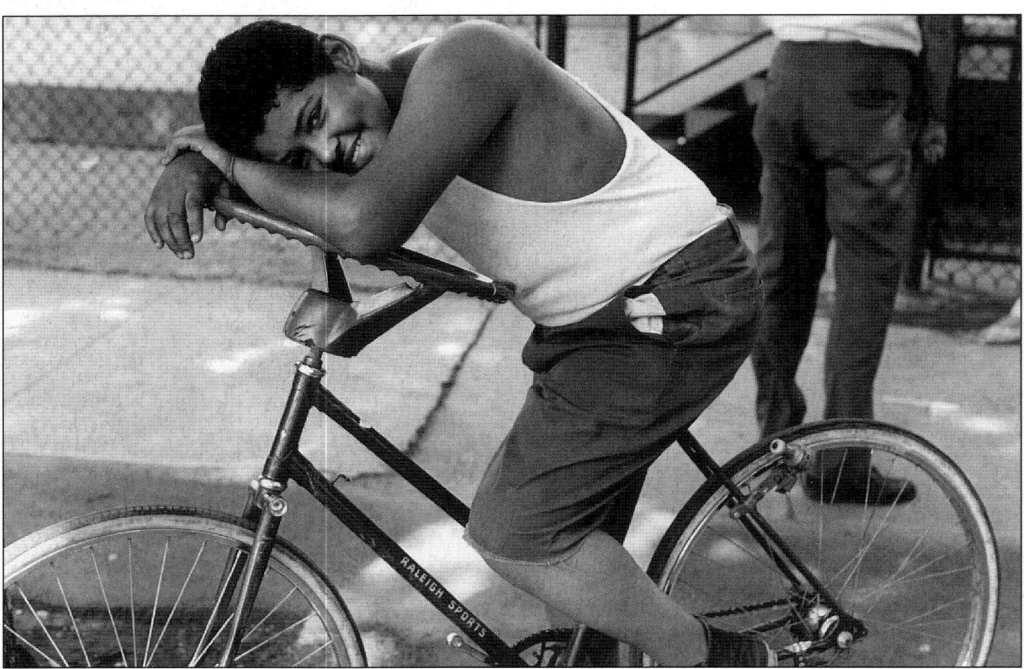

An unidentified Puerto Rican boy is pictured on Oakley Street in the Humboldt Park neighborhood in 1972. He gathered spare bicycle and car parts and put together a bike for himself. He rode the bike even though the bike was missing the right pedal. (Courtesy Jaime Rivera.)

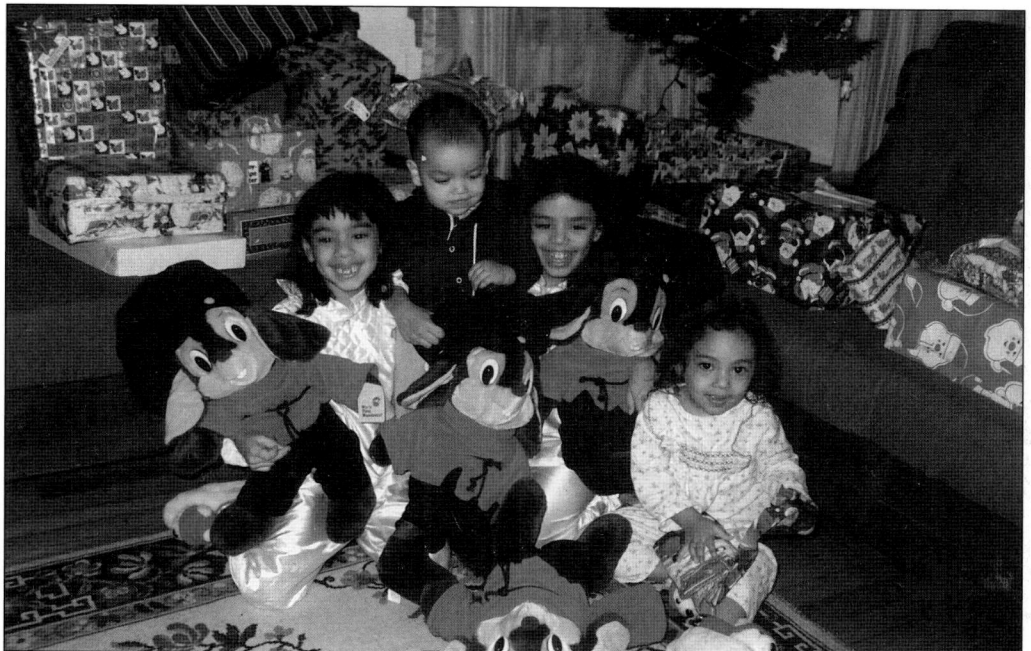

Three sisters and a cousin happily enjoy a 1987 Christmas at home. Pictured, from left to right, are Jennifer, Andy, Aby, and Jasmine. (Courtesy Jose and Wanda Betancourt.)

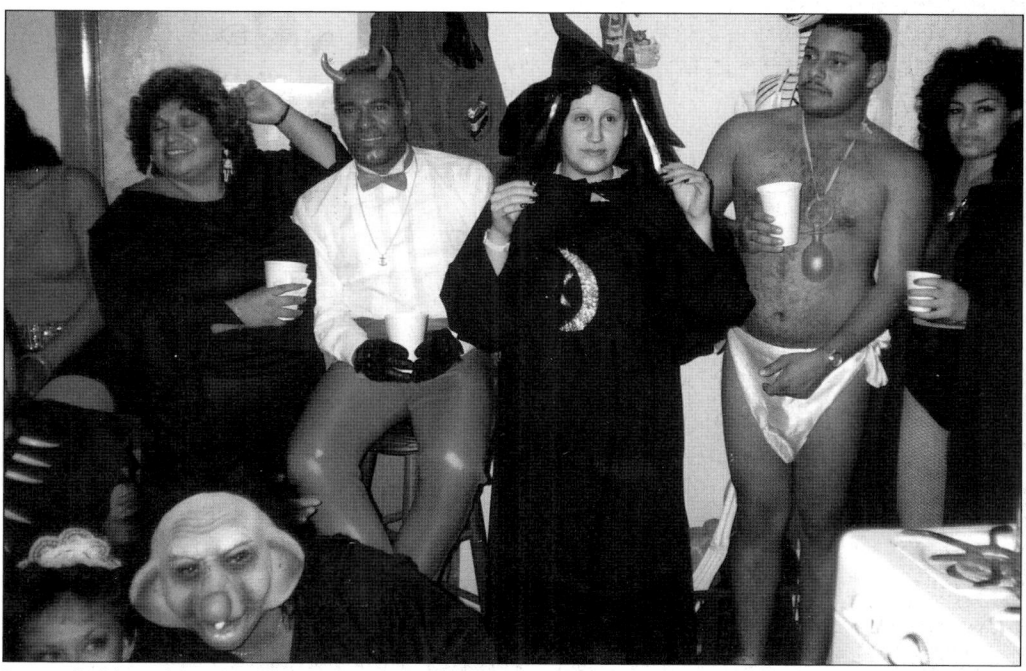

Irene (left) and her husband, Jose Peña (devil's costume), annually hold a Halloween party at their home in the Portage Park neighborhood. They are surrounded by unidentified friends in 1995. (Courtesy Jose and Irene Peña.)

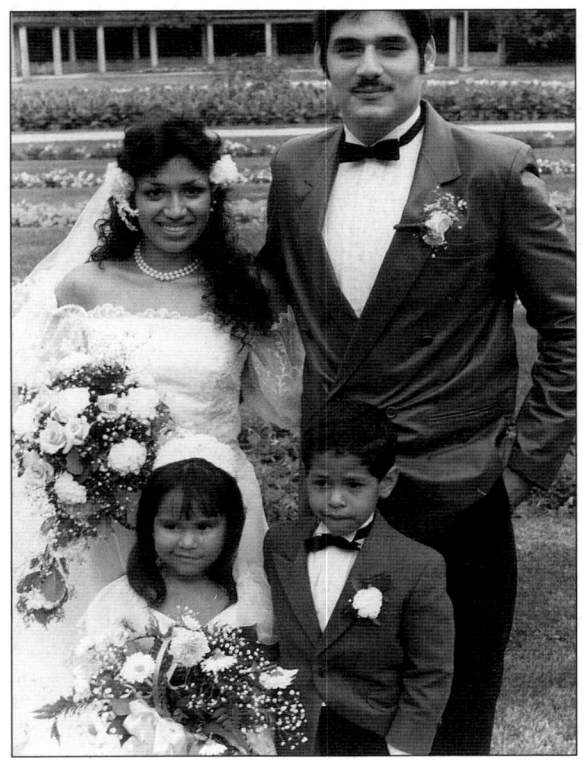

Mildred and Ray Rodriguez married in 1985. Acting as flower girl and ring bearer are Christina L. Peña and Alexis Rodriguez. This photo was taken in Humboldt Park in front of the park's flower garden. (Courtesy Jose and Irene Peña.)

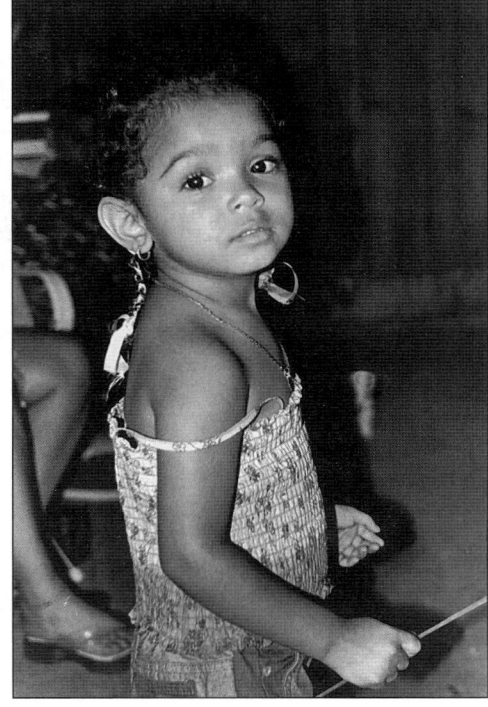

Three-year-old Artasia Gusman is the child of a Puerto Rican father and African American mother. Marriages between Puerto Ricans and African Americans are common in Chicago. Artasia waves the American flag on the Fourth of July, 2002. (Courtesy Alexandra Cruz.)

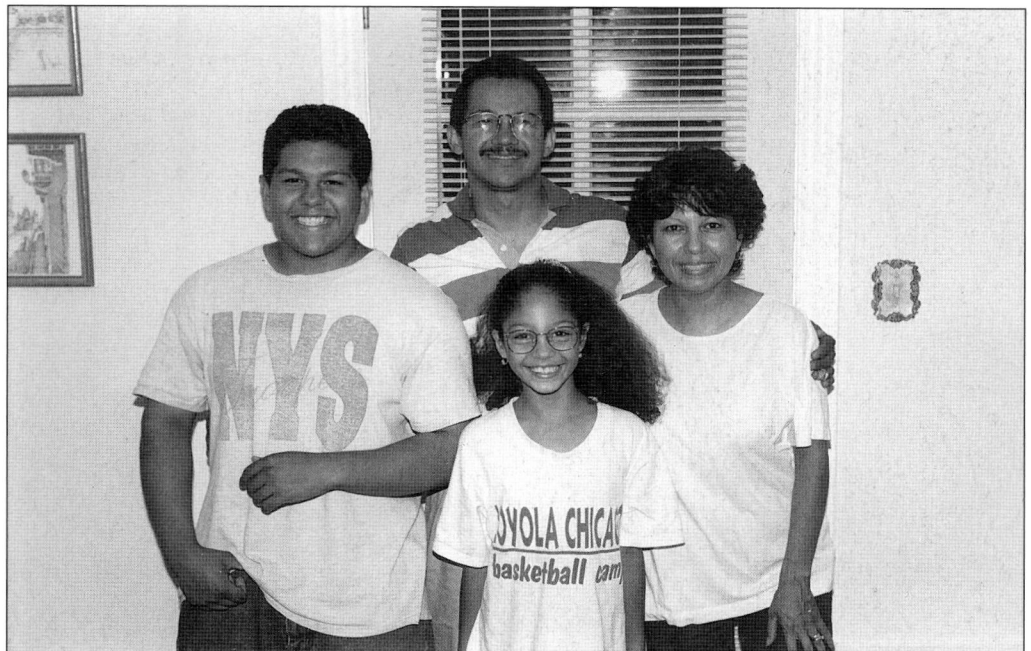

Rafael Anglada is pictured with his wife, Olga, and children, Rafael Javier and Karina, in their home in 2001. The family lives on the far north side in the Edison Park neighborhood. The parents of Rafael and Olga migrated to New York in the early 1950s, where they currently reside. The family makes periodic visits to New York to see their parents. Rafael works in the community policing department of the Chicago Police Department. Olga works as a social worker for the Chicago Public Schools. (Photo Wilfredo Cruz.)

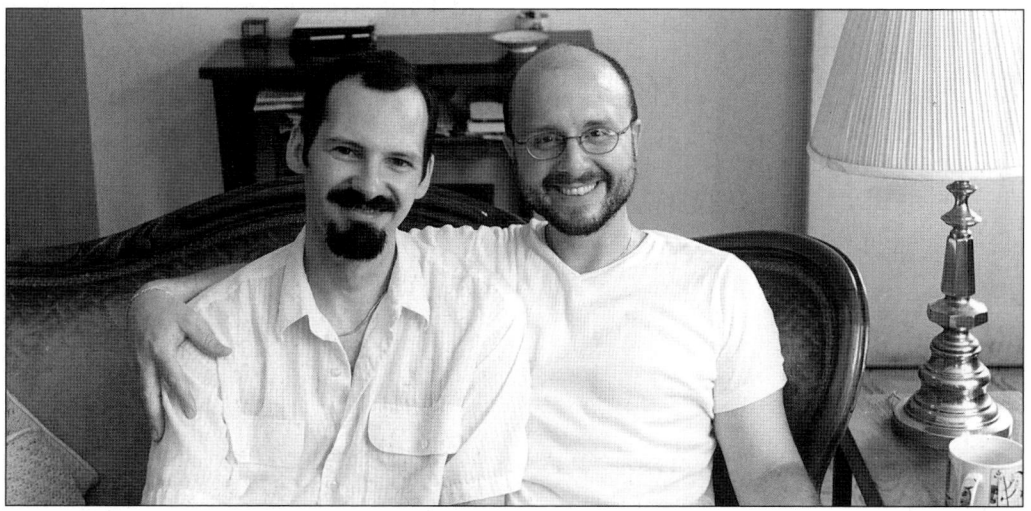

Carmelo Esterrich (right) came to Chicago in 1987 from Rio Piedras, Puerto Rico. He is shown here in 2000, with his partner, Joseph Myers. The couple has been together for 17 years. Carmelo is a professor of Spanish at Columbia College Chicago. Joseph is an acoustics consultant. They are in the home they own in Downers Grove, Illinois. (Courtesy Carmelo Esterrich and Joseph Myers.)

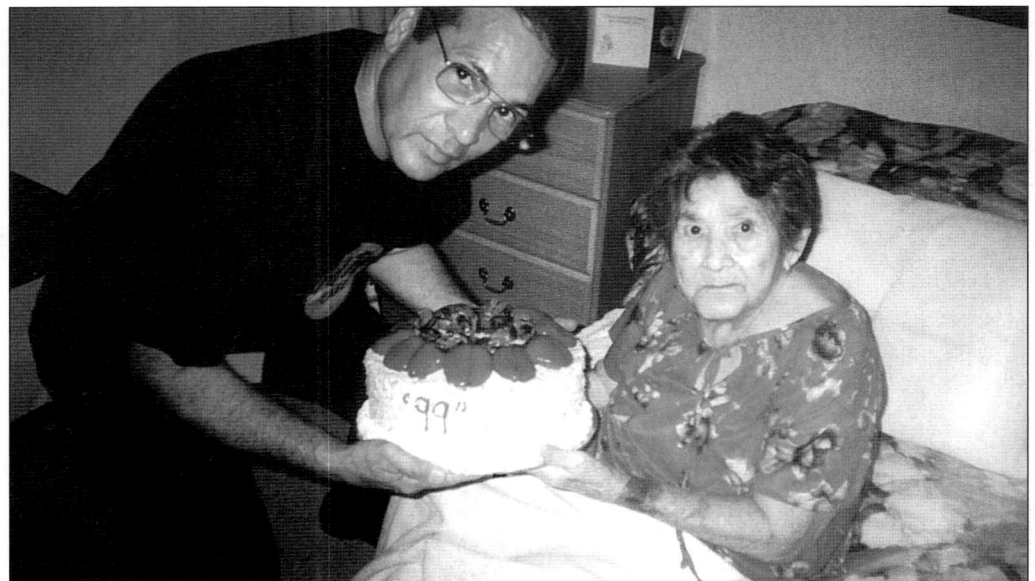

Efrain López presents his mother, Crecencia, with a homemade cake on her 99th birthday, in 2002, in a nursing home. Crecencia passed away later in 2002, four months shy of her 100th birthday. Efrain is one of four brothers who were police officers for the Chicago Police Department. See pages 76 and 77. (Courtesy Efrain López.).

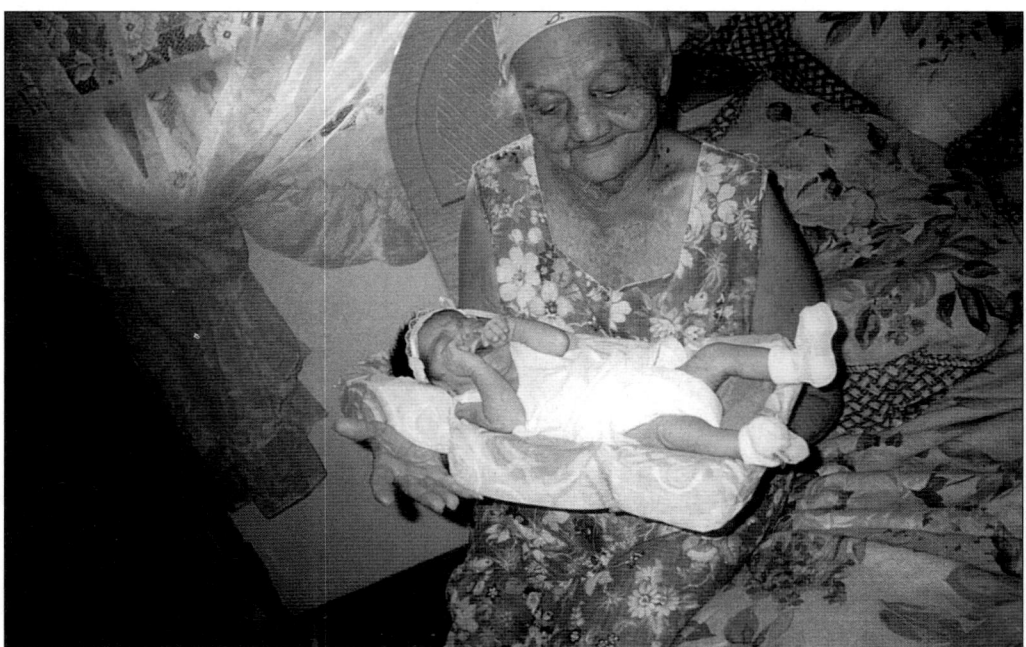

Rosa Lea Rivera celebrated her 99th birthday in September 2004. She is shown here in 1995, holding her newborn great-granddaughter, Naryln Rivera Rivera. She has one daughter and a grandson. She lives in a coach house behind her daughter's house. Rosa is still active and cooks, cleans, and takes care of herself. (Courtesy Anna Rivera.)

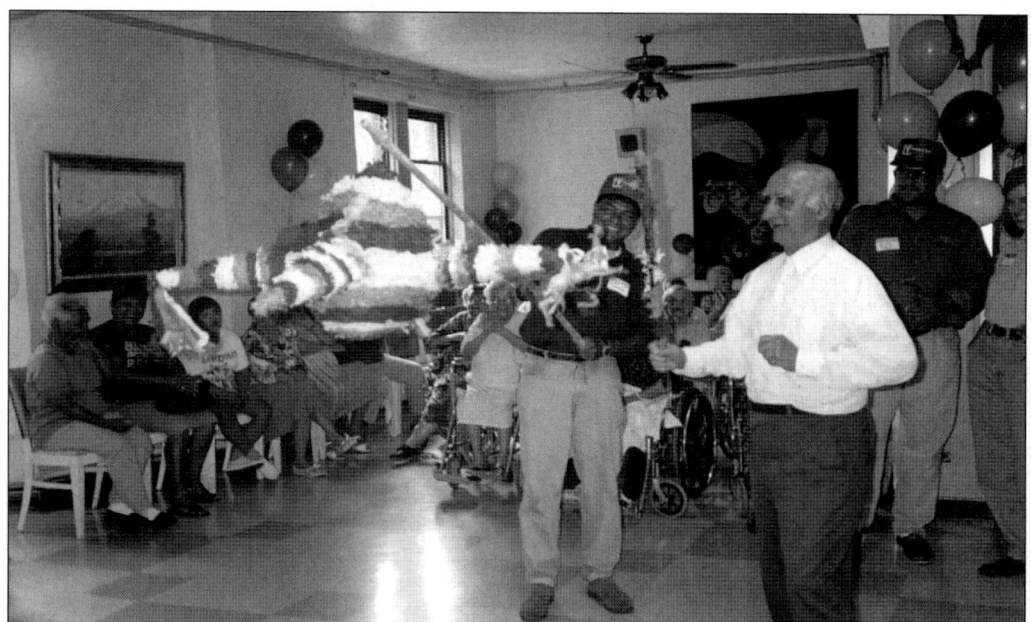

Frank Rodriguez, a Puerto Rican resident of the Casa Central's Center Home for Hispanic Elderly, tries to break a piñata in 1994, while staff and other nursing home residents cheer him on. He passed away in 2002. He was in his late 80s. Casa Central, founded in 1954, is one of the largest Latino social service agencies in Chicago. The organization has various programs for children, youth, adults, and elderly. Ann Alvarez, who is Cuban and Puerto Rican, runs the organization. (Courtesy Casa Central.)

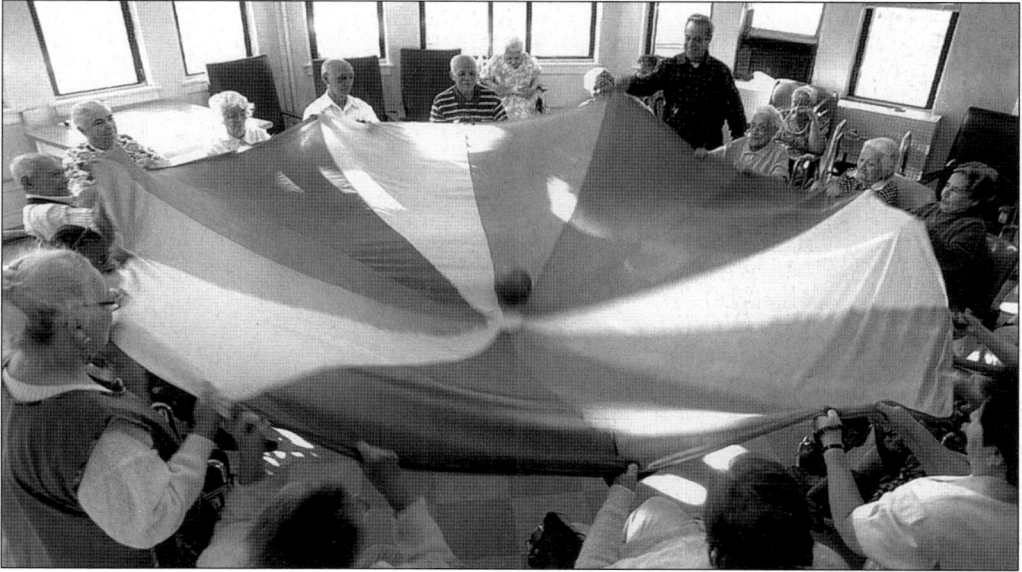

Various unidentified Puerto Rican and Cuban residents of Casa Central's Center Home for Hispanic Elderly participate in a parachute game in 1998. The game is intended to promote sociability among the residents, and also provides the residents with healthy exercise. (Courtesy Casa Central.)

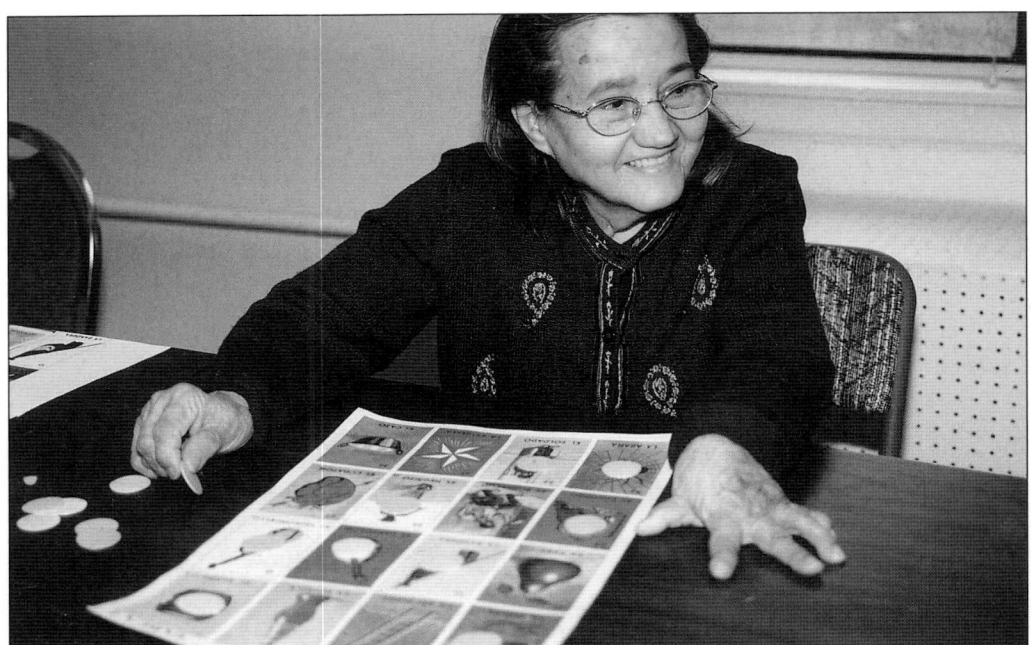

Cecilia Barreto is a current resident of Casa Central's nursing home along with her husband, Gregorio. Cecilia is 79 and Gregorio is 83. They have been residents since 2001. She and other residents are playing Loteria, a Spanish style bingo with pictures on the squares instead of numbers. Residents who win are awarded items such as lotions, perfumes, socks, soap, shaving lotion, etc. (Courtesy Casa Central.)

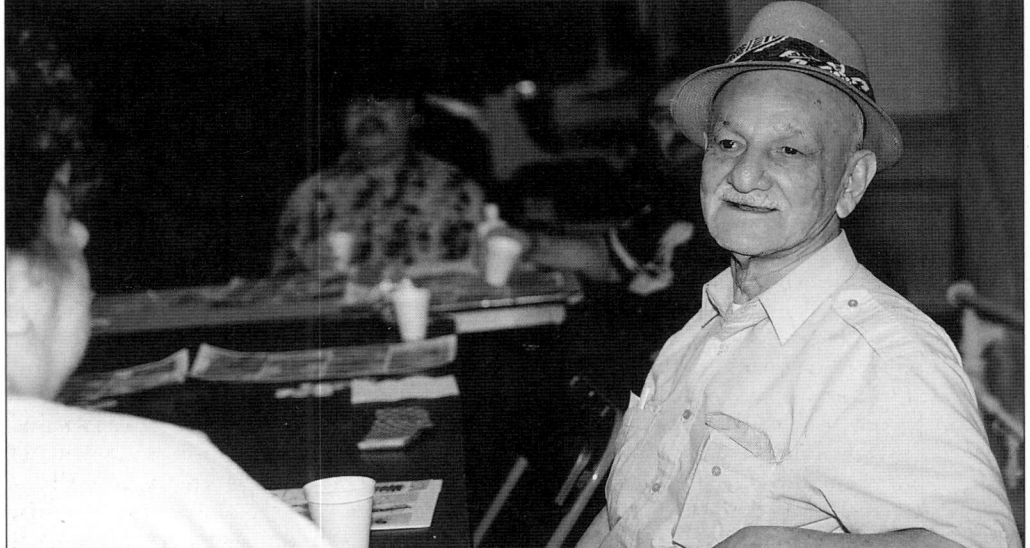

Antonio Batiz, 68, is a nursing home resident of Casa Central. Residents enjoy being around people their own age and cultural background. The residents play games together, watch movies, participate in arts and crafts, and read books and newspapers. Residents also enjoy talking to each other about their lives, their grown children and grandchildren, and about memories of Puerto Rico. (Courtesy Casa Central.)

Three

COMMUNITY LIFE

Some early Puerto Rican migrants to Chicago lived in Chicago's downtown Loop area in cheap, cramped apartment buildings and old, transient hotels. Many worked in fancy downtown hotels and restaurants as janitors, busboys, dishwashers, and cooks.

"When I arrived in Chicago in 1954, I lived near the center of the city on Harrison and Ashland," recalls Raul Cardona, who established one of the first Puerto Rican radio programs in Chicago. "There were a lot of multi-buildings in the area and the rents were low. Puerto Ricans were not making a lot of money so obviously the rents were low. More Puerto Ricans began moving into that neighborhood and around Madison, Washington, and Jackson Streets."

Besides Chicago's downtown area, Puerto Ricans found affordable housing in neighborhoods like Uptown and Lakeview. Yet landlords on the north side of the city often refused to rent to dark-skinned Puerto Ricans, who they viewed as blacks. While Puerto Ricans did not face the extreme housing segregation experienced by African Americans, they were not welcomed in certain neighborhoods. Some Puerto Rican families found affordable shelter in public housing projects alongside African Americans.

Other Puerto Ricans settled in south side neighborhoods. In the 1950s, many south side neighborhoods were undergoing racial change as African Americans moved in and white ethnics fled to the suburbs. Some white landlords in the East and West Garfield Park neighborhoods preferred renting apartments to Puerto Ricans instead of to African Americans. But Puerto Ricans still paid high rents.

Following their displacement from Lincoln Park, most Puerto Ricans moved west to Division Street to West Town, Bucktown, and Wicker Park. However, during the last 20 years, these communities have also undergone gentrification. Many Puerto Ricans moved out as young, white middle-class professionals moved in. Trendy, upscale restaurants, bars, shops, and coffee houses now dot the commercial strips of these neighborhoods. Today, even the Humboldt Park neighborhood, a Puerto Rican community for many years, is now encountering the forces of gentrification.

Being moved from neighborhood to neighborhood surely hurt the ability of Puerto Ricans to establish solid, lasting communities. Nevertheless, despite the setbacks and hardships, Puerto Ricans did establish a strong sense of community wherever they settled. While the climb was not always easy, many early Puerto Ricans realized the American dream of home ownership.

They realized the dream of seeing many of their children college educated.

Second and third generation Puerto Ricans have made important contributions to the progress of Puerto Ricans. Through the years, Puerto Ricans have established viable cultural, social, and political community organizations. These organizations have fostered a sense of community. Some took the lead in advocating for the rights of Puerto Ricans, fighting against social injustice. Additionally, Puerto Ricans have established sports teams, ethnic newspapers, radio programs, and a growing number of businesses.

Even today, as the photographs in this chapter demonstrate, Puerto Ricans gather in public places as neighbors and friends. They proudly celebrate their cultural heritage, and have a deep concern for the welfare of their families. Like other struggling communities, Puerto Ricans still face major social problems like drugs, gangs, low high school graduation rates, and poverty. But there is no denying that the Puerto Rican community has made significant progress since the first major group of Puerto Ricans came to the city in the 1950s. Undoubtedly, there exists a strong sense of a comunidad Puertorriqueña.

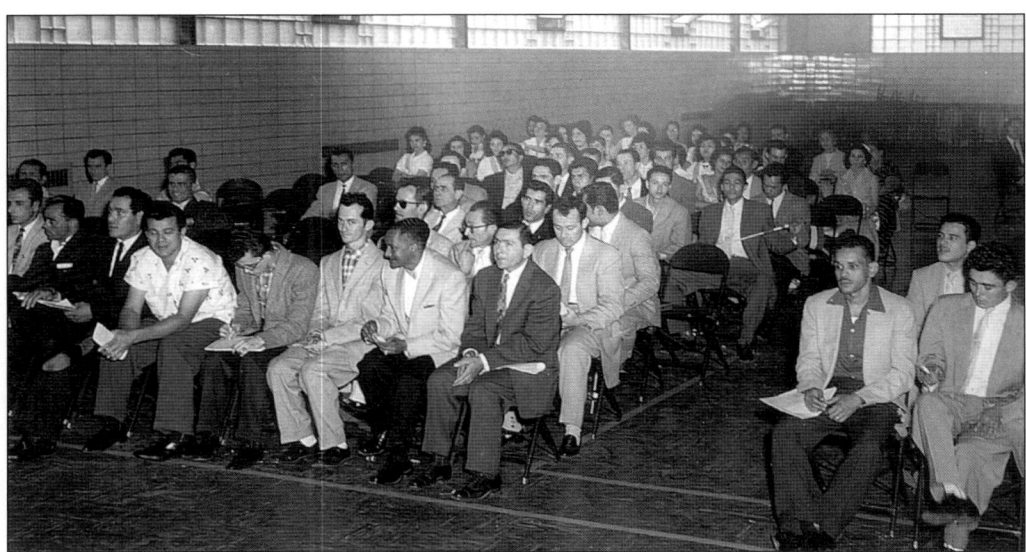

Roman Catholic priests helped form the Puerto Rican community's first large organization, Los Caballeros de San Juan (Knights of St. John), in 1954. Named after the patron saint of Puerto Rico, Los Caballeros formed 12 affiliated councils in various Catholic parishes. The organization served the religious and recreational needs of Puerto Ricans. Shown here is an early 1960s meeting of the councils. Leadership of the organization was mostly male; the wives are sitting in the back rows. (Courtesy Cesareo and Luz Maria Rivera.)

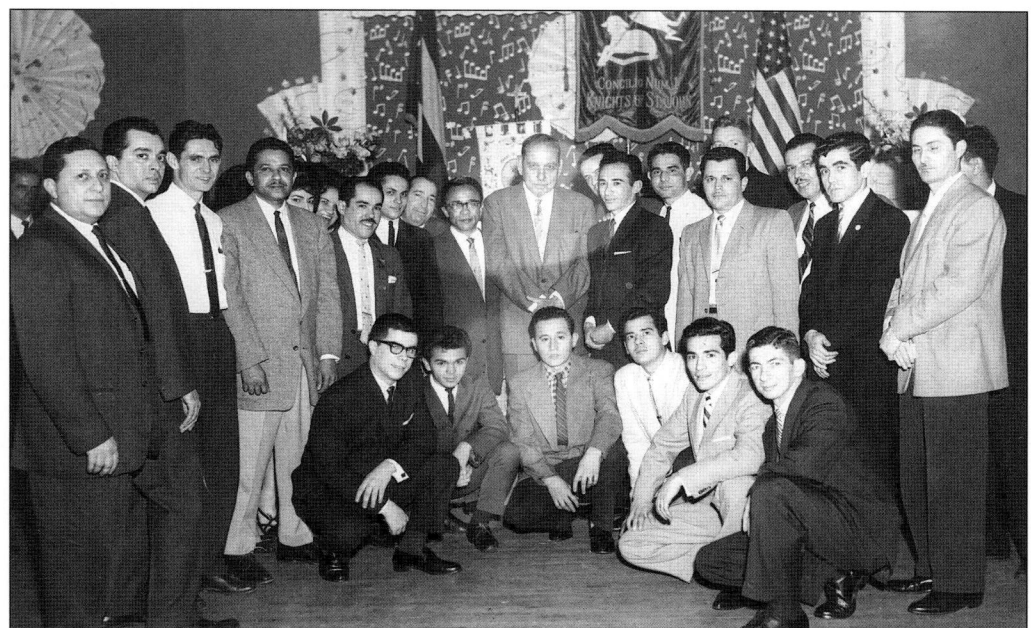

Leaders of the 12 councils of Los Caballeros de San Juan meet in 1960 in the main headquarters of the organization, located at 1300 South Wabash. Pictured in the center (standing) is Luis Muñoz Marín, the first former governor of Puerto Rico. Los Caballeros sponsored church services, dances, pool rooms for men, picnics, and banquets. Today, Los Caballeros de San Juan still exists, but solely as an independent credit union. (Courtesy Antonio Villalobos.)

Rev. Leo T. Mahon (right), an Irish priest who spoke Spanish, was director of the Chicago Catholic Archdiocese's Cardinal's Committee for the Spanish Speaking in the 1950s and 1960s. He was instrumental in founding Los Caballeros de San Juan. The organization helped Puerto Rican men prepare for the Chicago police test. In 1962 Puerto Rican Governor Luis Muñoz Marín (left) joined Los Caballeros de San Juan at Chicago's Hilton Hotel to celebrate Puerto Ricans who were becoming Chicago police officers. (Courtesy Leo T. Mahon.)

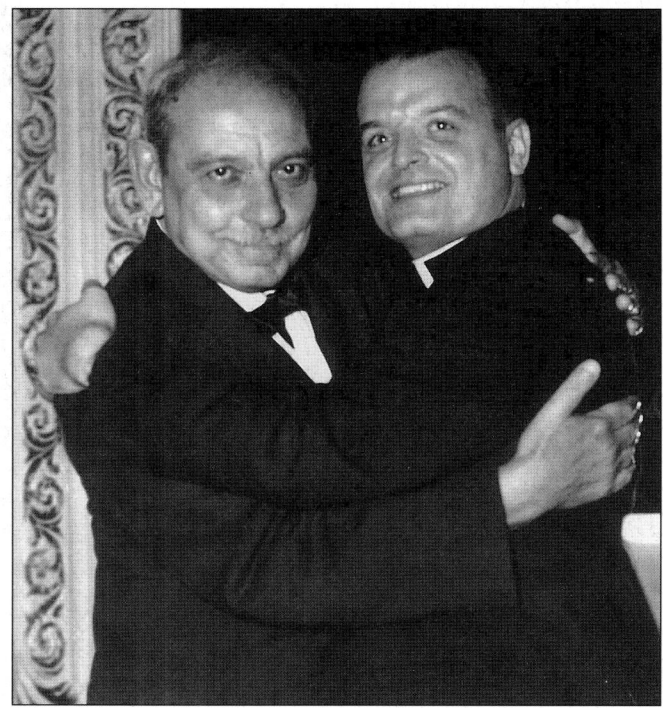

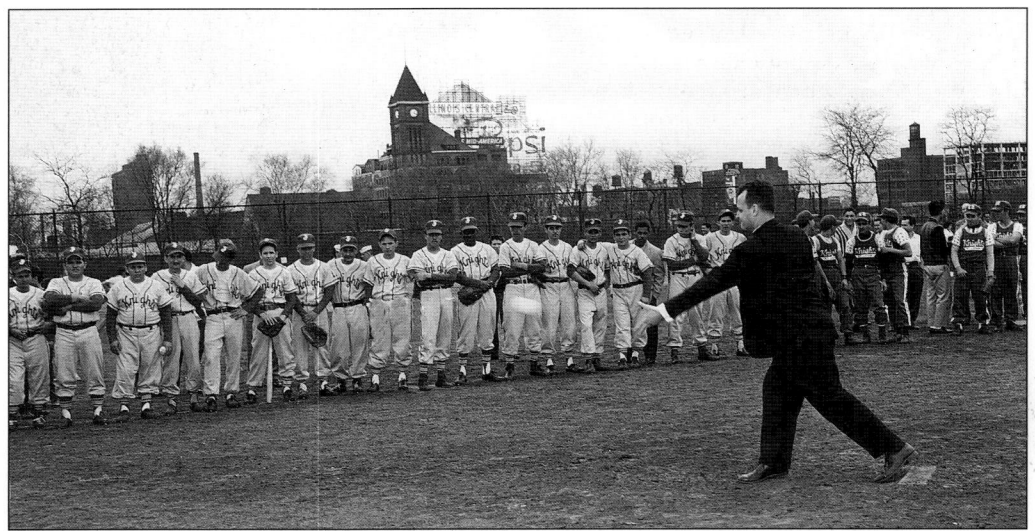

The different councils of Los Caballeros de San Juan sponsored baseball teams. These mid-1950s teams played against each other. The teams usually played in Garfield Park. Rev. Leo T. Mahon throws out the first pitch. The organization used baseball teams as a healthy outlet for young Puerto Rican men. The organization tried to keep Puerto Rican men off the streets and focused on religion, family, and recreation. (Courtesy Los Caballeros de San Juan Credit Union.)

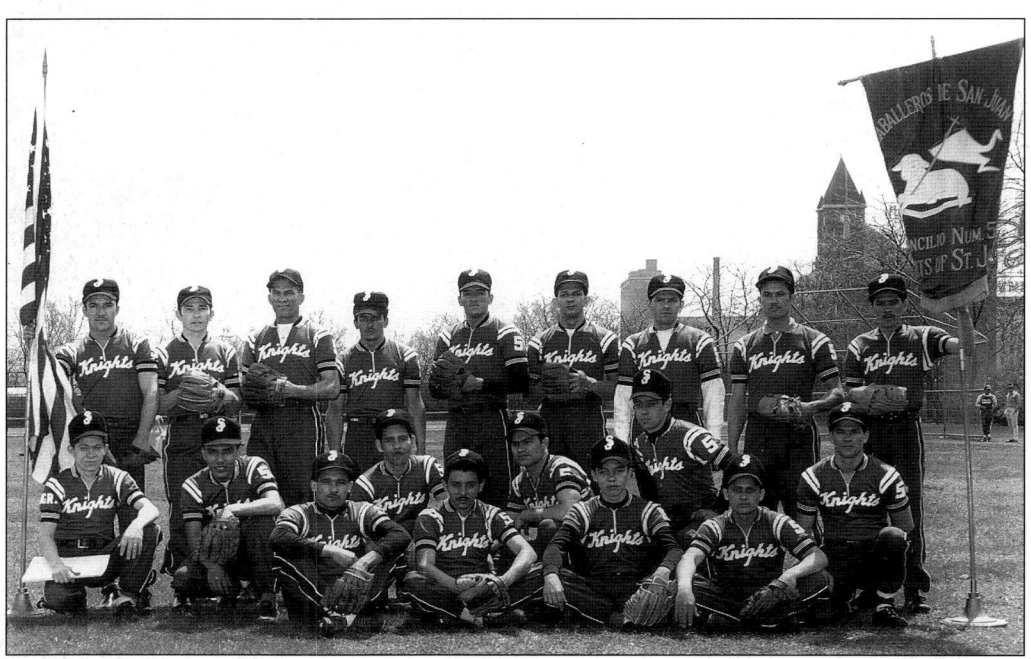

One of the baseball teams of Los Caballeros de San Juan. The team is holding the organization's banner along with the American flag. The organization was devoted to assimilating Puerto Ricans to American ways, and to adopting an American style of Catholicism. The organization worked hard to convince Chicagoans that newly arriving Puerto Ricans were decent, religious, family-oriented people. (Courtesy Los Caballeros de San Juan Credit Union.)

Cafe Central opened in 1954 and is one of the first Puerto Rican restaurants in Chicago. The restaurant catered to single Puerto Rican men working as factory laborers in the 1950s. The restaurant extended credit to the men. Pictured here is Rafael Cruz. His uncle and father owned the restaurant previously. Today, Rafael Cruz and his wife are the owners. The restaurant is located on Chicago and Bishop, and while few Puerto Ricans live in the gentrified neighborhood, they still patronize the restaurant. (Photo Wilfredo Cruz.)

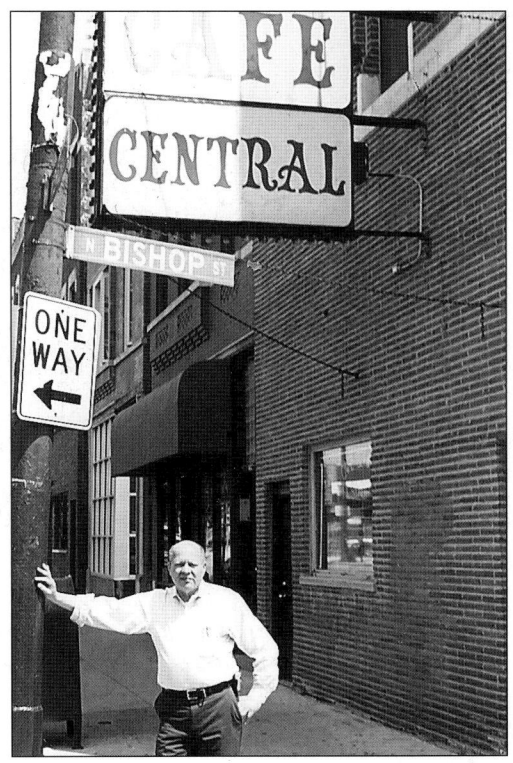

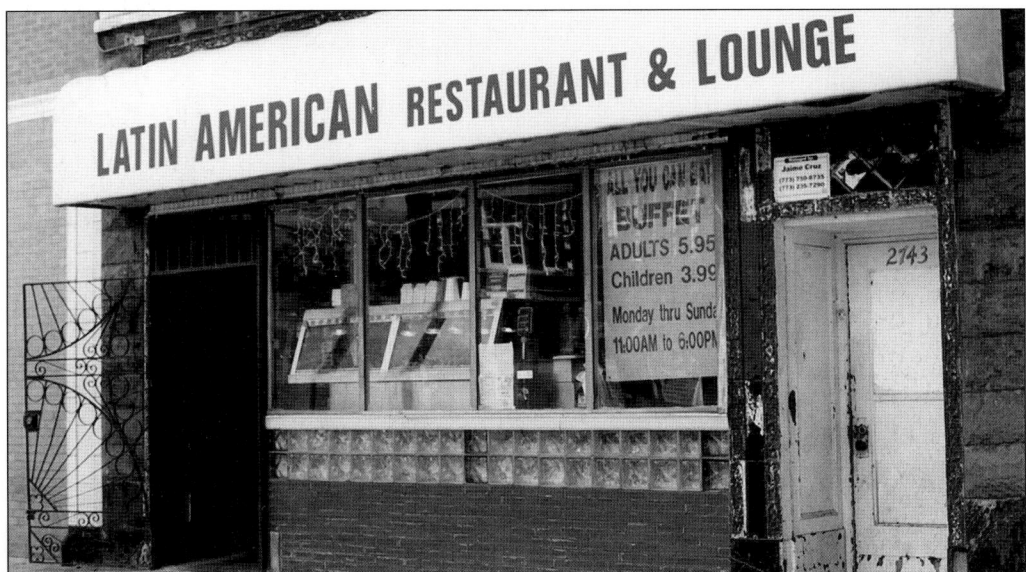

A favorite Puerto Rican restaurant is Latin American Restaurant in the Humboldt Park neighborhood. The restaurant was founded in 1959, and has been open at the same location ever since. It is popular for its delicious inexpensive Puerto Rican cuisine. Three generations have owned the restaurant. The current owners are Jaime and Yolanda Cruz. The owners completely renovated the restaurant's inside, and soon plan to renovate the outside. (Photo Wilfredo Cruz.)

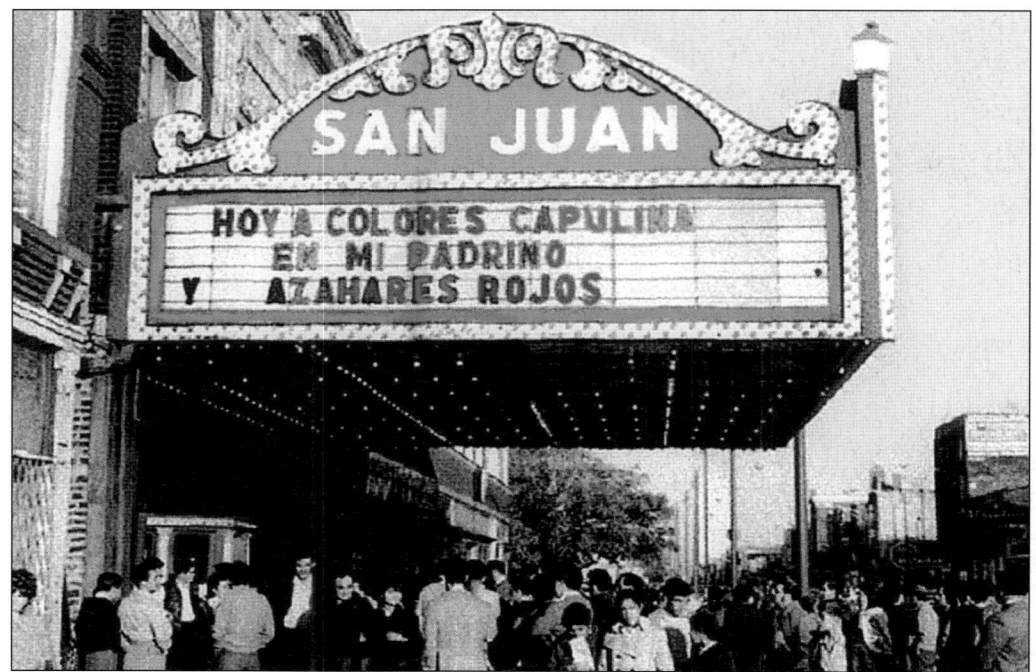

The San Juan was a popular Puerto Rican neighborhood theater on Division Street near Damen Avenue. The theater featured Spanish films from Puerto Rico and Mexico. The theater also featured live performances by famous Puerto Rican and Mexican musicians. This photo was taken in 1970. The theater no longer exists. (Courtesy Carlos Flores.)

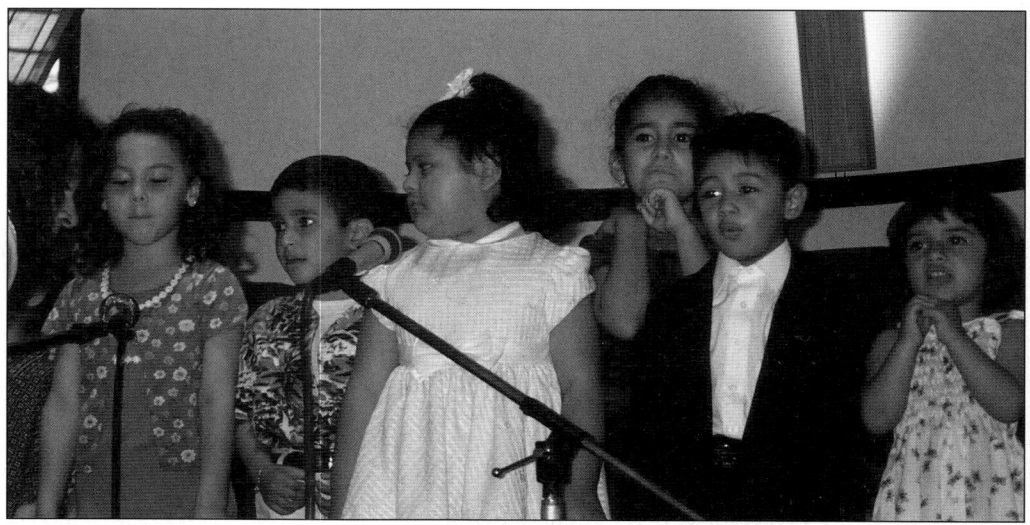

Puerto Rican children learn to appreciate other Latino cultures in Chicago. The children are from La Progresiva Pre-School, housed in the Primera Iglesia Hispana Unida de Cristo in the Logan Square neighborhood. The children are participating in a Christmas Party in 2000. Pictured, from left to right, are: Jenal Ortiz, of white and Puerto Rican background; Norma Reyes, Puerto Rican; Kathenne Flores, Guatemalan; Shelice Cartagena, Puerto Rican; Jeffery Medrano, Mexican; and Carmen Rodriguez, Columbian. (Courtesy Ivette Rosario.)

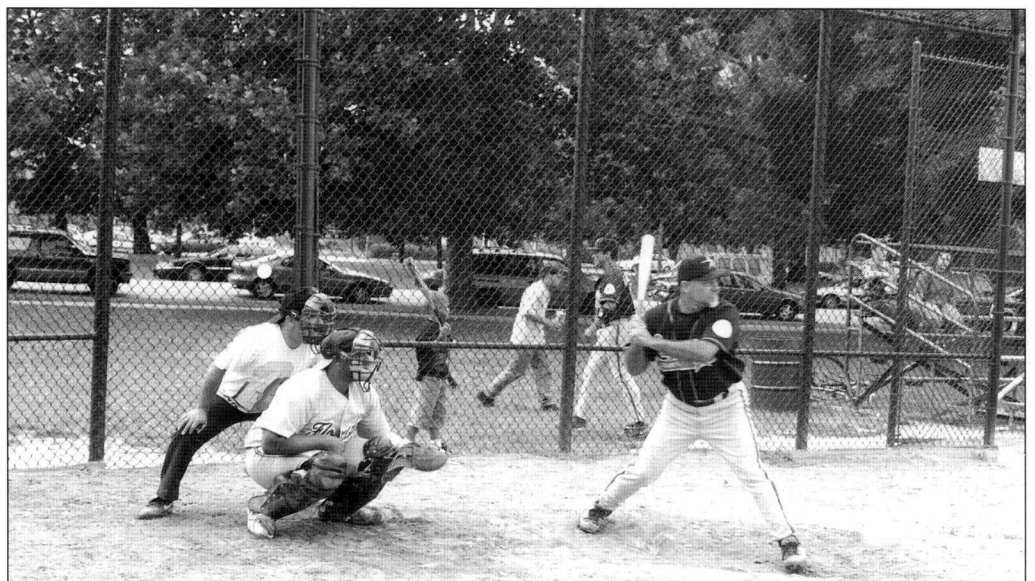

During the summer months, organized Puerto Rican baseball teams play against each other on baseball diamonds throughout Humboldt Park. Friends and family in the bleachers cheer them on. In the middle of the Humboldt Park neighborhood sits Humboldt Park with 206 acres of lagoons, trees, and gardens. The park was named for Alexander von Humboldt, a German naturalist and author. (Photo Wilfredo Cruz.)

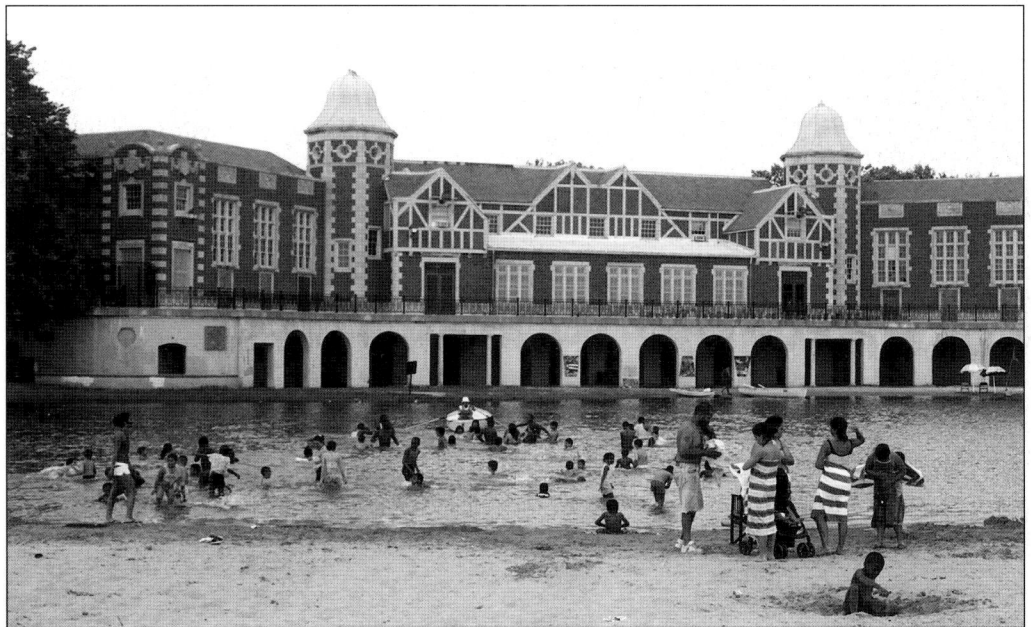

Puerto Rican and African American families enjoy a swim at the man-made beach in Humboldt Park. The park's distinctive field house is in the background. Famous park planner, Jens Jensen, played a big role in designing the park, which opened in 1877. (Photo Wilfredo Cruz.)

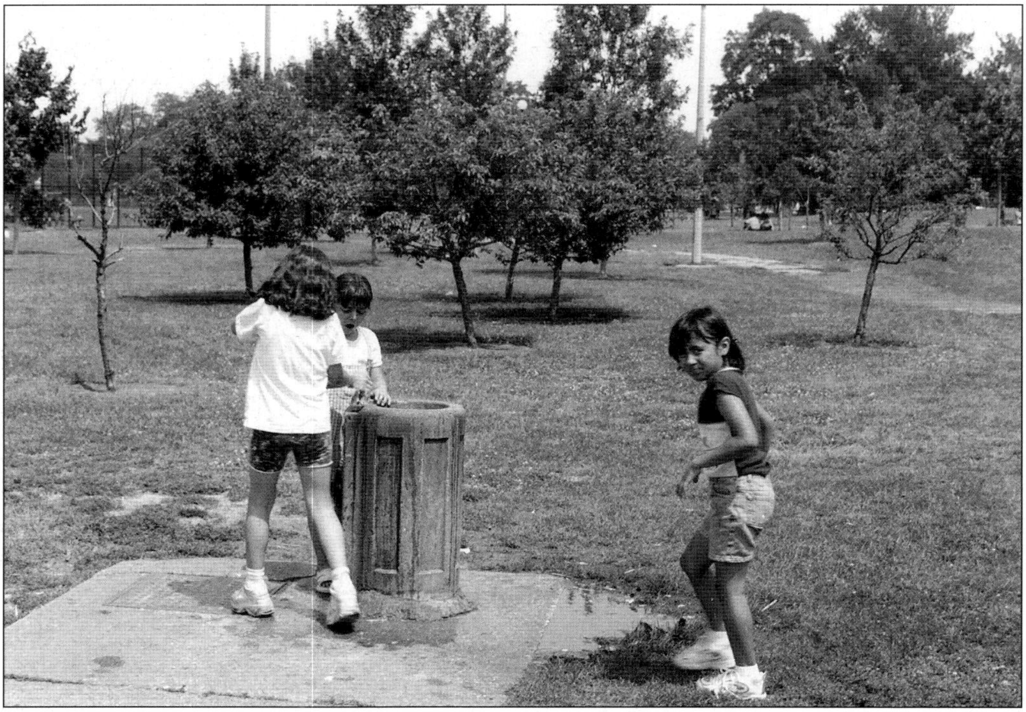

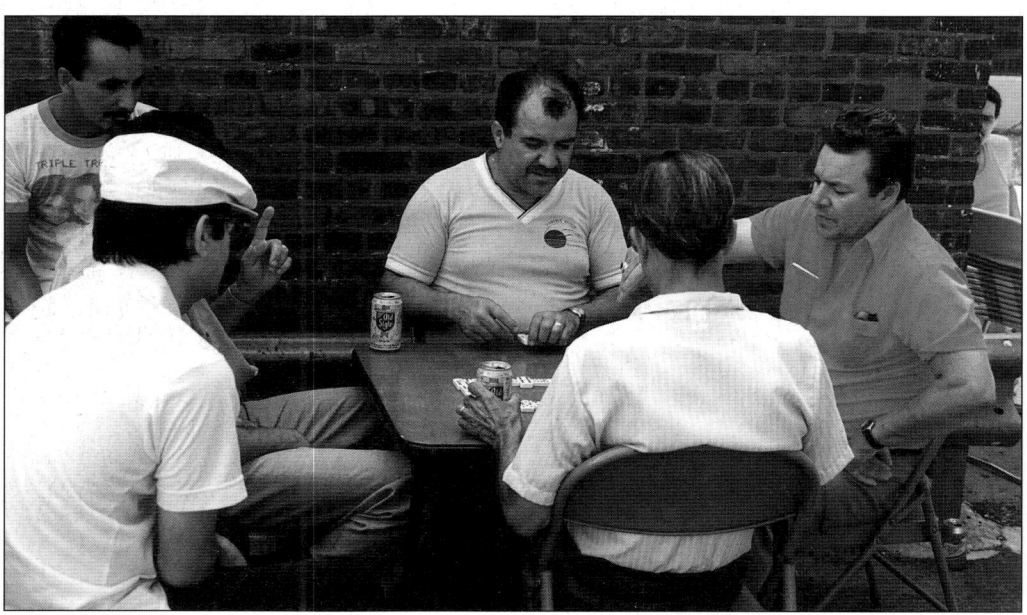

Unidentified Puerto Rican and Mexican girls drink water and splash each other to cool off on a hot 2000 summer in Humboldt Park. (Photo Wilfredo Cruz.)

Unidentified Puerto Rican and Cuban men play dominoes and drink beer in Humboldt Park in the 1980s. Puerto Ricans love playing dominoes with family and friends. The men play either as teams or against each other. (Courtesy Antonio Villalobos.)

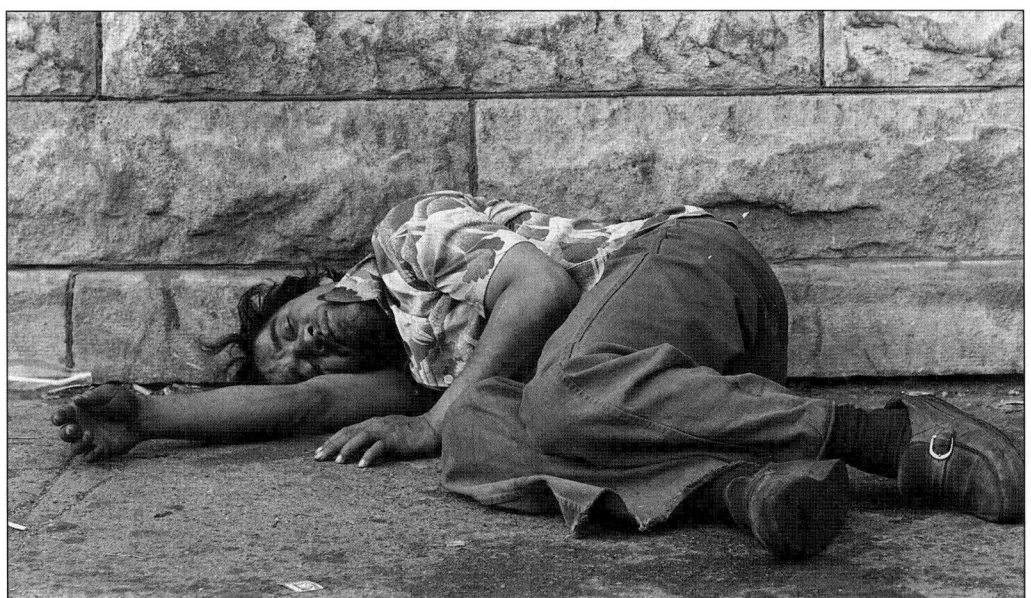

An unidentified man sleeps on the sidewalk in the Humboldt Park neighborhood in the early 1970s. Alcoholism, homelessness, and drug abuse are still social problems that affect some members of the Puerto Rican community. (Photo Jaime Rivera. Courtesy Aspira Inc. of Illinois.)

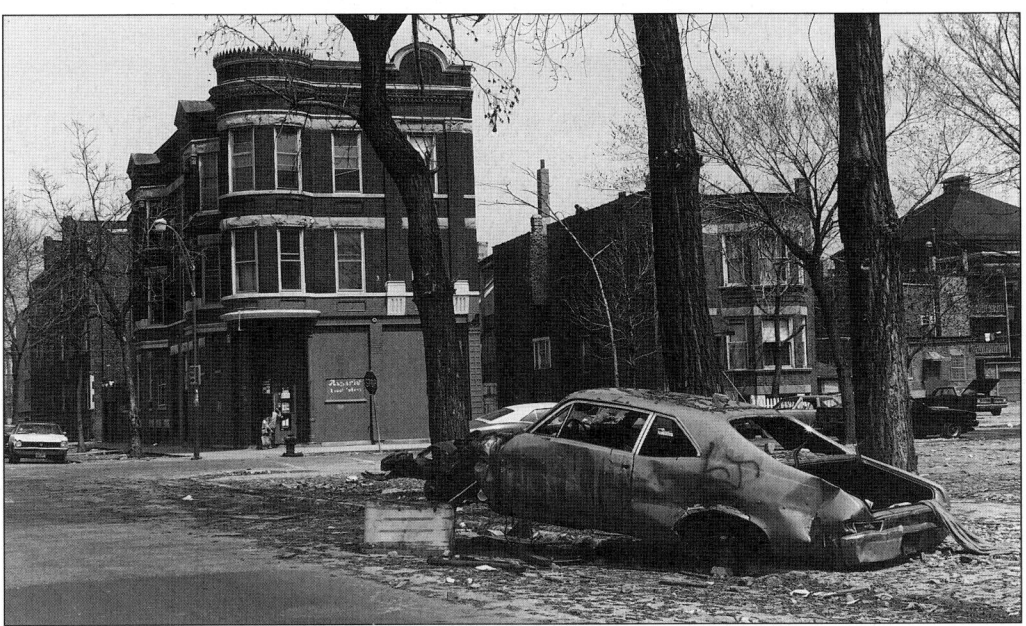

A burned car sits on an empty lot where a large apartment building once stood. In the late 1970s, many buildings were burned throughout the Humboldt Park neighborhood. Many suspected it was an "arson for profit" scheme, in which slum landlords paid individuals to deliberately torch the buildings. By burning the buildings the landlords rid themselves of dilapidated property and collected large sums of money from insurance companies. (Photo Jaime Rivera. Courtesy Aspira Inc. of Illinois.)

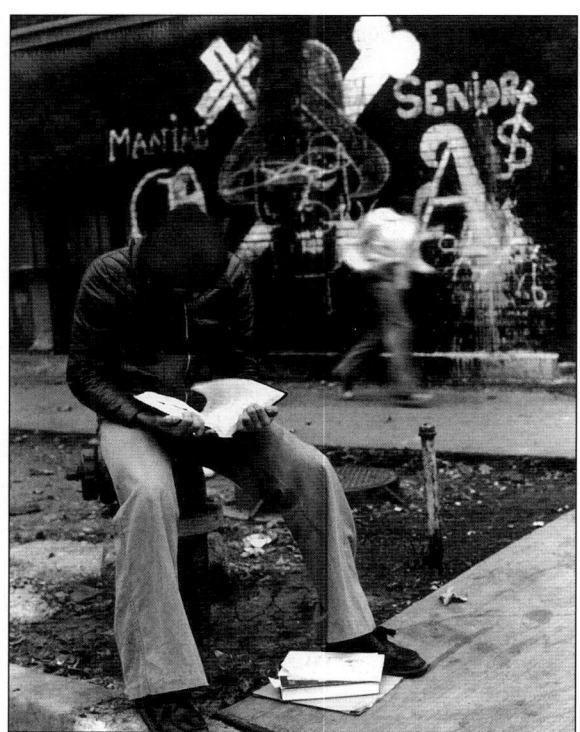

A student from Tuley High School in the Humboldt Park neighborhood reads a book in the early 1970s. He is surrounded by dirty lots, broken glass, gang graffiti, and broken sidewalks. (Courtesy Jaime Rivera.)

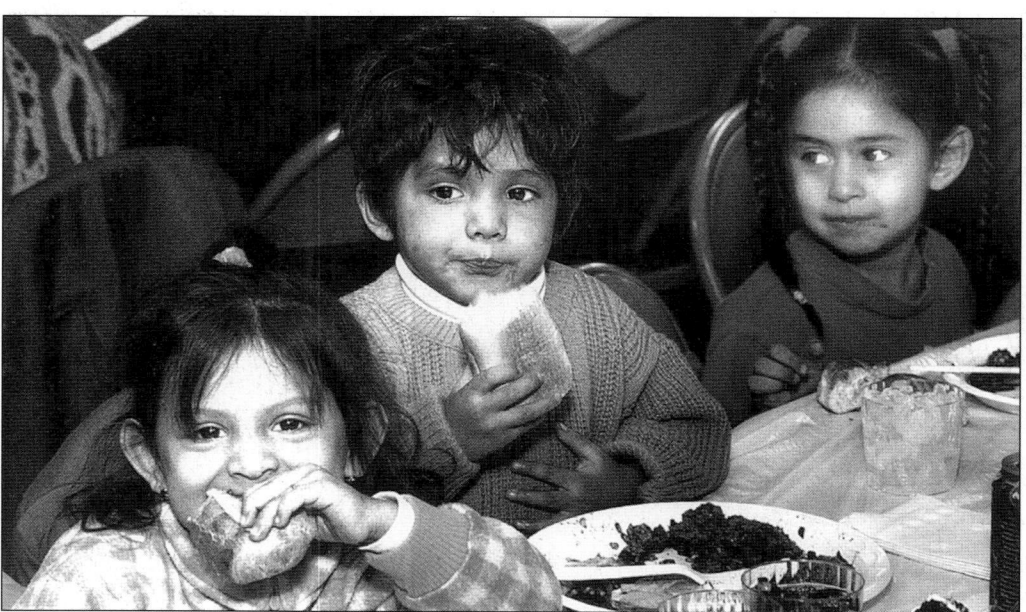

Puerto Rican children have dinner in a church basement. The event was an all-day "feed the needy and homeless," sponsored by San Lucas United Church of Christ in the Humboldt Park community, held on January 6, 1998. January 6 is "Dia De Los Reyes Magos" (Three Kings Day) when families in Puerto Rico traditionally observe Christmas. (Courtesy Carmen Flores and San Lucas United Church of Christ.)

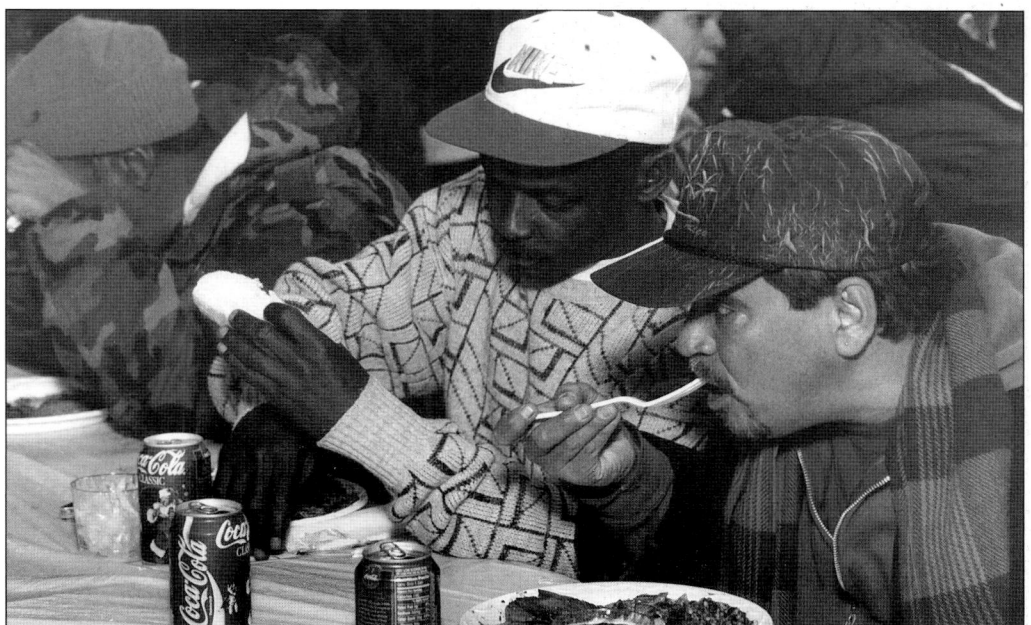

Puerto Rican and African American men eat dinner at the all-day "feed the needy and homeless," sponsored by San Lucas United Church of Christ on January 6, 1998. (Courtesy Carmen Flores and San Lucas United Church of Christ.)

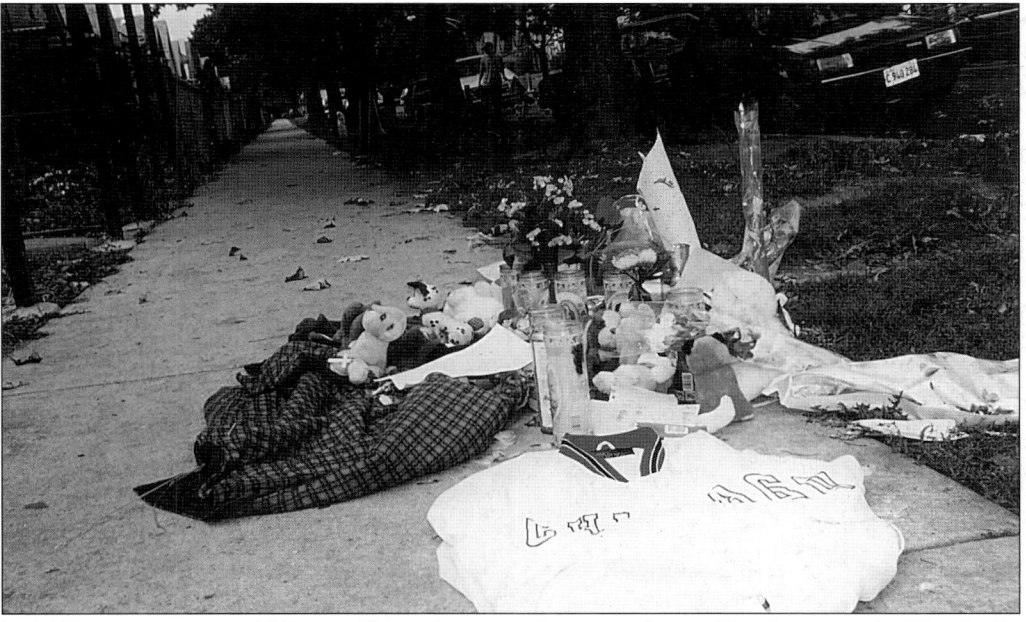

In 1998, a seven-year-old Puerto Rican boy was playing in front of his home in the Humboldt Park neighborhood. A group of gang members in a car shot at young men walking on the sidewalk. The bullets missed them, but one bullet struck and killed the innocent boy. Community residents place gifts on the spot where the boy was killed. The gifts include poems, candles, flowers, teddy-bears, and a jacket. (Courtesy *La Raza*.)

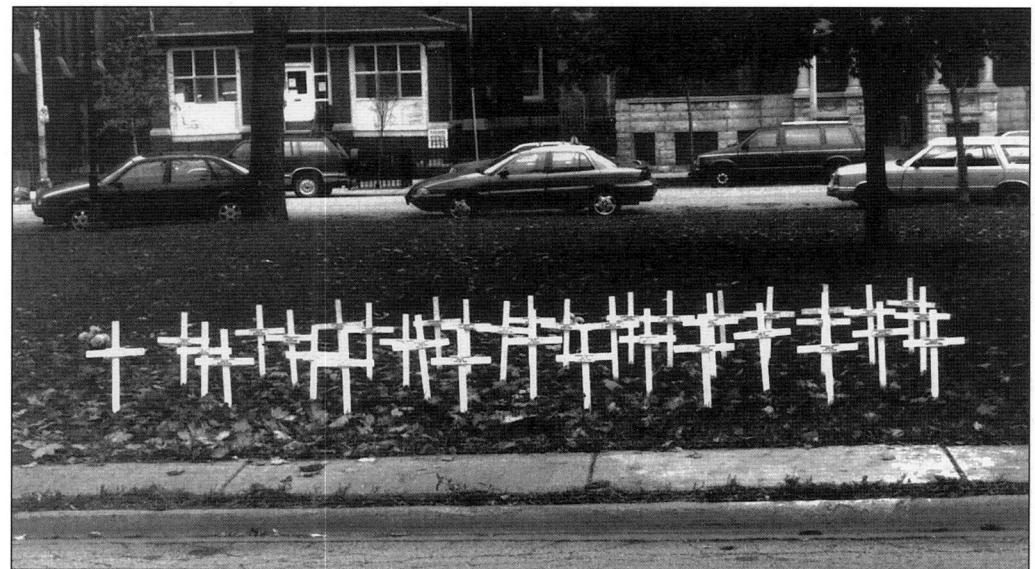

A memorial is placed near St. Sylvester's Catholic parish in the Logan Square neighborhood in 1998. The crosses represent people in the neighborhood killed by acts of violence during the year. The violence includes gang violence as well as domestic and family violence. The Alliance of Logan Square Organizations (ALSO) sponsors the annual memorial. ALSO is a coalition of agencies serving children and families in the area. (Photo Wilfredo Cruz.)

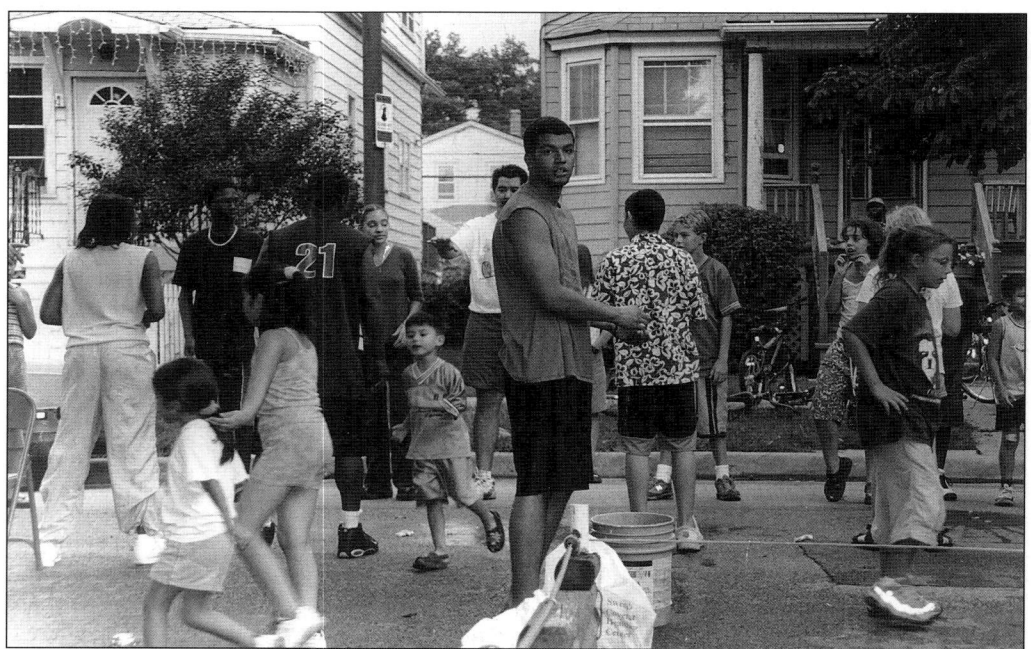

Puerto Rican, African American, and Mexican families enjoy an annual 2002 block party on the 4200 block of Central Park. The block party is an opportunity for neighbors to become better acquainted. The party featured kids' games, rides, hotdogs, hamburgers, pastries, and soda. (Courtesy Alexandra Cruz.)

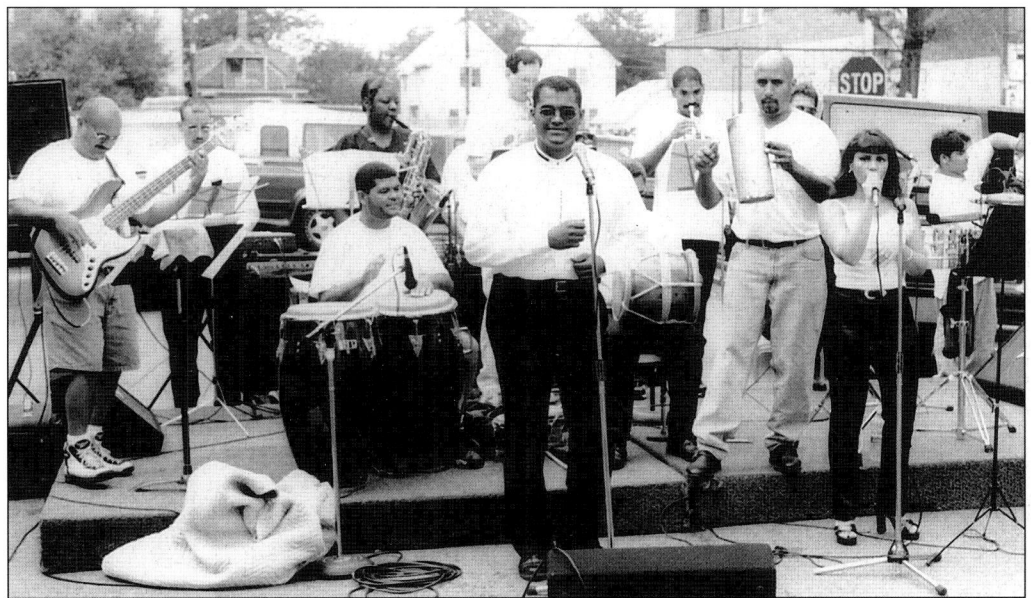

A local Puerto Rican music group entertains the crowd with the hot sounds of salsa. The group was playing music as part of a 1998 block party in the 2500 block of West Haddon in the Humboldt Park neighborhood. Many residents got out of their chairs and danced in the streets. (Photo Wilfredo Cruz.)

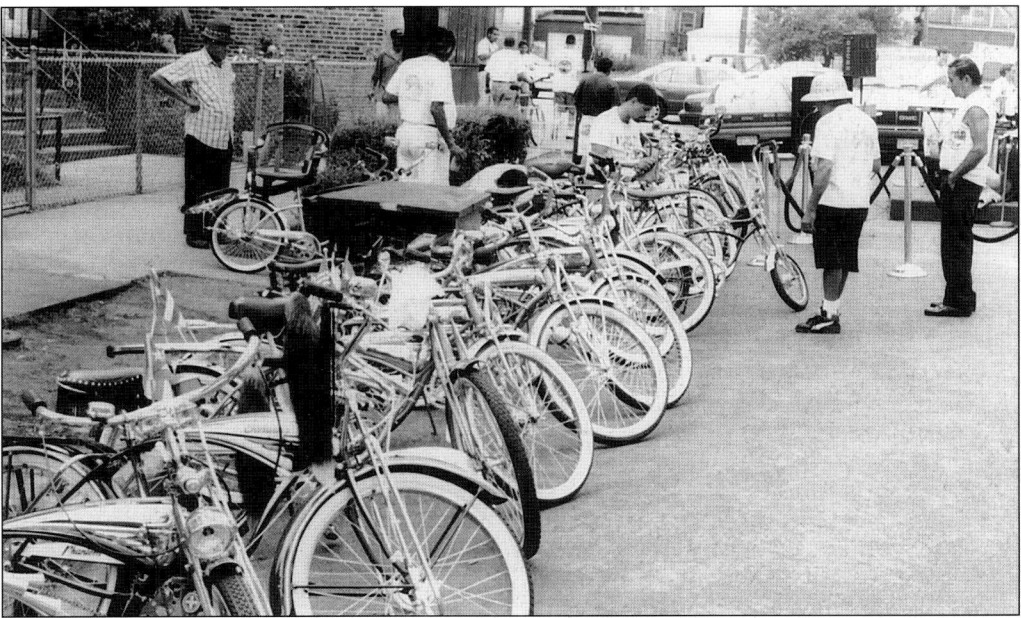

Renovated bicycles of the Just Cruising Bicycle Club are seen here during a 1998 block party in the 2500 block of West Haddon. The club's members are mainly middle-aged Puerto Ricans who enjoy renovating and riding older bikes. All the bicycles were made by the Schwinn Bicycle Company, which for years was based in Chicago. The Chicago office closed and moved the business to Colorado. (Photo Wilfredo Cruz.)

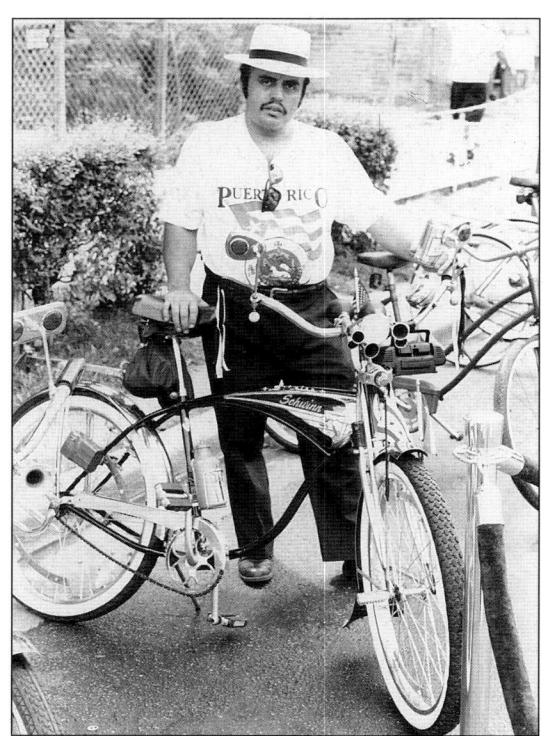

Isac Pacheco is a member of the Just Cruising Bicycle Club. He proudly shows off his renovated classic 1960s Schwinn bicycle. Members invest hundreds, sometimes thousands, of dollars in upgrading and renovating the bicycles. Pacheco enjoys riding with fellow members in ethnic parades, or by himself throughout the community. (Photo Wilfredo Cruz.)

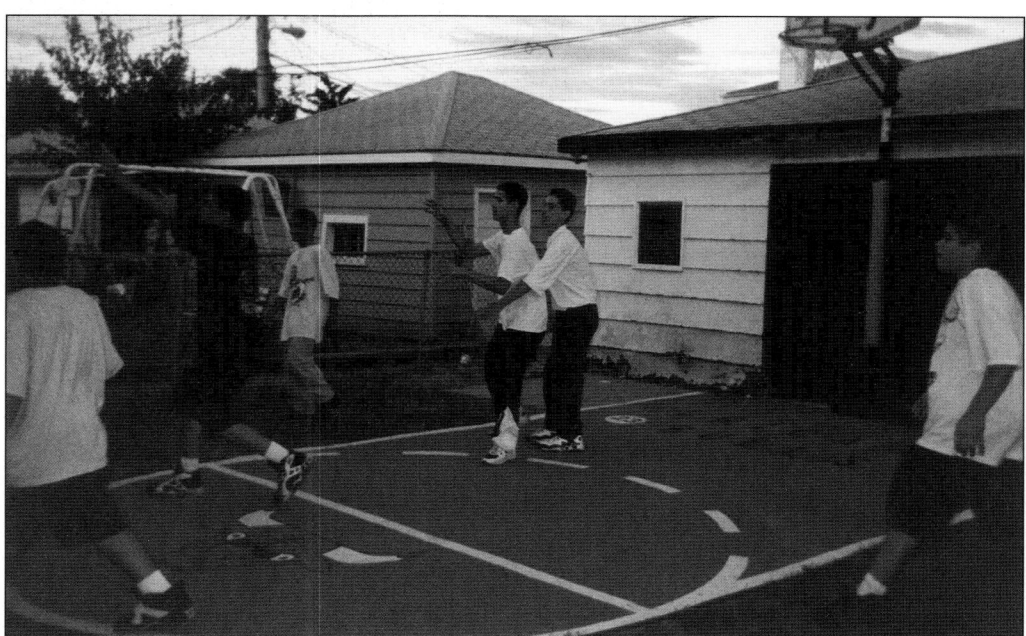

Jose Peña, a Puerto Rican father, designed this basketball court in his backyard. Playing basketball in the yard keeps his children close by and off the streets. The home is in the 2100 block of North Mulligan. Neighborhood youth are invited to drop by and play basketball. (Courtesy Jose and Irene Peña.)

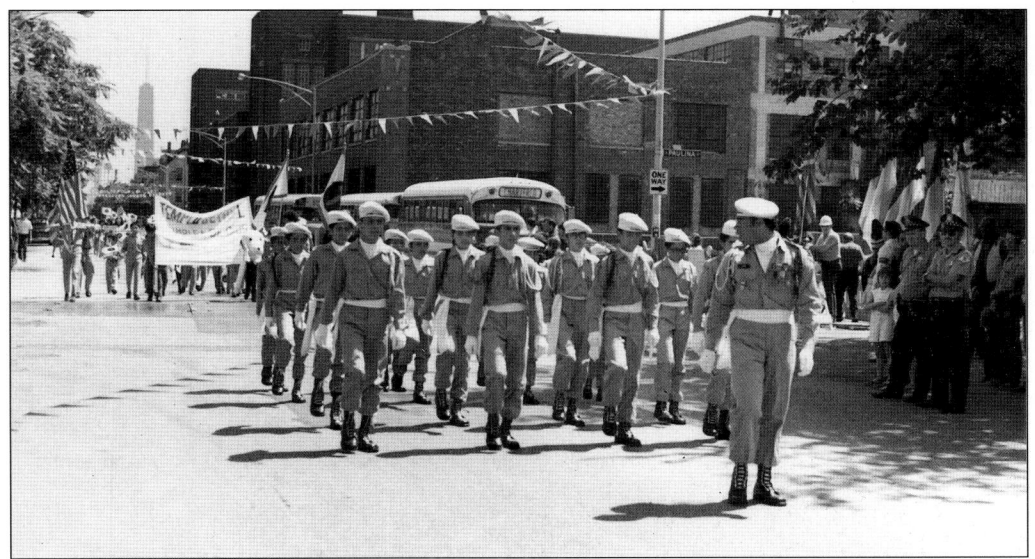

Jose Peña (lead marcher) is a former Chicago Public School teacher and currently a Chicago police officer. He has always enjoyed working with neighborhood children, and steering them in positive directions. He organized neighborhood youth into a drill team called the Junior Berets. The group is shown here marching in a local parade in 1972. (Courtesy Jose and Irene Peña.)

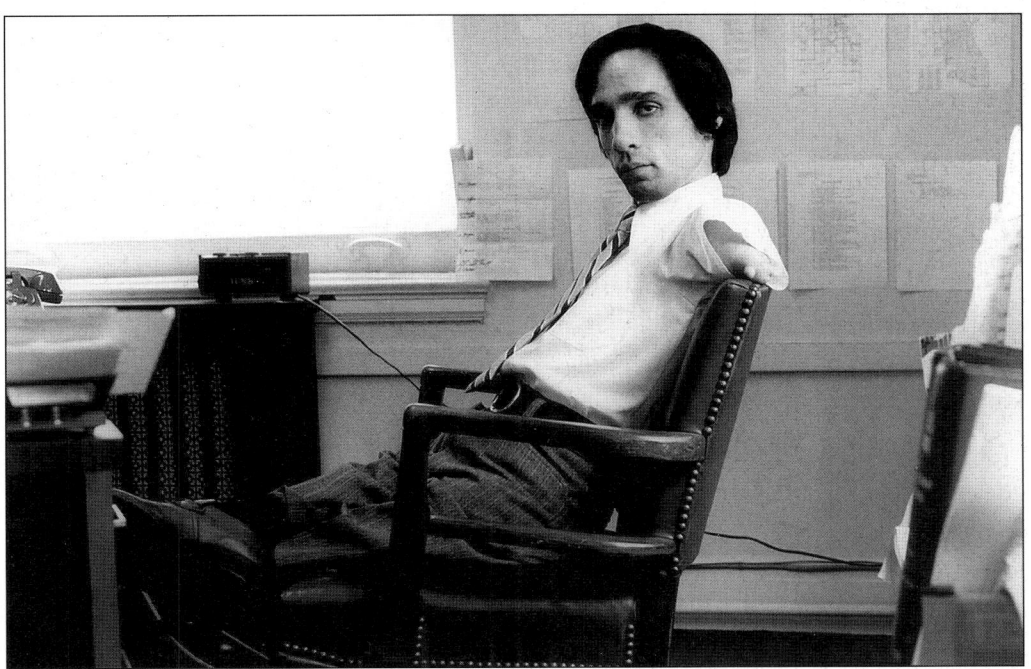

Hiram Zayas, shown here in 1970, was born with physical disabilities. He lived for many years in Chicago. Zayas graduated from college and writes and uses a computer with his feet. He designed a steering wheel device and pedals which allows him to drive his van. He now lives in Buffalo, Michigan where he runs a residential center for people with mental and physical disabilities. (Courtesy Tomas V. Sanabria.)

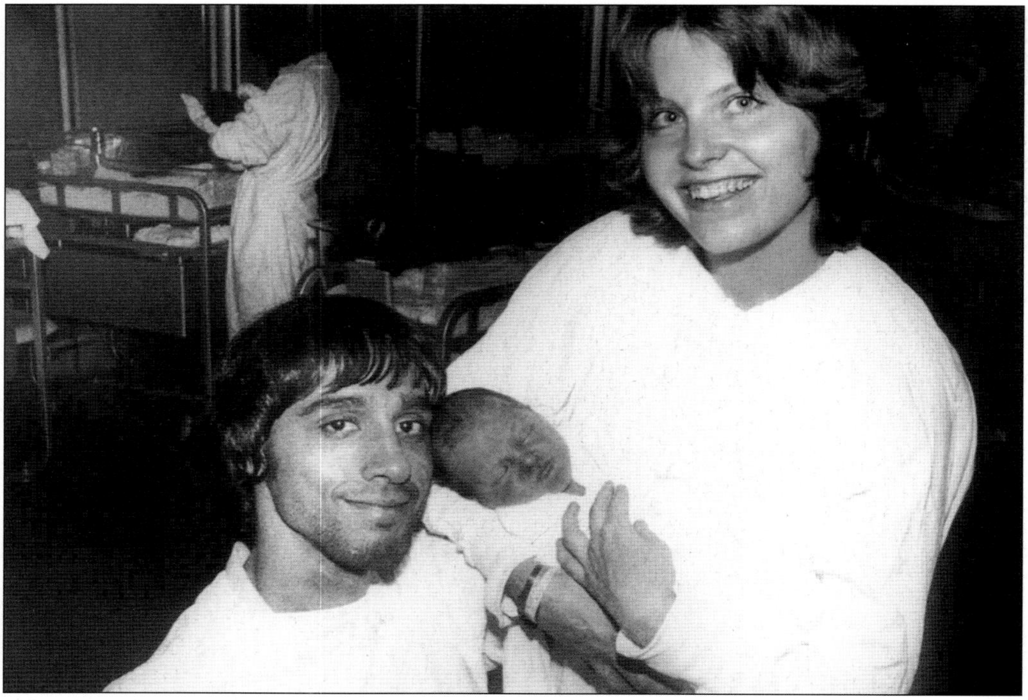

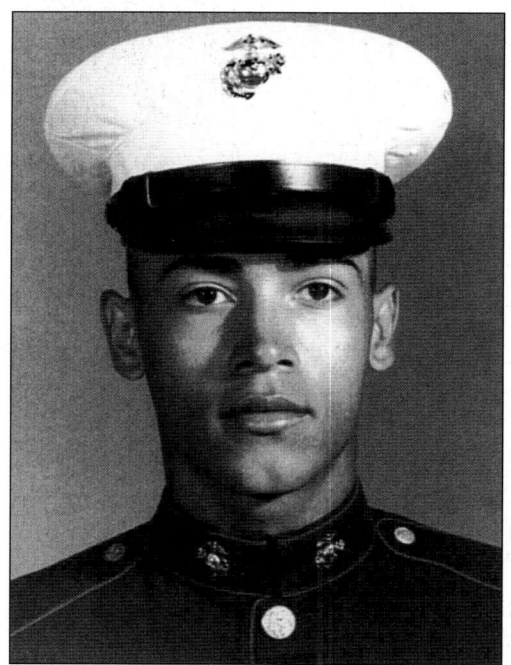

Hiram Zayas never used his physical disabilities as an excuse for not trying to accomplish his life's goals. He is pictured here with his former wife and newborn daughter in the late 1980s. He has three children. He enjoys sailing his boat and on weekends he drives from Michigan to Chicago to visit family and friends. (Courtesy Tomas V. Sanabria.)

Puerto Ricans have served with distinction in all branches of the United States military. Johnny Lopez served in the United States Marine Corps. He did four years in Vietnam and participated in two tours of battle. He was awarded two Purple Hearts for being wounded in battle. He made the rank of sergeant. He worked for 32 years in the federal bank reserve. He retired in 2004. (Courtesy Efrain López.)

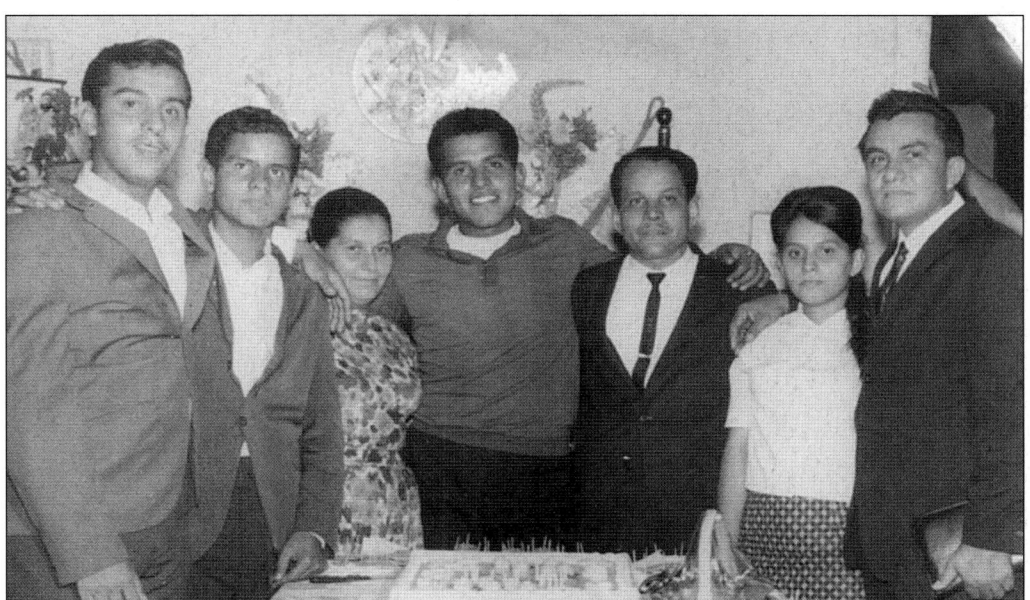

Jose Velgrara (center) joined the United States Marine Corps at age 17 in 1964. He served for four years and did three tours of battle in Vietnam. He was a helicopter machine gunner. He made the rank of sergeant. Velgrara is shown here in 1965 with his mother, father, brothers, sister, and uncle. The family is celebrating his safe return home after a year in Vietnam. (Courtesy Jose Velgrara)

Pictured here in the early 1960s are three brothers who served in the United States military. From left to right, are Edwin, Monserrate, and William Diaz. Edwin served in the U.S. Air Force for 30 years, obtaining the rank of chief master sergeant. He saw action in Vietnam and Desert Storm. Monserrate served for eight years in the U.S. Air Force, and retired from the Army National Guard with the rank of sergeant. William served for 14 months in Vietnam with the U. S. Marine Corps. He served another four years in the Marine reserves, and earned the rank of sergeant. (Courtesy Hilda Frontany.)

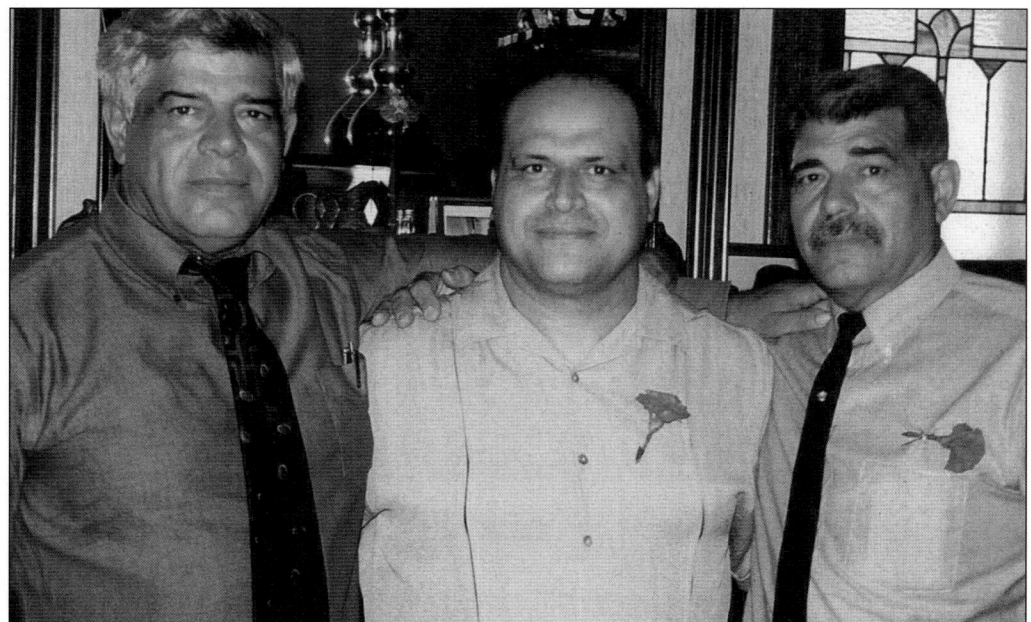

The three brothers, pictured on the previous page, are seen here as they appear today. Pictured, from left to right, are William, Monserrate, and Edwin Diaz. William and Edwin live in Florida. Monserrate lives in New Hampshire. (Courtesy Hilda Frontany.)

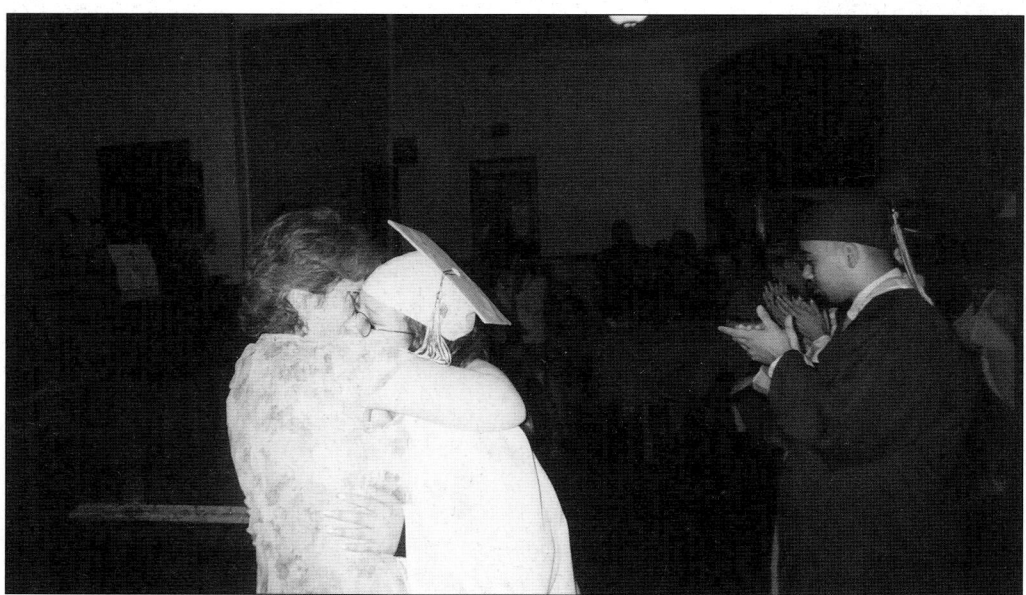

A mother proudly hugs her daughter, Leonarda Lazo, after she receives her high school diploma from the Antonia Pantoja High School. The alternative high school is run by Aspira Inc. of Illinois for youth who drop out of regular high school but decide to return to school. Aspira helps Puerto Rican youth finish high school and enter college. Antonia Pantoja, a Puerto Rican educator, started Aspira in New York in the1960s. Other Aspira chapters were formed later in six major cities, including Chicago. (Courtesy Aspira Inc. of Illinois.)

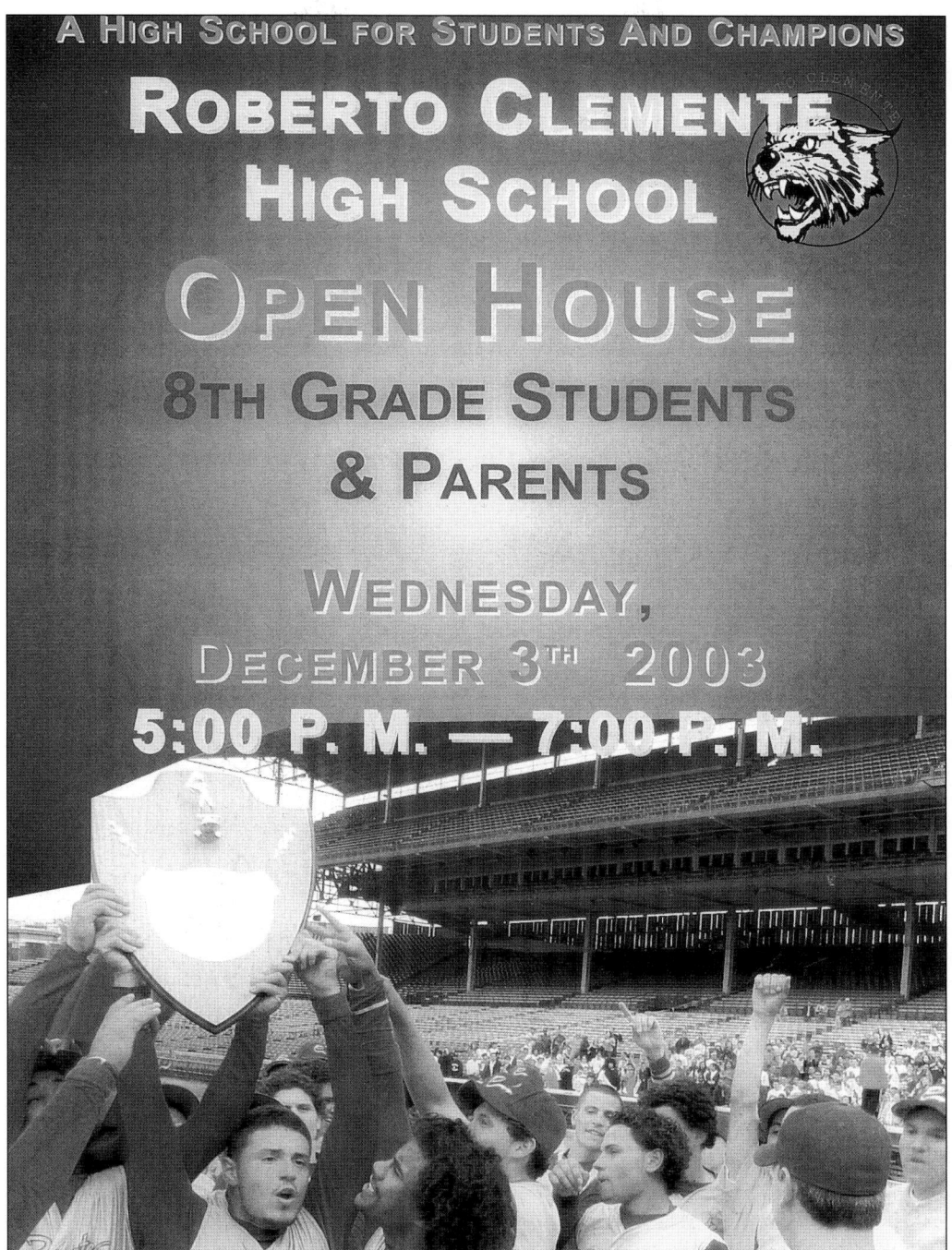

Ever since Roberto Clemente High School opened in 1973, it has put together a formidable baseball team. The school's team has won ten city championships since 1974. The majority of the youth on the baseball team are Puerto Rican. Pictured here is a recruitment poster for the school, showing the school's team winning the city championship in baseball in 2003 at Wrigley Field. (Courtesy Roberto Clemente High School.)

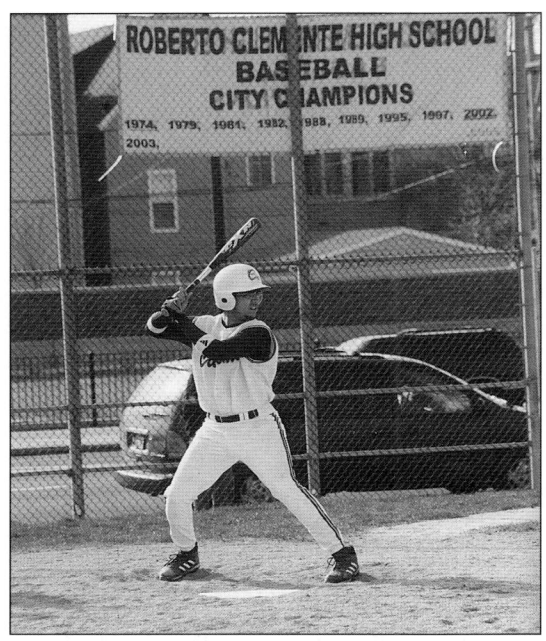

An unidentified member of the Roberto Clemente High School baseball team takes batting practice in the baseball diamond adjacent to the school. The banner displays the school's ten city championships. "Our baseball coaches, Rich Tomleoni and Dave Bain, have done wonders with our baseball team and our kids. We are so proud of our kids," says one administrator at the school. (Courtesy Roberto Clemente High School.)

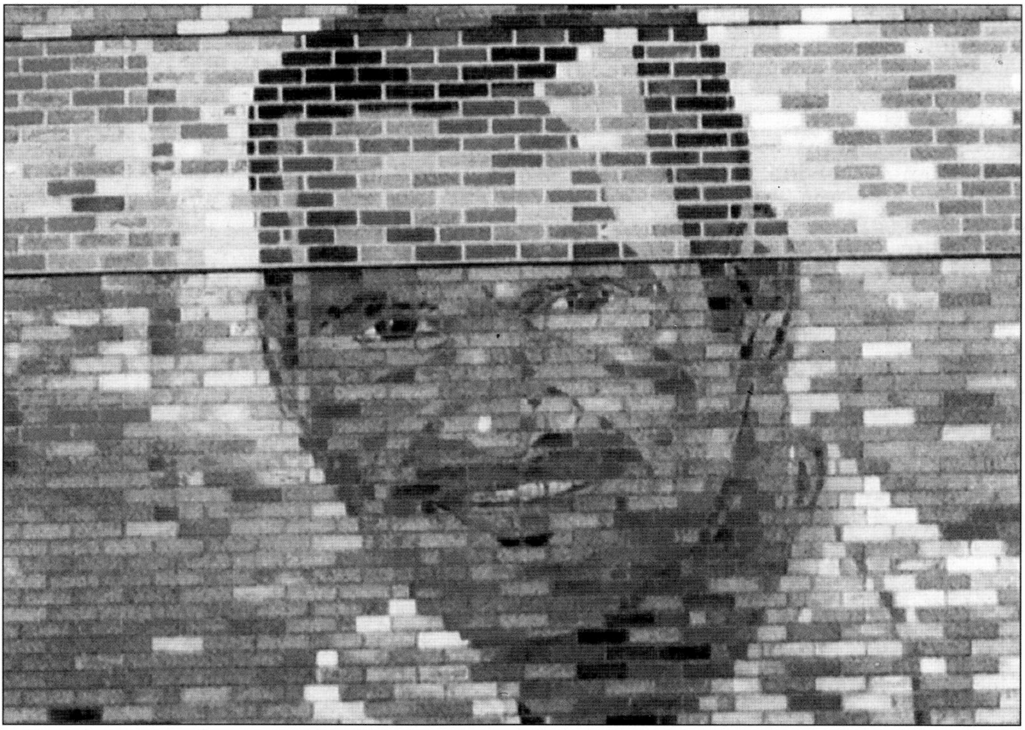

This is an artistic rendering of the late great baseball player and humanitarian, Roberto Clemente. The artistic mural is baked into the brick of the Roberto Clemente High School gymnasium at Division and Western Avenues. Pablo Marcano, an artist from Puerto Rico, created the mural. (Courtesy Puerto Rican Cultural Center.)

Four

RELIGION

Puerto Ricans are mainly Roman Catholic. The Archdiocese of Chicago first reached out to Puerto Ricans in Chicago in the late 1940s under the leadership of Auxiliary Bishop Bernard Sheil, founder of the Catholic Youth Organization. This group maintained its club house at Congress and Wabash Streets. The organization started a Puerto Rican project to deal with housing, employment, and health problems. It also provided recreational events, such as a weekly dance. By 1947 the Sociedad Catolica Puertorriqueña had been founded in Chicago under the auspices of the Catholic Youth Organization. It's not clear, however,

In 1955, the Archdiocese of Chicago set up the Cardinal's Committee for the Spanish Speaking. Under the direction of Rev. Gilbert Carroll and Rev. Leo T. Mahon, this group worked closely with Chicago's Puerto Rican community. However, to the great dismay of the Puerto Rican community, the first decision of the Cardinal's Committee for the Spanish Speaking was to rule out the building of any national parishes for Puerto Ricans. The Cardinal's Committee believed national parishes would prevent the assimilation of Puerto Ricans. They wanted Puerto Ricans to assimilate quickly into American Catholicism and culture. Also, after World War II, church officials were following their flock to the suburbs. Church officials believed any newly constructed city parishes might quickly become white elephants.

Unlike other ethnic groups, Puerto Ricans came to Chicago without their own priests. Thus, the Cardinal's Committee for the Spanish Speaking was composed mainly of white priests. Puerto Ricans found some of the white priests to be paternalistic. However Puerto Ricans respected other priests, such as Rev. Leo T. Mahon and Rev. Donald Headley. But even Rev. Mahon and Rev. Headley did not understand that Puerto Ricans, like previous waves of ethnic Catholic immigrants to the city, wanted their own ethnic parish—they wanted a national parish that provided a sense of community, maintained their language and culture, and validated their unique experience.

Traditionally, the ethnic parish was an effective institution that helped waves of immigrants adjust to a new and often hostile society. But Chicago's Catholic Church did not offer Puerto Ricans—American citizens by birth—a single ethnic parish of their own. Instead, Puerto Ricans were encouraged to attend existing neighborhood parishes. During the 1950s and 1960s, some white parishes refused to welcome Puerto Ricans. They viewed Puerto Ricans as foreigners who did not speak English or assimilate to American ways. Puerto Ricans wandered around the city looking for parishes that would welcome them.

Despite misunderstandings with the Catholic Church, the majority of Puerto Ricans remained loyal Catholics. But a good number of Puerto Ricans drifted from a Catholic Church they saw as cold and distant. Even today, Puerto Ricans are increasingly converting to Protestant denominations, becoming Adventists, Jehovah's Witnesses, and evangelical Pentecostals.

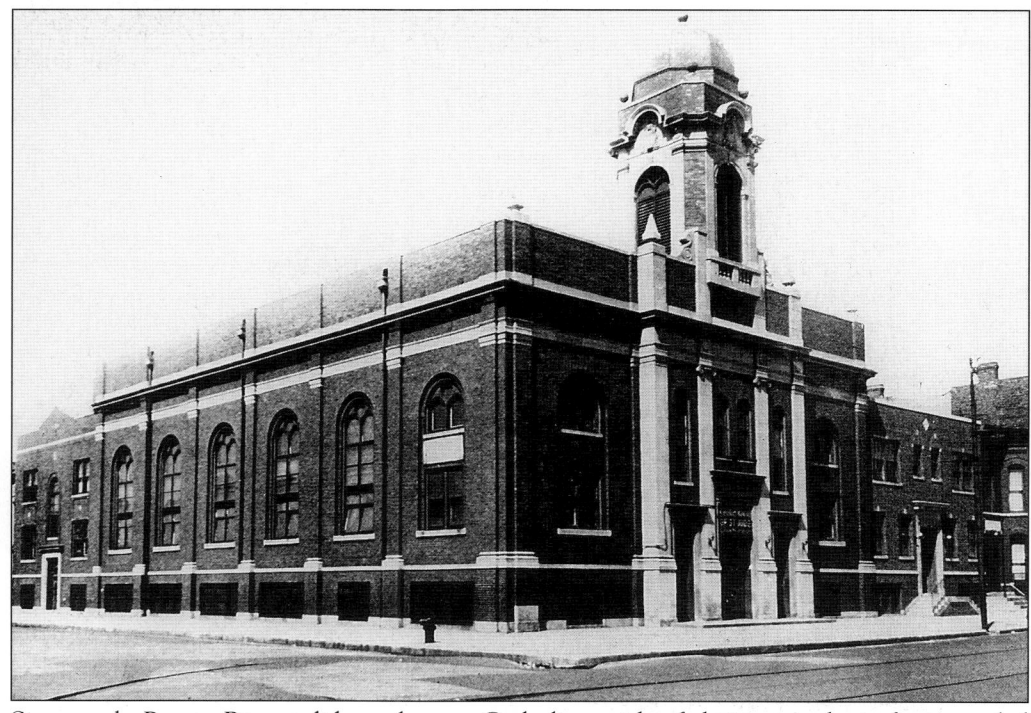

Since early Puerto Ricans did not have a Catholic parish of their own, they often traveled across the city to attend Sunday mass at Our Lady of Guadalupe Church on 91st Street and Brandon in South Chicago. The parish, built in 1928, is one of the oldest Mexican parishes in the midwest. Puerto Ricans were pleased that priests at the church spoke Spanish. Numerous Puerto Ricans were married at the church. (Courtesy Southeast Historical Society.)

Some early Puerto Ricans attended St. Francisco of Assisi Catholic Church at 813 W. Roosevelt Road. The parish was once an Italian church, but by the early 1930s, Mexicans had claimed it as their own. Puerto Rican couples were married in the church. Others attended Spanish language masses and received the Catholic sacraments. Even today, some Puerto Rican families attend Sunday mass at the parish. (Courtesy St. Francisco of Assisi.)

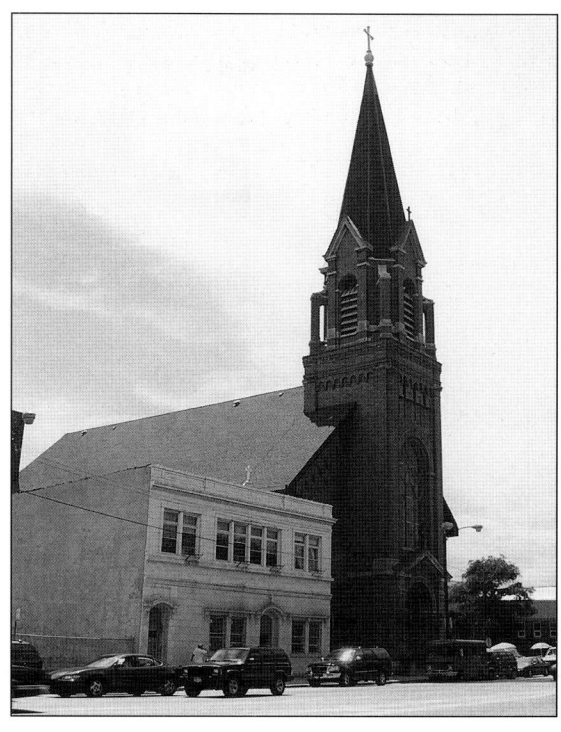

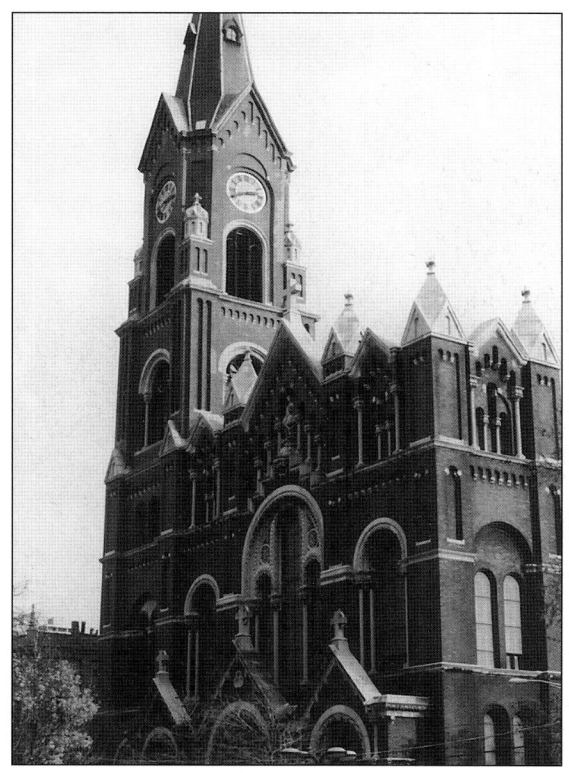

Puerto Ricans living in the Lincoln Park neighborhood in the late 1950s and early 1960s attended St. Michael's Roman Catholic Church at Cleveland and North Avenue. For a brief time, Puerto Ricans were provided Sunday mass in the church's hallway, away from white parishioners in the main church. Some families still come from across the city to attend the parish's Sunday mass. (Photo Wilfredo Cruz.)

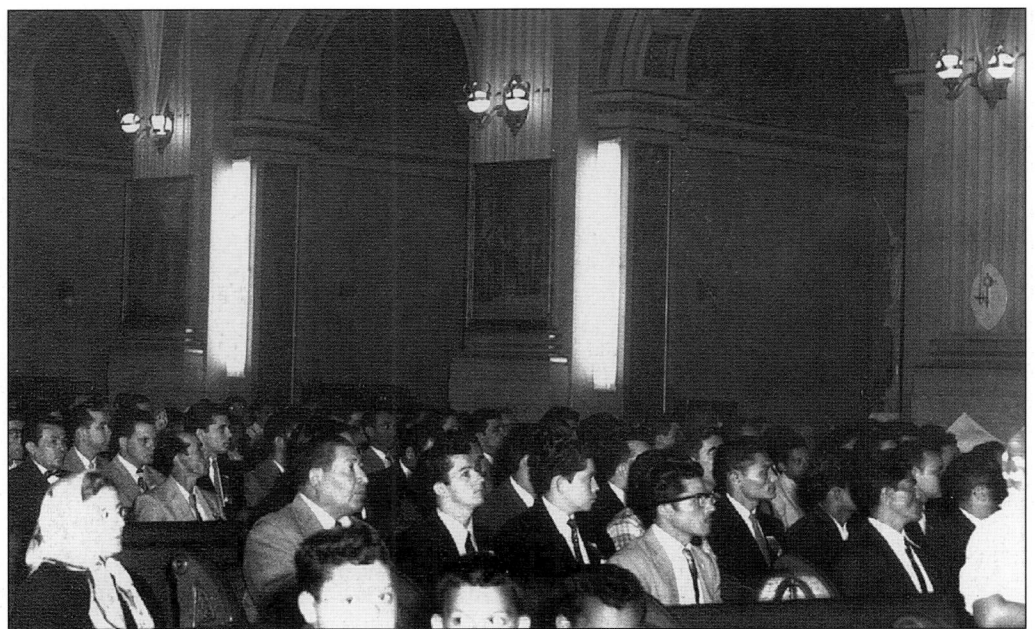

Members of Council Three of Los Caballeros de San Juan attend mass in 1961. The mass is at St. Michael's Church. Los Caballeros de San Juan was a Puerto Rican religious organization composed of 12 councils. (Courtesy Cesareo and Luz Maria Rivera.)

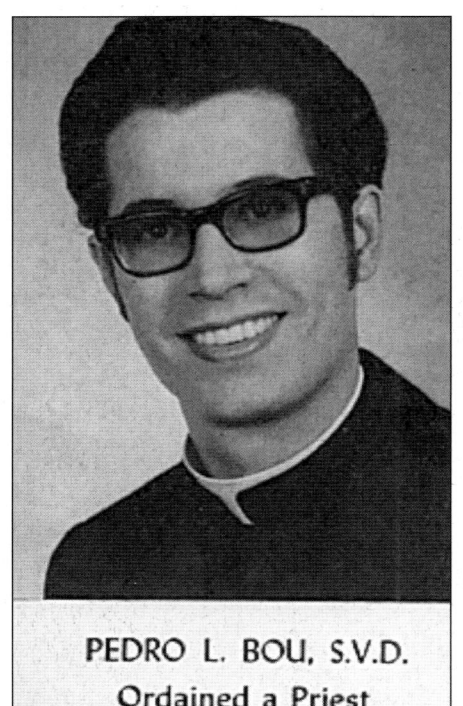

PEDRO L. BOU, S.V.D.
Ordained a Priest
December 21, 1974

Rev. Pedro L Bou was probably the first Puerto Rican ordained as a priest in Chicago. He was ordained in 1974, and lived for many years in the Humboldt Park neighborhood. He is still a priest, serving in New Jersey. Of over 500 parish priests in the Archdiocese of Chicago, only a handful are Latino, and fewer yet are Puerto Rican. (Courtesy Antonio Villalobos.)

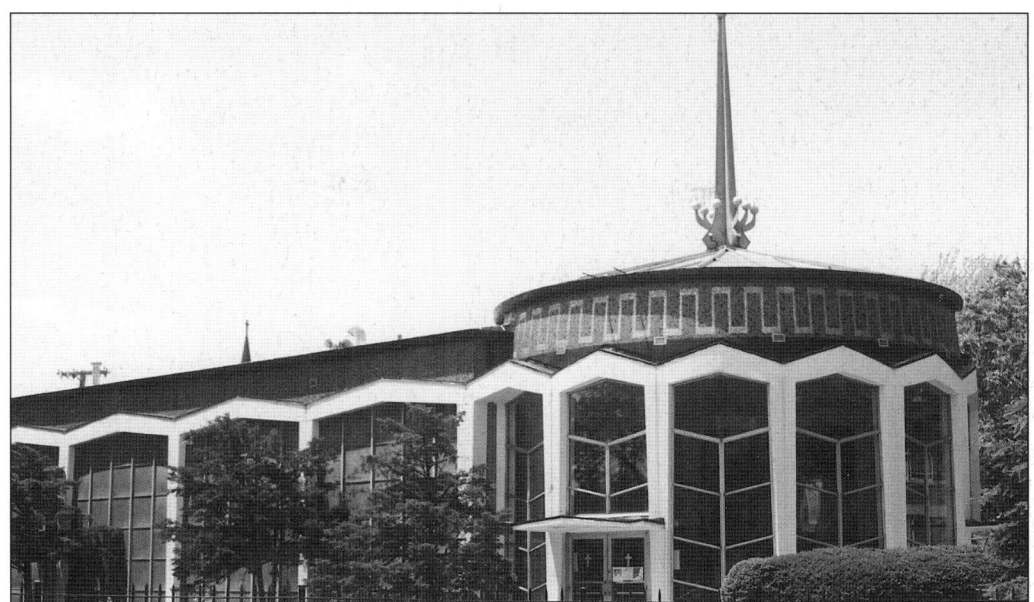

In the 1960s, Puerto Ricans tried to attend St. Mark Catholic Church, pictured here, at Augusta and Campbell Streets. But the pastor adamantly refused to accept Puerto Ricans. "Some parishes refused to accept Puerto Ricans, others put them in the basement," recalls Rev. Leo T. Mahon. "Parishes said Puerto Ricans didn't have money to give to the church. Or they would scare the whites away. Some parishes told Puerto Ricans, 'Don't come here; go to your own church; go to St. Francis of Assisi.'" (Photo Wilfredo Cruz.)

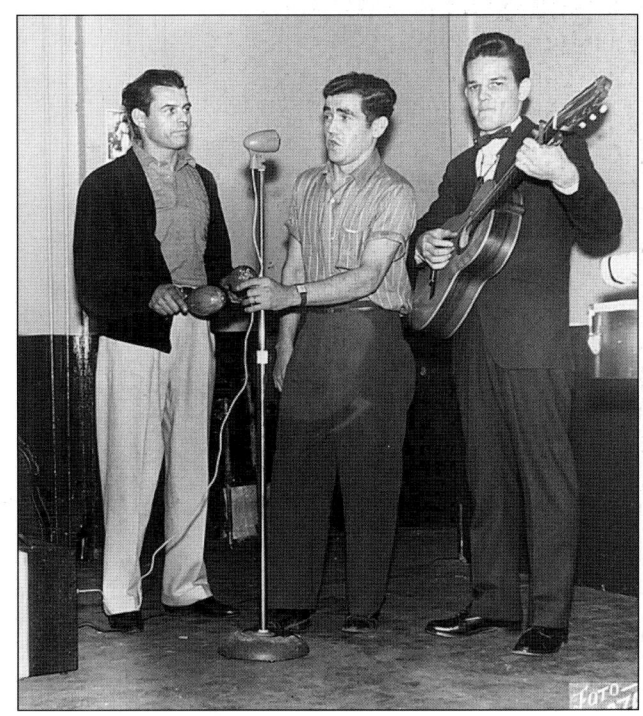

In 1961, Puerto Ricans asked the pastor at St. Mark Church if they could meet in the church basement to socialize and play music. The pastor once again refused to have Puerto Ricans in his church. Instead, Puerto Ricans rented a small hall nearby where they could meet and play traditional Puerto Rican music. Pictured, from left to right, are Agustin Toledo, Antonio Villalobos, and Juan Ocasio. (Courtesy Antonio Villalobos.)

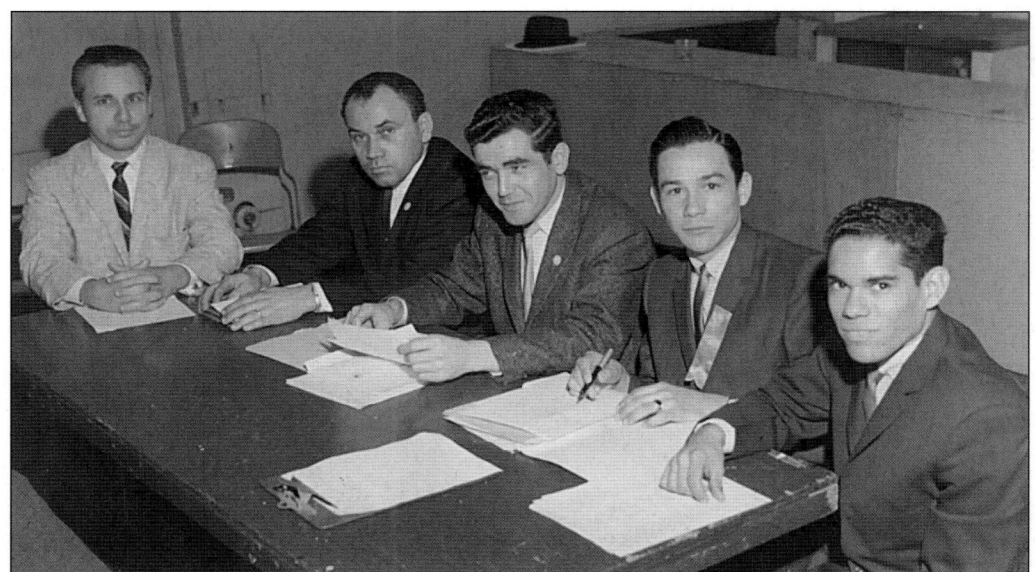

High ranking Catholic officials forced the pastor at St. Mark Church to accept Puerto Ricans as parishioners in the early 1960s. Council Eight of Los Caballeros de San Juan, a religious Puerto Rican group, was formed at St. Mark. Pictured are unidentified council officials. Third from the left is Antonio Villalobos, president of the council. (Courtesy Antonio Villalobos.)

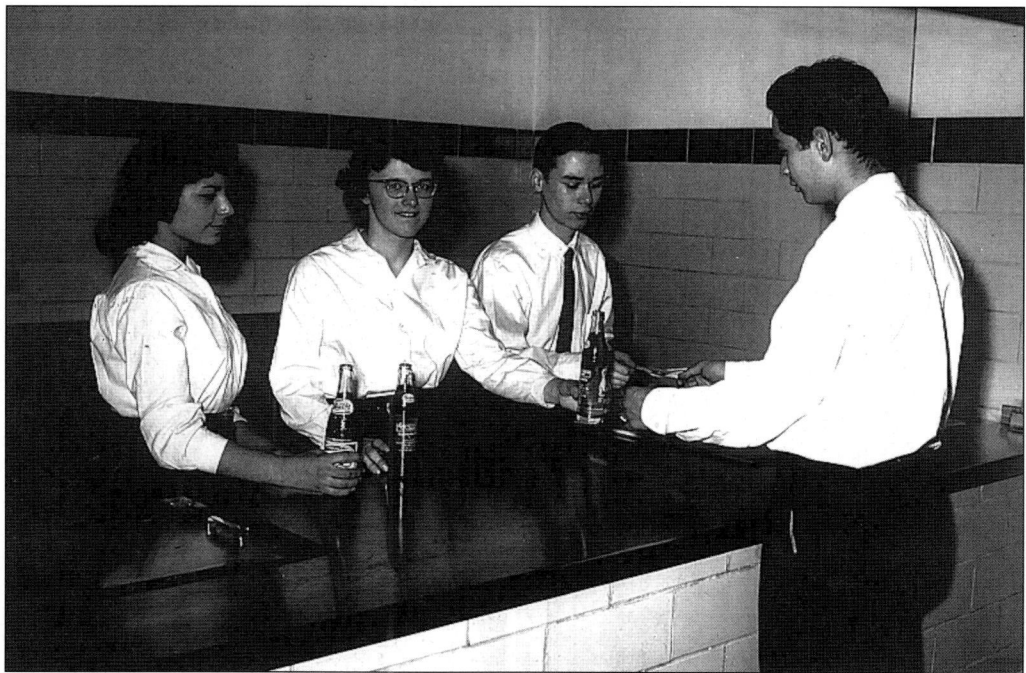

Hilda Frontany (left) is pictured with classmates at Cathedral High School in 1961. Frontany would later become a well-known community organizer and political activist in the Puerto Rican community. Puerto Rican families made sacrifices to send their children to expensive Catholic elementary schools and high schools. (Courtesy Hilda Frontany).

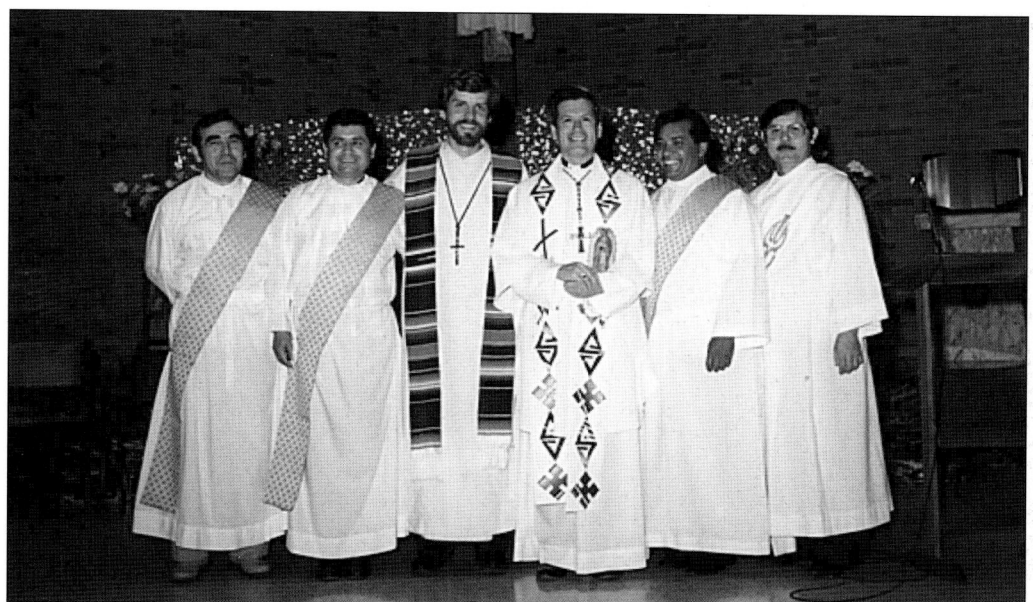

Most Catholic churches in Chicago lacked Puerto Rican deacons. St. Mark Church held a special ceremony in the early 1980s to honor its four deacons. Pictured, from left to right, are Antonio Villalobos; Jorge Gutierrez; Rev. Dave Public; former Auxiliary Bishop Placido Rodriguez; Sixto Rivera; and Abram Rosa. (Courtesy Antonio Villalobos.)

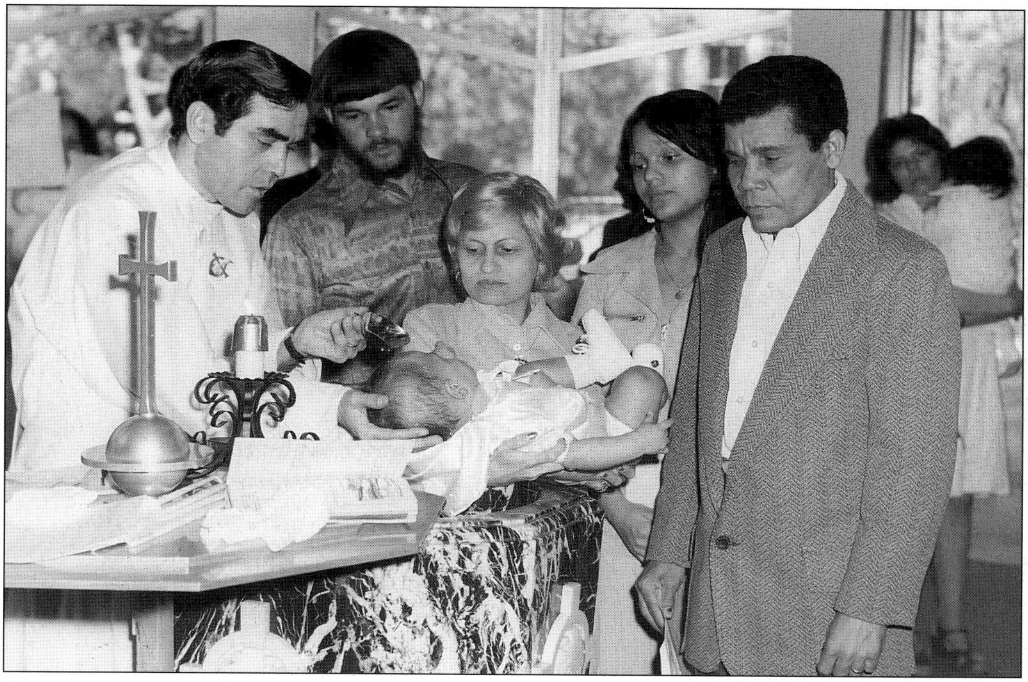

Deacon Antonio Villalobos baptizes a child at St. Mark Church in the early 1980s. The child's unidentified padrino (godfather) and madrina (godmother) are nearby. Deacons in the parish spoke Spanish and understood Puerto Rican culture. (Courtesy Antonio Villalobos.)

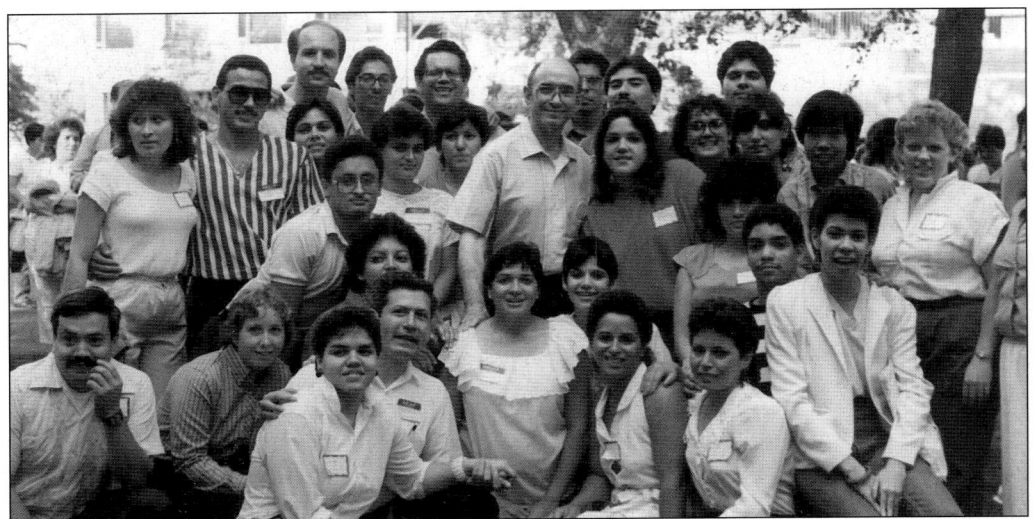

The late Cardinal Joseph Bernardin (center with glasses) met with a group of youth and parents from St. Mark Church in the mid-1990s. Also present was former Auxiliary Bishop Placido Rodriguez (second from left first row). Rodriguez was the first Mexican Bishop in the Archdiocese of Chicago. He later moved to Texas. (Courtesy Antonio Villalbos.)

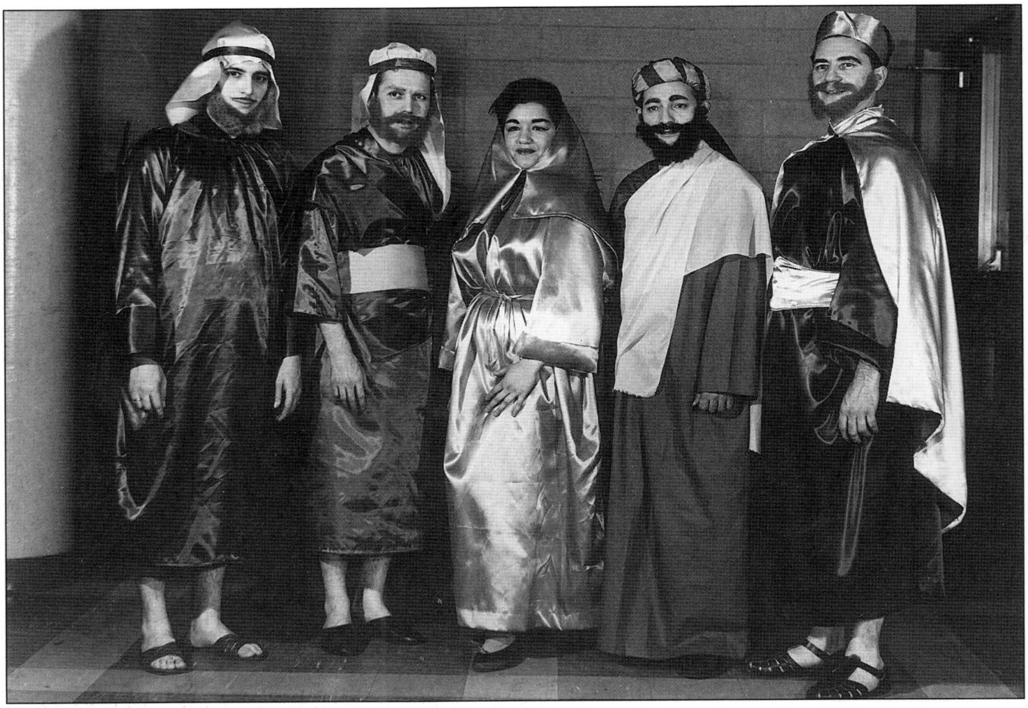

In the mid-1960s, Puerto Ricans from various Catholic parishes formed a Catholic lay group, Hermanos de La Familia de Dios (Brothers of the Family of God). The group met regularly to reflect on the Catholic faith and discuss how to better serve the community. Unidentified members of the group performed a play in the mid-1960stelling the story of the life of Jesus Christ. About 300 people attended the event. (Courtesy Antonio Villalobos.)

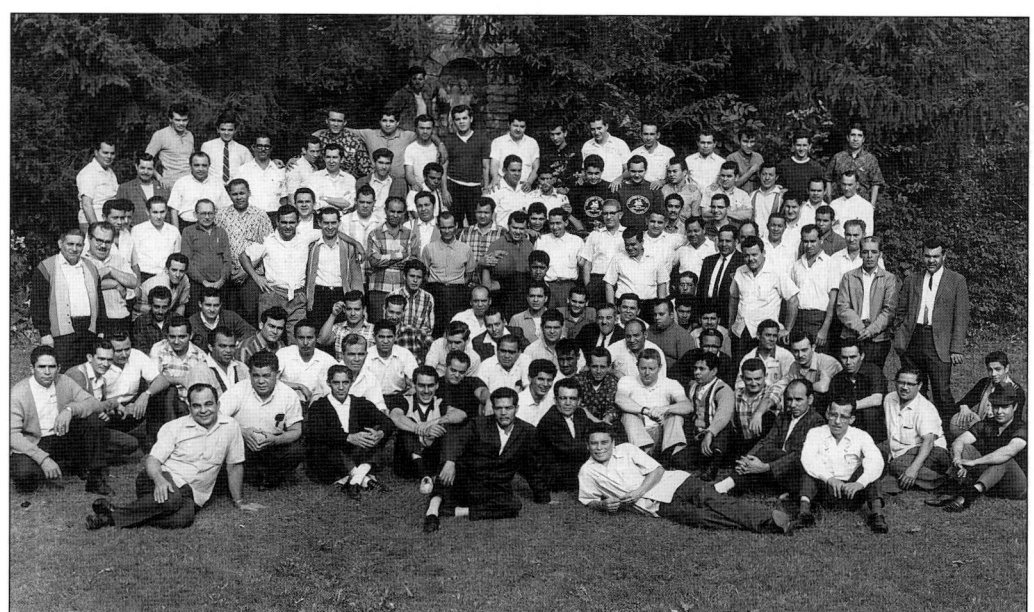

Hermanos de La Familia de Dios (Brothers of the Family of God), a Puerto Rican Catholic lay group, regularly sponsored religious retreats. The group had two retreats a year, one for female members, and another for men. Shown here is a 1975 retreat in Libertyville, Illinois. The purpose of the retreats was to reflect on Catholicism and the spiritual life. (Courtesy Antonio Villalobos.)

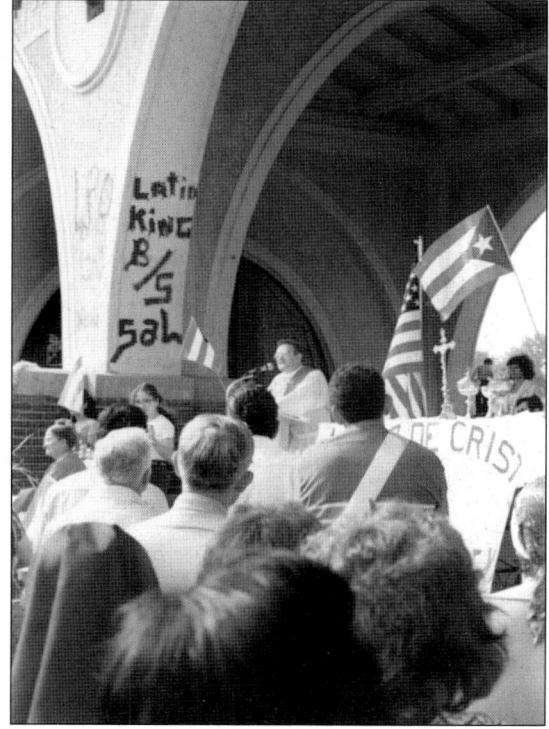

In 1976, parishioners from five Catholic churches in the Humboldt Park neighborhood got together for an outdoor mass in the Humboldt Park boathouse. The mass, attended by more than 1,000 people, was held to kick off the celebration of the Puerto Rican parade. Gang graffiti can be seen on the walls of the boathouse. (Courtesy Antonio Villalobos.)

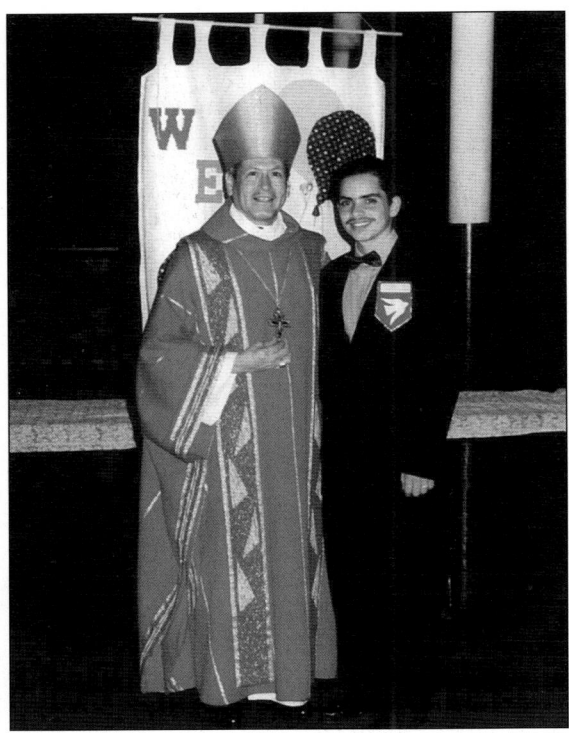

Jose Lugue Jr. celebrates his confirmation at St. Philomena Church in the Humboldt Park neighborhood in 1993. He stands with former Auxiliary Bishop Placido Rodriguez. (Courtesy Anna Rivera.)

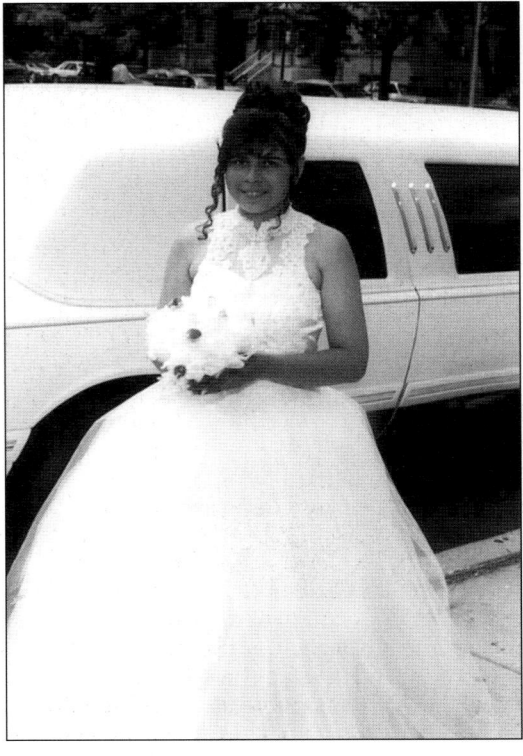

Some Puerto Rican families have adopted the Mexican tradition of a quinceañera to celebrate a girl's 15th birthday. The quinceañera is the social debut of a young woman and has both religious and cultural significance. Nicole Maria Rivera celebrated her quinceañera in 1998. The ceremony took place at St. Philomena Church. Her parents bought her an expensive dress, rented a limousine, and had a large catered banquet for friends and family. (Courtesy Norma Rivera.)

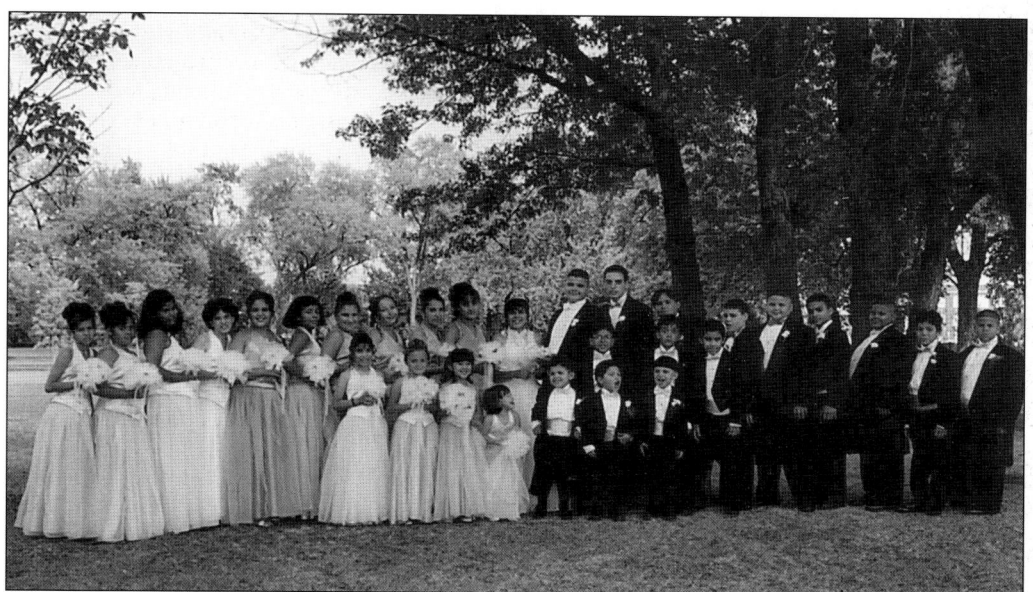

The damas (female attendants) and chambelanes (male escorts) dressed up in elegant dresses and tuxedos to celebrate the quinceañera of Nicole Maria Rivera (center) in 1998. (Courtesy Norma Rivera.)

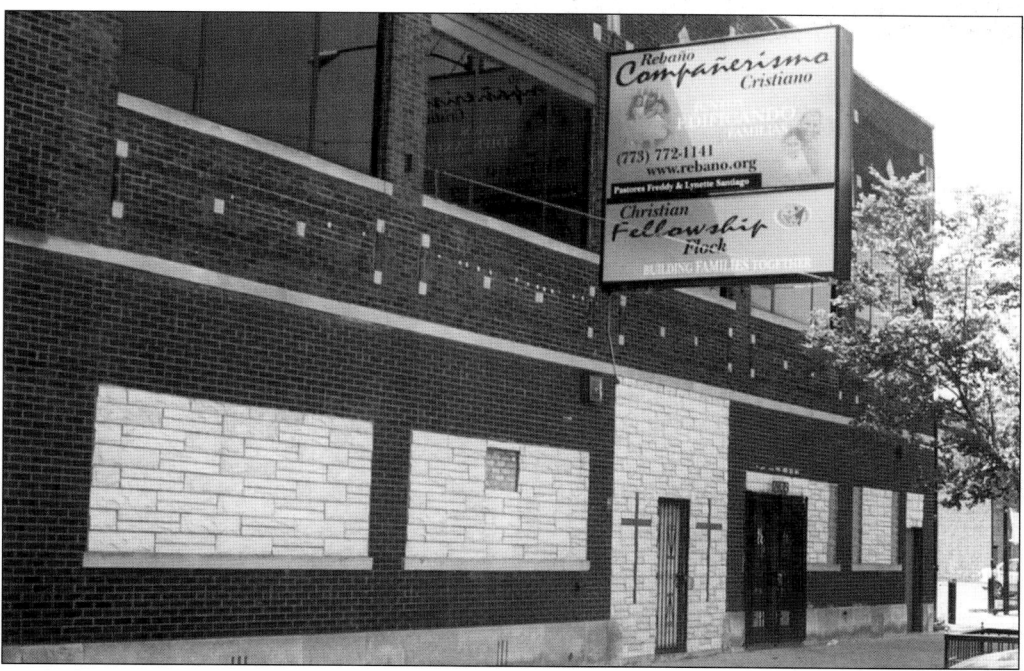

Many Puerto Ricans attend Christian nondenominational churches. Pictured here is the Rebano Compañerismo Cristiano Church on Division Street. Over 1,000 people, mainly Puerto Ricans, Mexicans, and South and Central Americans, attend Sunday services at the church. The church began as a small storefront 27 years ago. The co-pastor of the church is a woman—Christian churches permit women to become pastors. (Photo Wilfredo Cruz.)

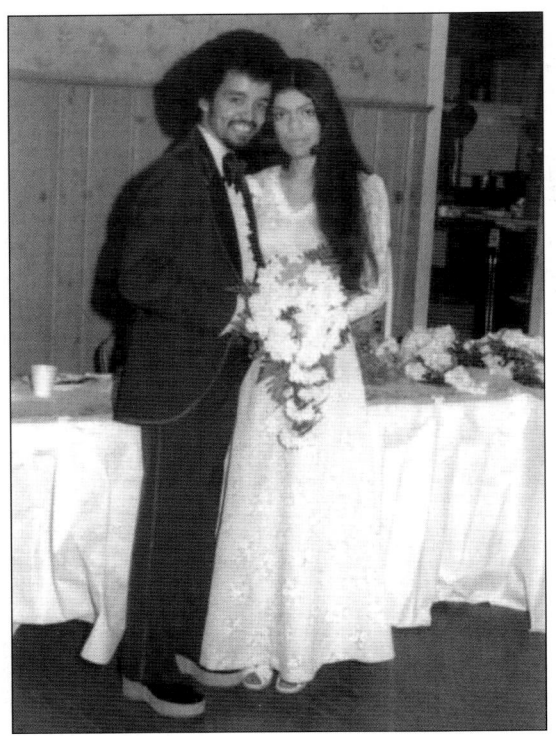

The 1977 wedding of Rolando Jr. and Vilma Ithier is shown here. Rolando is currently a reverend at New Dimension Christian Center, a small Christian church in the Belmont Cragin neighborhood. Vilma runs the church's Seeds of Hope program. The program is a yearlong recreational and educational program for youth. (Courtesy Rolando Jr. and Vilma Ithier.)

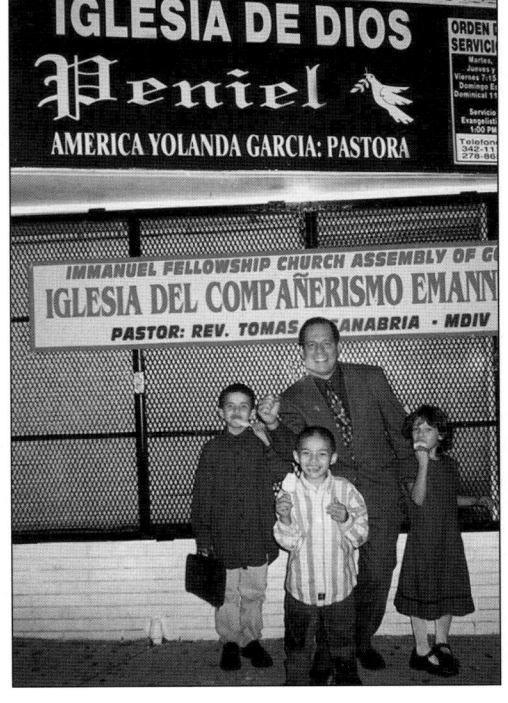

Many small, storefront Pentecostal churches are springing up in Puerto Rican neighborhoods. The small churches give Puerto Ricans a sense of belonging and solace. Pictured here is Rev. Tomas V. Sanabria with young members of his storefront Pentecostal church on the corner of Maplewood and Division Streets in the summer of 2000. Members attend small churches like this as often as four times a week to pray, chant in ecstatic rituals, and socialize. (Courtesy Tomas V. Sanabria.)

Five
BUSINESS AND
PROFESSIONS

The first generation of Puerto Ricans to come to Chicago arrived without many skills and without much capital to start businesses. Most were concerned with finding decent jobs, adjusting to a new culture and language, and raising their families. Most had the added burden of trying to learn English. They had entered a city and economy that required higher education, but most came with little or no education. Lack of education prevented them from moving into high-paying professions.

Nevertheless, some of the early Puerto Rican used their ingenuity and hard work to start small businesses. Some Puerto Ricans opened up small mom-and-pop grocery stores, restaurants, barbershops, liquor stores, music shops, and bakeries. Daniel Ramos, an early Puerto Rican migrant to Chicago used to sell produce to Puerto Rican families from the trunk of his car. He saved his earnings and started Ramos Movers, a moving company that helped move many Puerto Rican families who were searching for affordable housing. His daughters currently operate the small business.

Other Puerto Ricans were not business owners in the traditional sense of owning an established business—but they were clever entrepreneurs who found ways of supplementing their often meager wages. Puerto Rican men acted as weekend barbers cutting the hair of friends in their basement apartments. Some men worked overtime or held two jobs. Some became street vendors, selling snow cones or fruit. Women added to the family income by working in factories, sewing clothes at home, or by babysitting for friends and neighbors.

The community has made much progress since those humble beginnings. Subsequent generations of Puerto Ricans have acquired the requisite skills and higher education to progress in business and in the professional world. Growing numbers of Puerto Ricans have achieved the American dream of self-employment. Puerto Ricans own a variety of businesses, including record shops, restaurants, bakeries, barber shops, clothing stores, jewelry stores, furniture stores, taverns, and grocery stores. Puerto Ricans have made great strides in professional radio, the building trades, criminal justice, teaching, higher education, law, and the medical profession.

There is room for even further improvement. Certain professions still lack a significant number of Puerto Ricans. However, as the following photographs illustrate, Puerto Ricans have come a long way since their parents first came to this city. No doubt future generations will continue to make significant inroads.

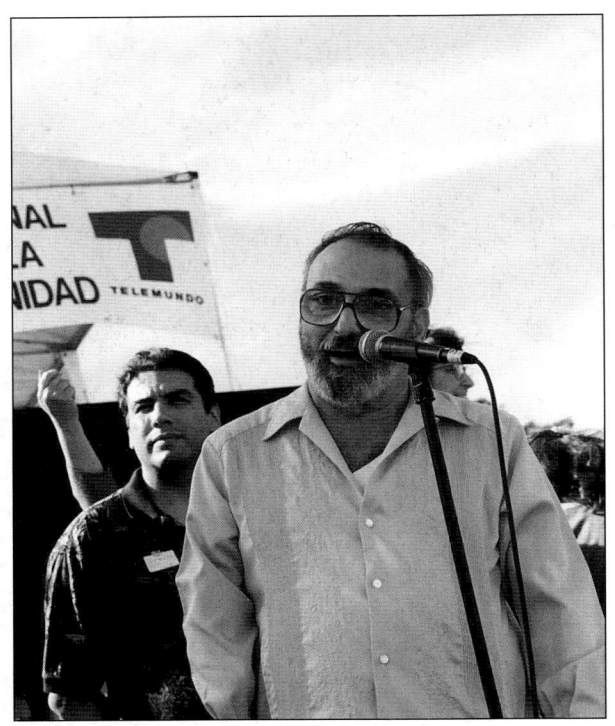

Elias Dias y Perez was one of the first Puerto Ricans to broadcast Puerto Rican music, news, and sports on a major radio station. His popular Spanish language program, Radio Club Familiar, played on the radio for over 50 years. He passed away in 2002. A large medallion honoring Perez was placed on the sidewalk on Paseo Boricua, a commercial strip on Division Street. (Courtesy Puerto Rican Parade Committee.)

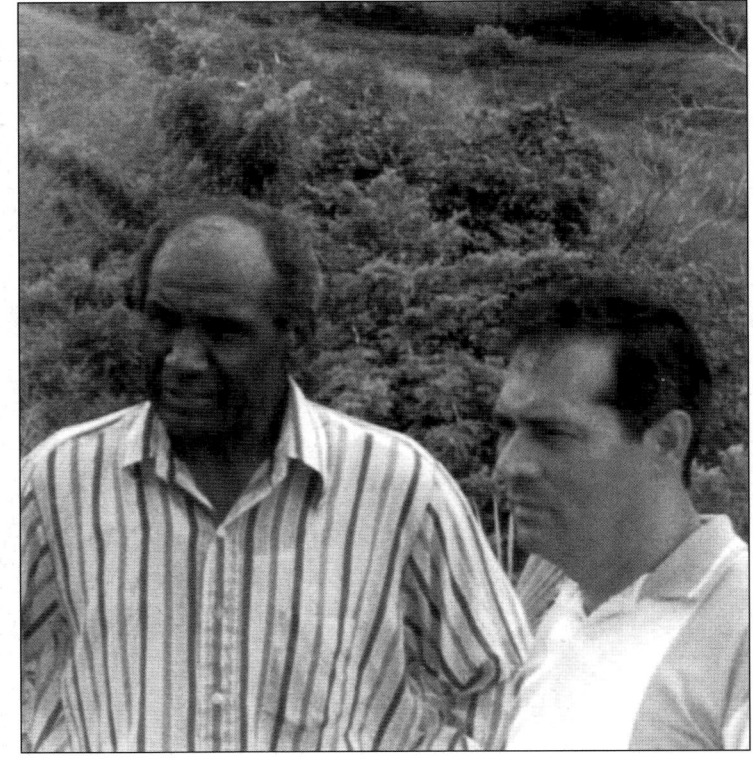

Juan Abedo Gomez (left) is believed to be the first Puerto Rican to become a police officer with the Chicago Police Department. Gomez joined the department in 1960, worked on the force for over 27 years, and earned the rank of sergeant. Opposite Gomez is Efrain Lopez, a longtime Chicago police officer. Lopez says Gomez, a dark skinned Puerto Rican, had a difficult time joining the department because of prejudice within the department during the 1960s. Gomez passed away in 2003. (Courtesy Efrain López.)

Raul Cardona and a handful of other Puerto Ricans joined the Chicago Police Department in 1961. For years, the Chicago Police Department had height requirements that excluded many Puerto Rican from joining the force. The courts struck down arbitrary height requirements in Chicago. (Courtesy Raul Cardona.)

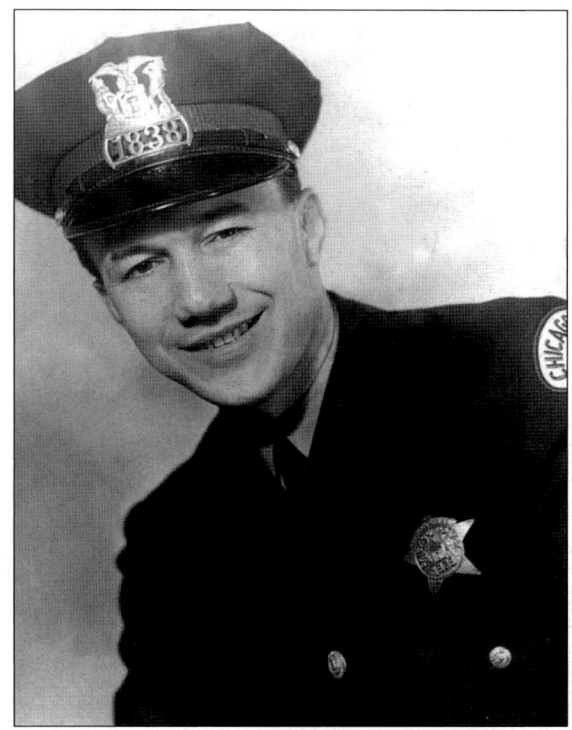

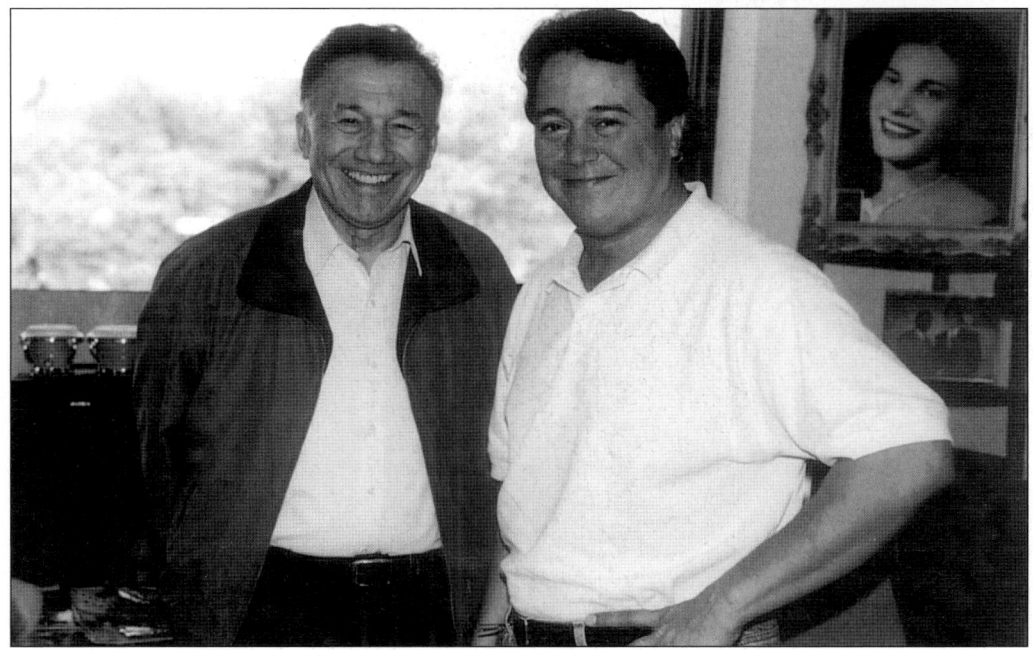

Raul Cardona (left) is a well-known Puerto Rican radio personality. For many years he played Puerto Rican and Spanish music and news on his popular "Raul Cardona" radio program. Also pictured is his son, Felix. The two are businessmen who own record stores, dance halls, and apartment buildings in the Logan Square neighborhood. (Photo Wilfredo Cruz.)

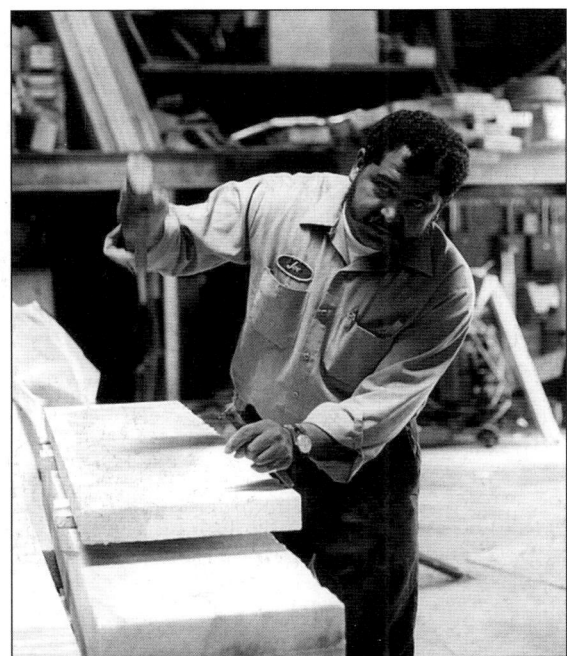

Jose Anibal Rivera is pictured in 1972. Rivera was a skilled Puerto Rican stone cutter for Galassi Cut Stone Company in Worth, Illinois. He worked for the company for many years. He came from Puerto Rico to Chicago in 1950. (Courtesy Jaime Rivera.)

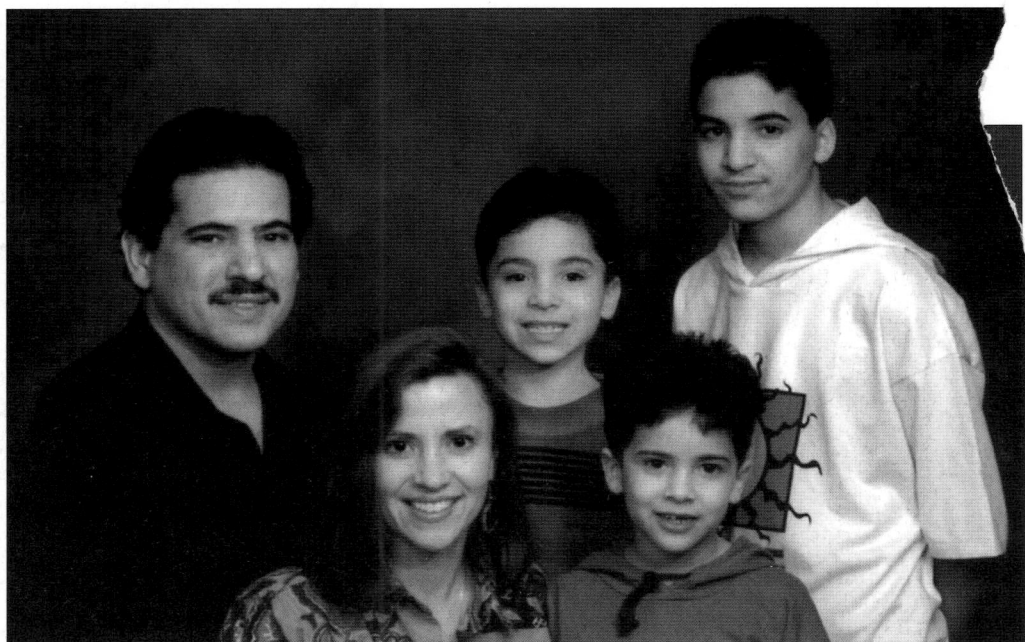

Noel and wife Marcia Ruiz are seen here with their three sons, Nathan Anthony (front), Joel Brian (center), and Noel Ryan. Noel is a journeyman carpenter and Marcia is an elementary school teacher for the Chicago Public Schools. For many years Puerto Ricans could not enter apprenticeship training programs in the building trades in Chicago due to favoritism and discrimination in the unions controlling the programs. Even today there is a severe shortage of Puerto Ricans in the building trades. (Courtesy Noel and Marcia Ruiz.)

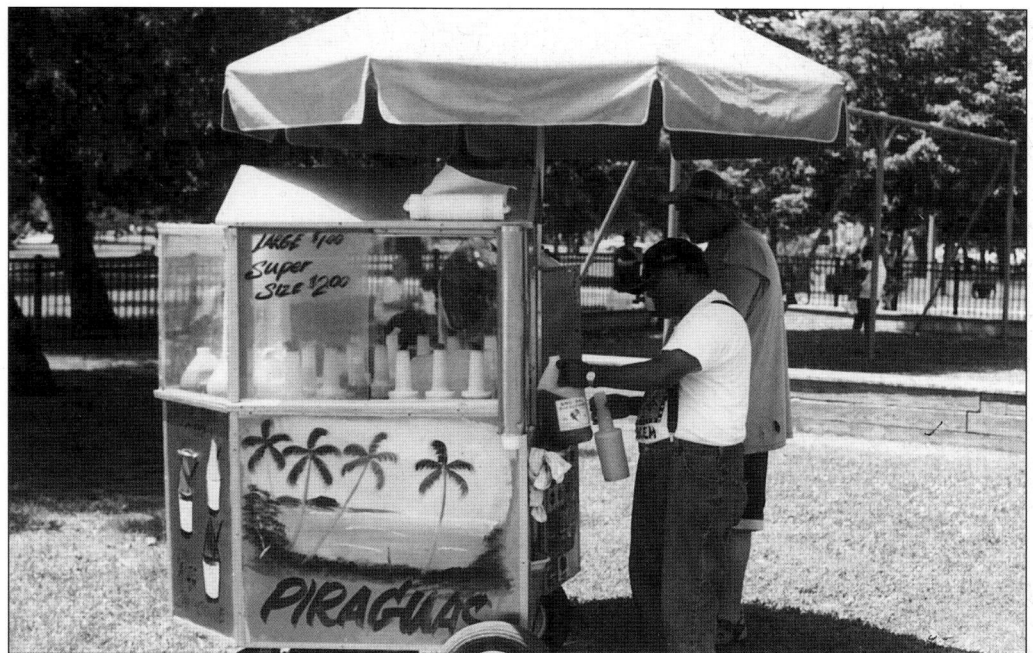

Angel Ortiz makes his living selling piraguas (snow cones) in Humboldt Park near North Avenue. Ortiz came to Chicago in 1953 from Caguas, Puerto Rico. He worked for over 29 years in a small photo frame company, until the company shut down. He has seven children. (Photo Wilfredo Cruz.)

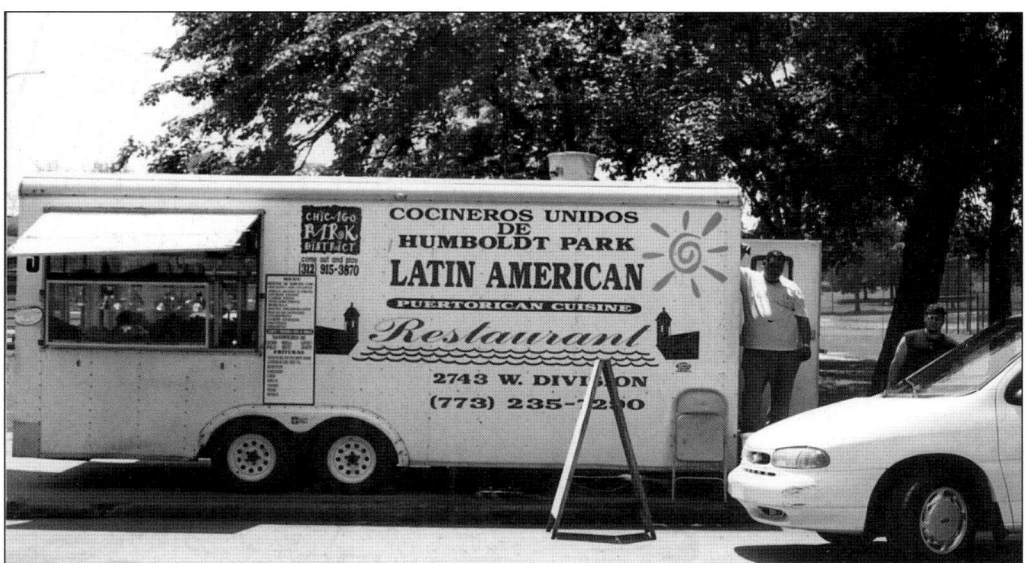

Jose Pagan takes a cigarette break after working all morning selling Puerto Rican food from a power-generated mobile restaurant in Humboldt Park. The restaurant belongs to his brother-in-law, Jaime Cruz. Over a dozen Puerto Rican vendors sell food in the park from mobile restaurants. They are an organized business group called Cocineros Unidos de Humboldt Park (United Cooks of Humboldt Park). (Photo Wilfredo Cruz.)

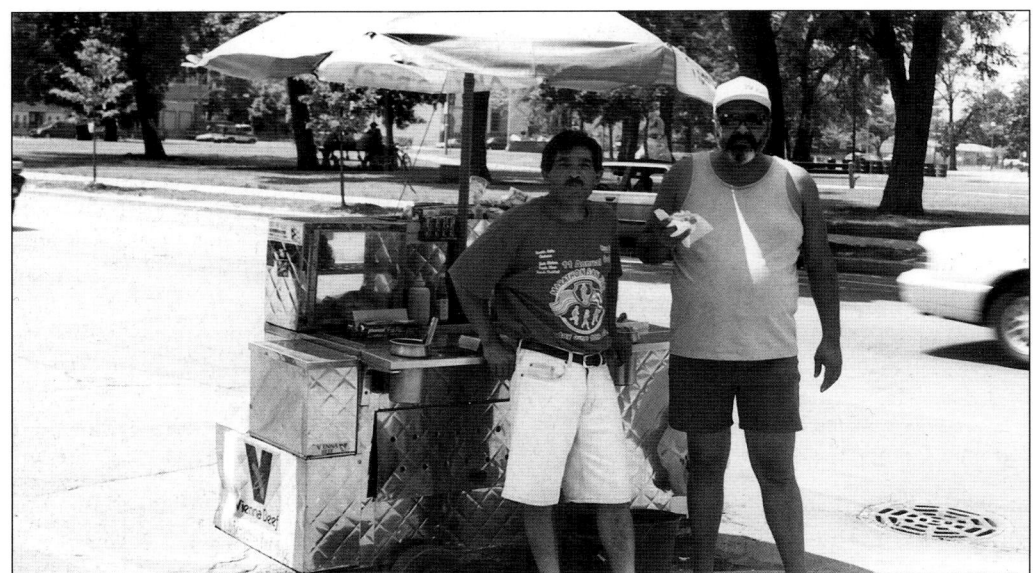

Hector DeJesus (left) makes his living selling hotdogs and soda pop on Crystal and California Avenues. An unidentified customer savors a hotdog. Hector has been selling on this corner for the last ten years. "I stopped drinking and smoking about ten years ago. That stuff is not good for you," says Hector. "Have a hotdog and soda instead of beer." (Photo Wilfredo Cruz.)

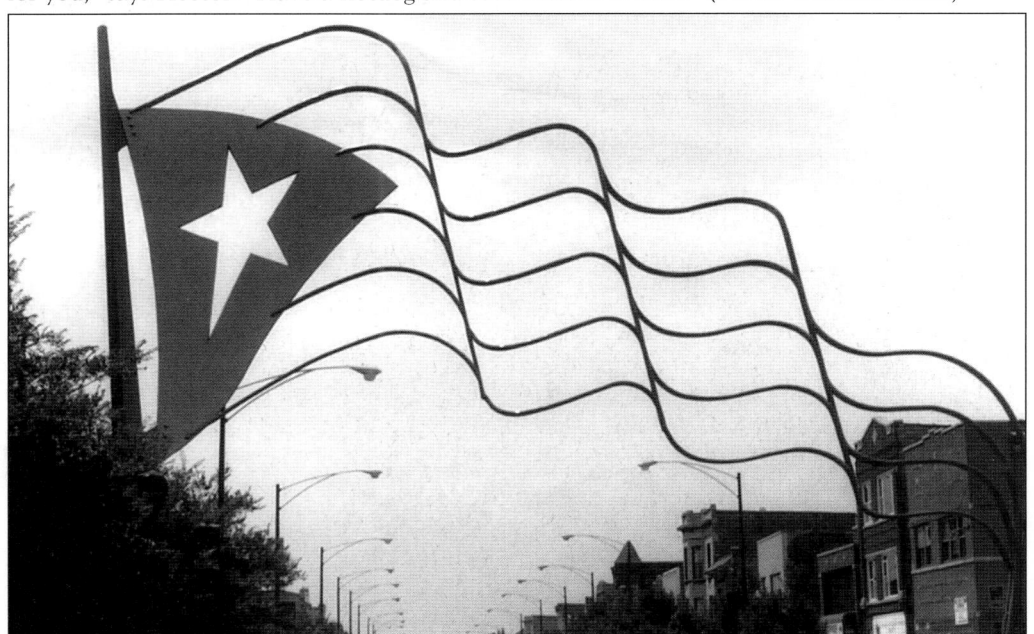

In 1995, Puerto Rican community leaders and politicians pressured the city of Chicago to build two steel, 59-foot Puerto Rican flags on Division Street. One flag is near Western Avenue and the other is about six blocks west on California Avenue. The area within the flags is a small commercial district called Paseo Boricua (Puerto Rican Public Square). Of about 120 businesses on the strip, 88 are Puerto Rican owned. Shown here is the flag on Western Avenue. (Photo Wilfredo Cruz.)

The city of Chicago invested over two and a half million dollars to beautify Paseo Boricua. The project included new streets, curbs, sidewalks, and street lights. Sixteen small plazas complete with benches, tables, trees, and flower pots were installed. Shown here is one of the many concrete planters on Paseo Boricua. The planters have the flags of the 78 towns of Puerto Rico painted on them. (Courtesy Puerto Rican Cultural Center.)

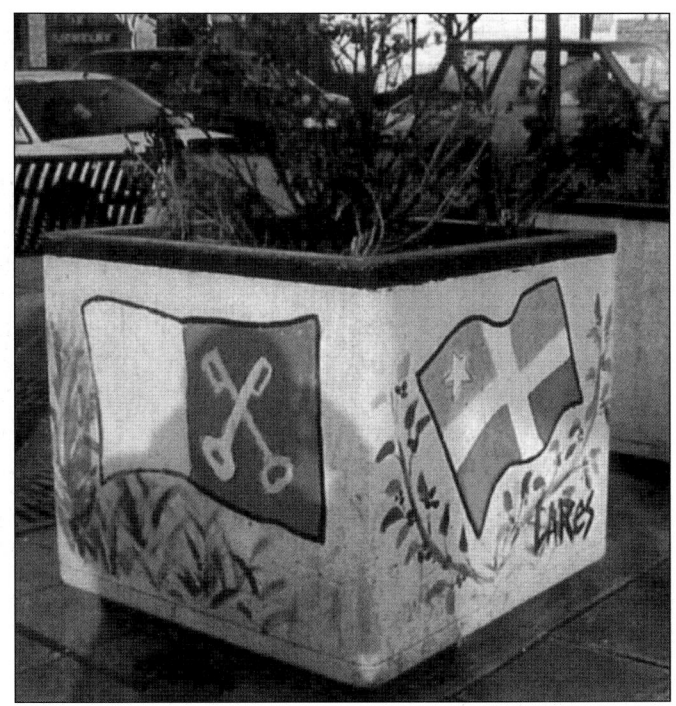

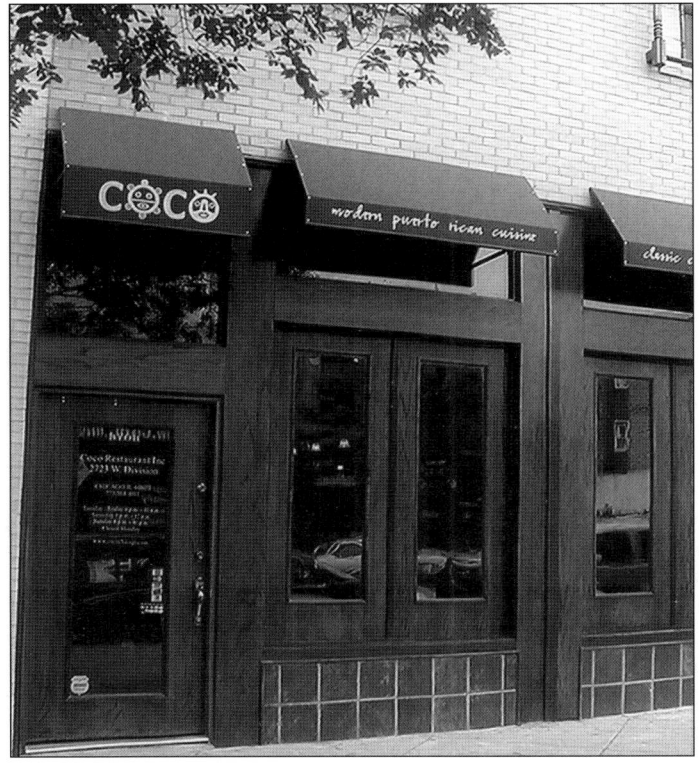

Coco is an elegant, upscale restaurant that opened its doors on Paseo Boricua in February 2004. It is the only high end Puerto Rican restaurant in Chicago. The restaurant is open only for dinner. Thus far business has been brisk. It is uncertain whether an expensive restaurant can prosper when they are several less expensive Puerto Rican restaurants on the same commercial strip. The owner is Jose Allende. (Courtesy Puerto Rican Cultural Center.)

71

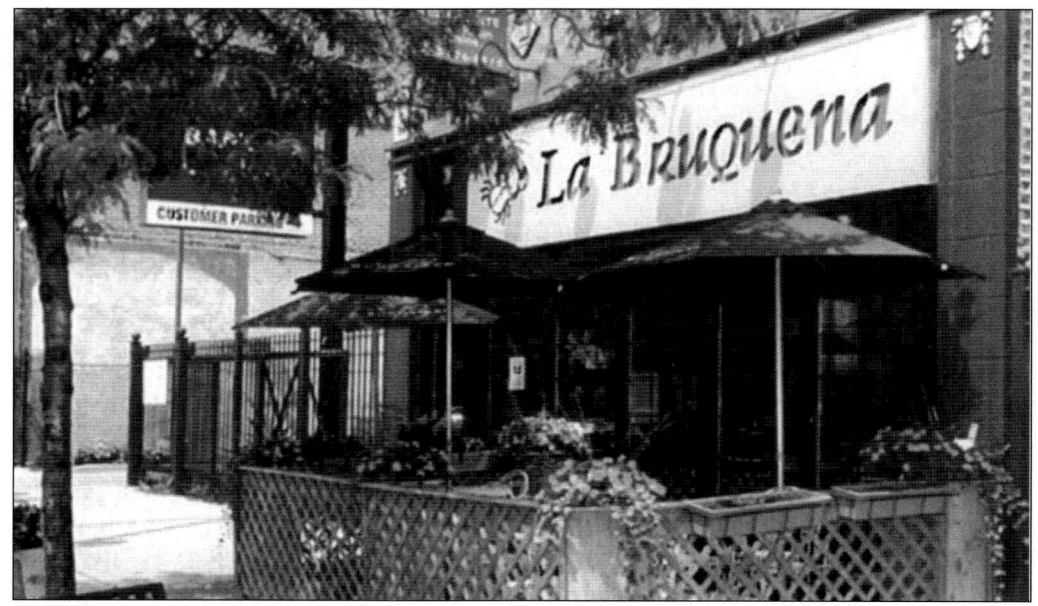

La Bruquena on Paseo Boricua is a well-known restaurant that is a favorite among Puerto Ricans, especially Puerto Rican professionals and politicians. The restaurant serves delicious, inexpensive Puerto Rican dishes. The restaurant has a lounge on the second floor. The owner is Roberto Tañon. (Courtesy Puerto Rican Cultural Center.)

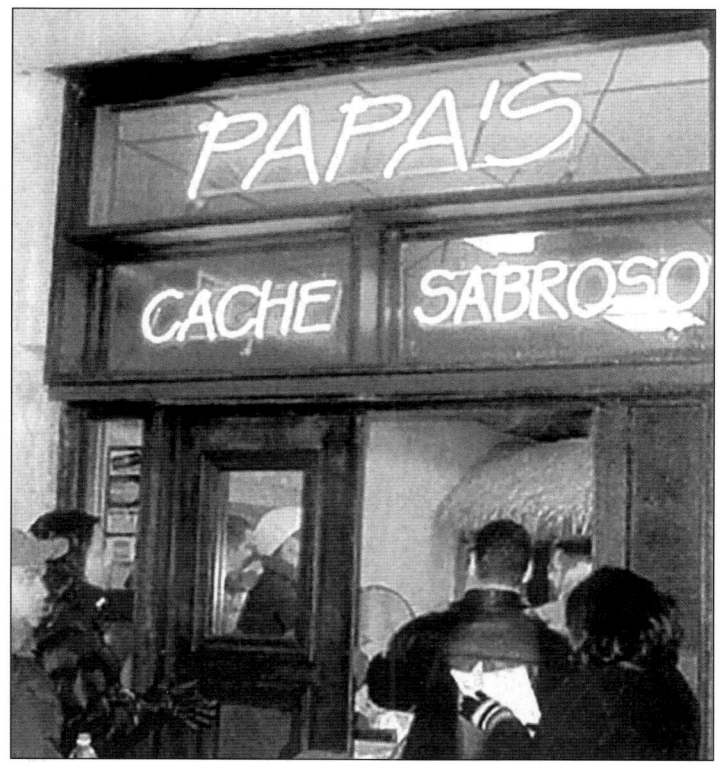

Papa's Cache Sabroso on Paseo Boricua is a favorite restaurant among many local Puerto Ricans. The business moved to Division Street in 2002. The restaurant serves many popular, traditional Puerto Rican dishes, including its specialty, roasted chicken. The owners are Victor and Nancy Garcia. (Courtesy Puerto Rican Cultural Center.).

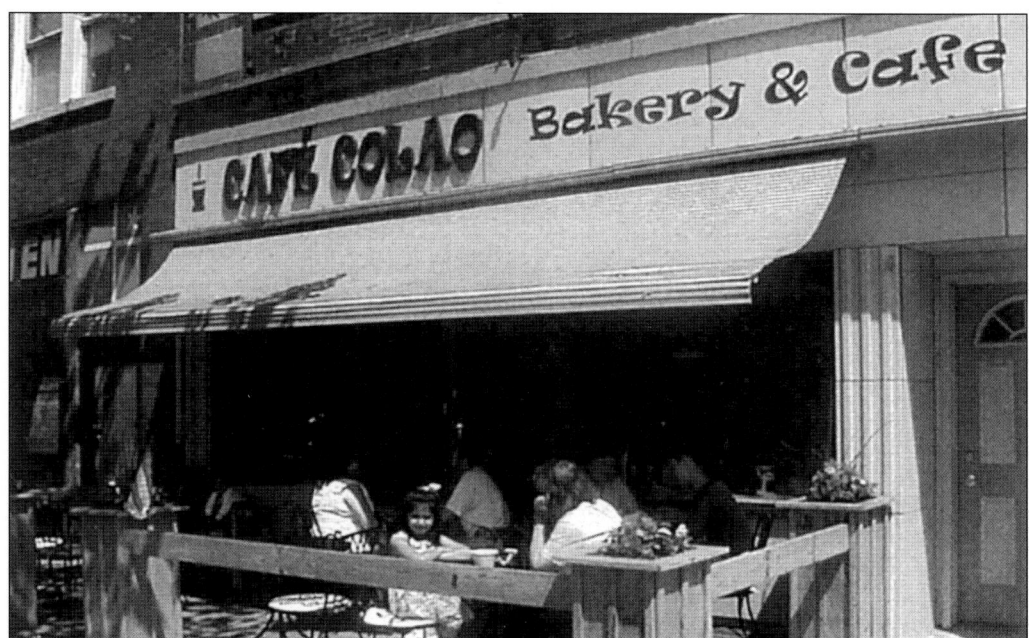

Café Colao is a popular bakery and café on Paseo Boricua. The café serves Puerto Rican pastries for breakfast and lunch, as well as Puerto Rican sandwiches. The owner is Wanda Colón. (Courtesy Puerto Rican Cultural Center.)

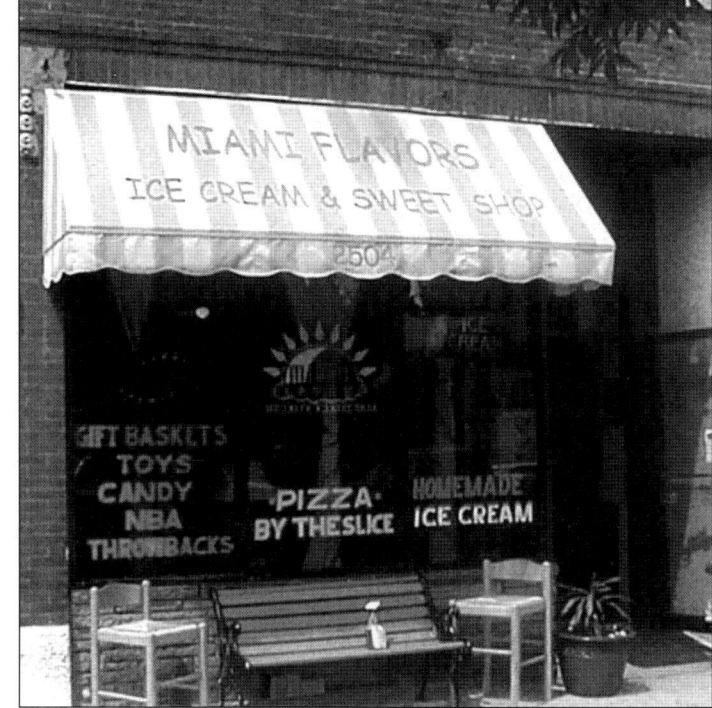

Miami Flavors, an ice cream shop, opened on Paseo Boricua in 2003. The shop serves ice cream made from sugar cane with Caribbean favors. The owner, Robert Bouyer, is part Dominican. He has similar ice cream shops in Miami, Florida, and New York. (Courtesy Puerto Rican Cultural Center.)

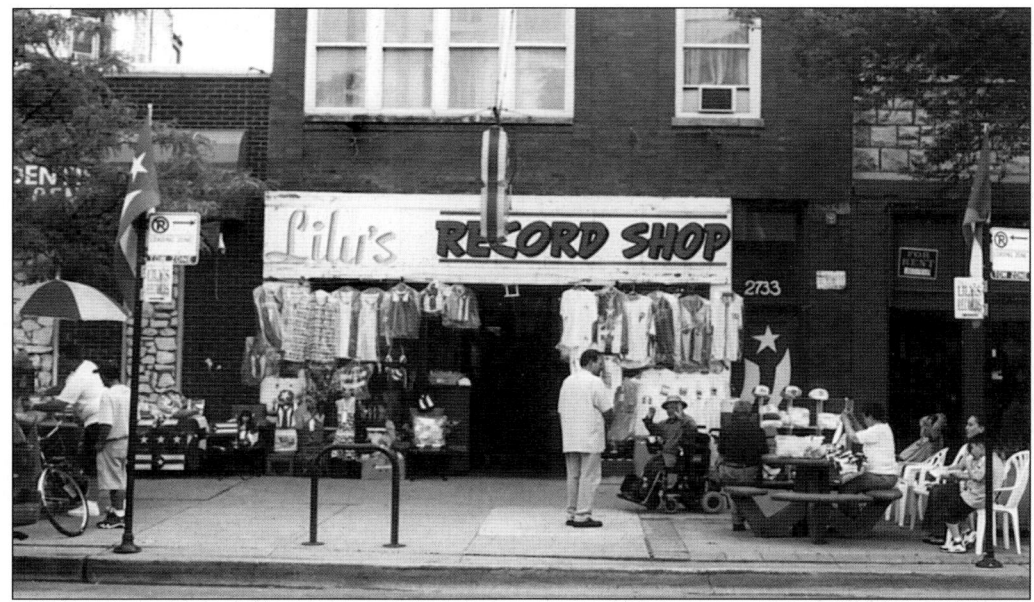

Lily's Record Shop on Paseo Boricua has been at the same location for over 25 years. It is a popular store for buying CDs, videos, dominoes, shirts, flags, and other Puerto Rican goods. The owner is Carmen Martinez. Pictured on the right is one of the numerous concrete tables and benches installed by the city along the commercial strip. (Photo Wilfredo Cruz.)

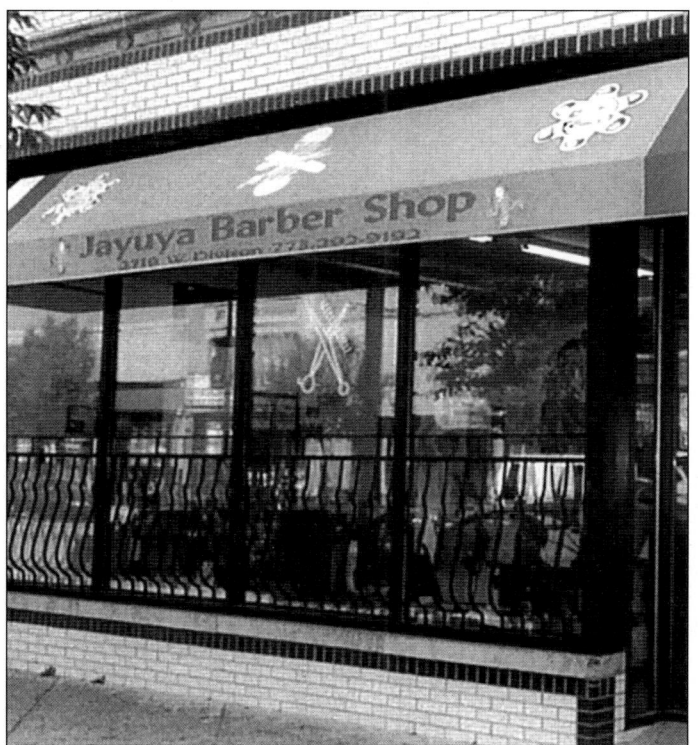

Jayuya Barbershop on Paseo Boricua is always full of customers. Even with 12 barbers working in the shop, patrons often have to wait to get a haircut. While waiting, customers can entertain themselves on the shop's pool tables or by playing dominoes or watching television. (Courtesy Puerto Rican Cultural Center.)

74

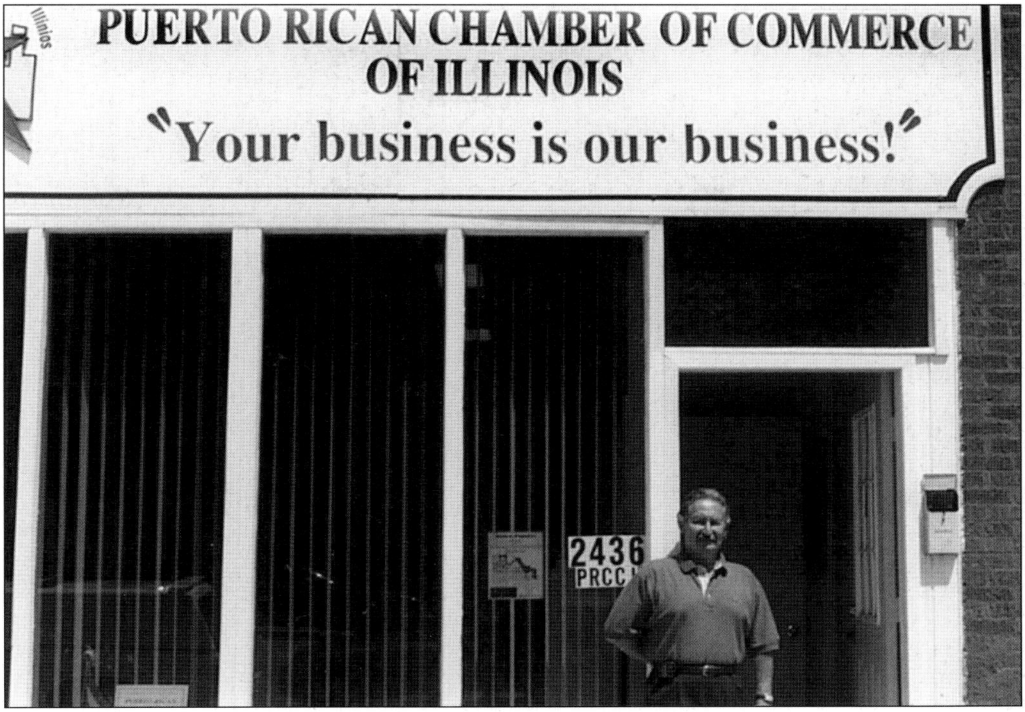

PUERTO RICAN CHAMBER OF COMMERCE OF ILLINOIS
"Your business is our business!"

Angelo Sanchez, former director of the Puerto Rican Chamber of Commerce (PRCC), stands outside the chamber's office on Paseo Boricua in 1998. The PRCC and the Division Street Business Development Association promote business development on Paseo Boricua, and throughout the city. (Photo Wilfredo Cruz.)

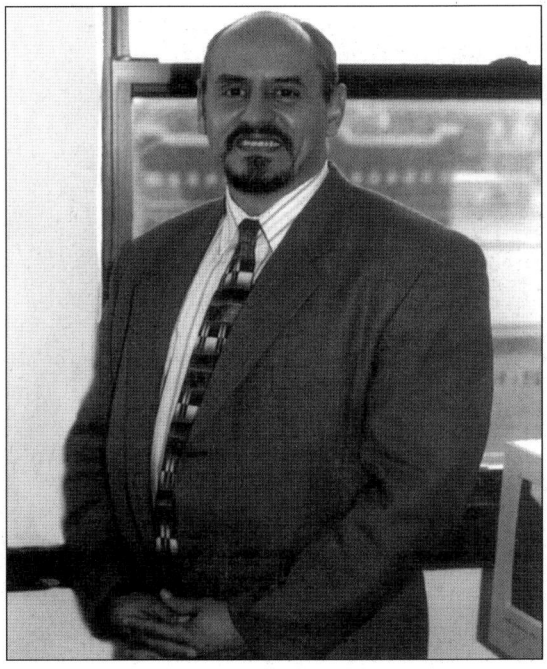

Kenny Ruiz is director of the Street Intervention program of the McCormick Tribune YMCA in the Logan Square neighborhood. Ruiz has dedicated his life to helping youth avoid gang life. He uses recreational activities, combined with religious instruction, to help youth leave the destructive world of gangs. He is pictured here in 1998. (Photo Wilfredo Cruz.)

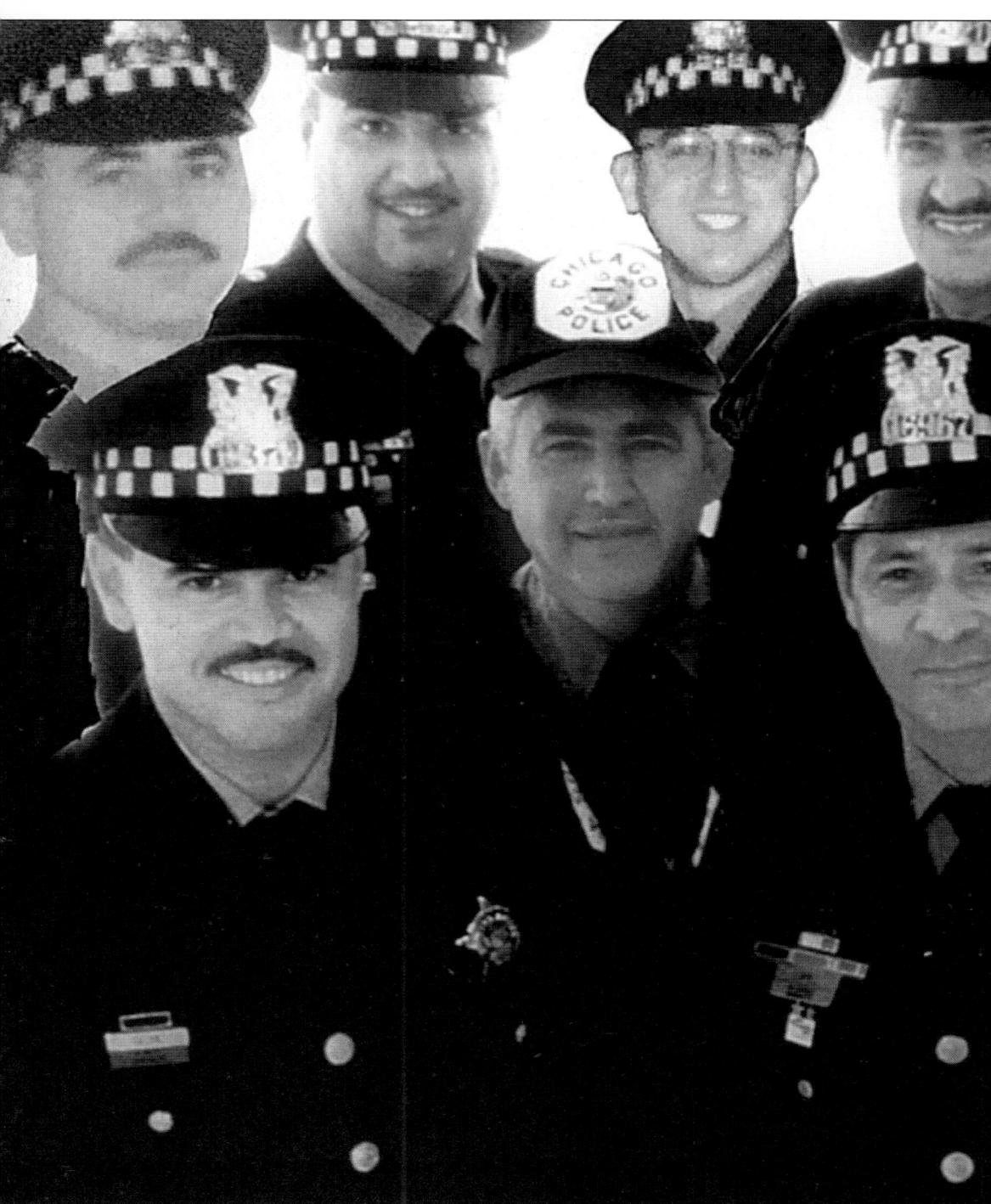

Thirteen relatives became police officers with the Chicago Police Department. Four retired from the department, one passed away, and eight are still serving. Pictured, from left to right, are (first row) Adolfo López, current police chaplain; (second row) Edwin Silva, Richardini López, Efrain

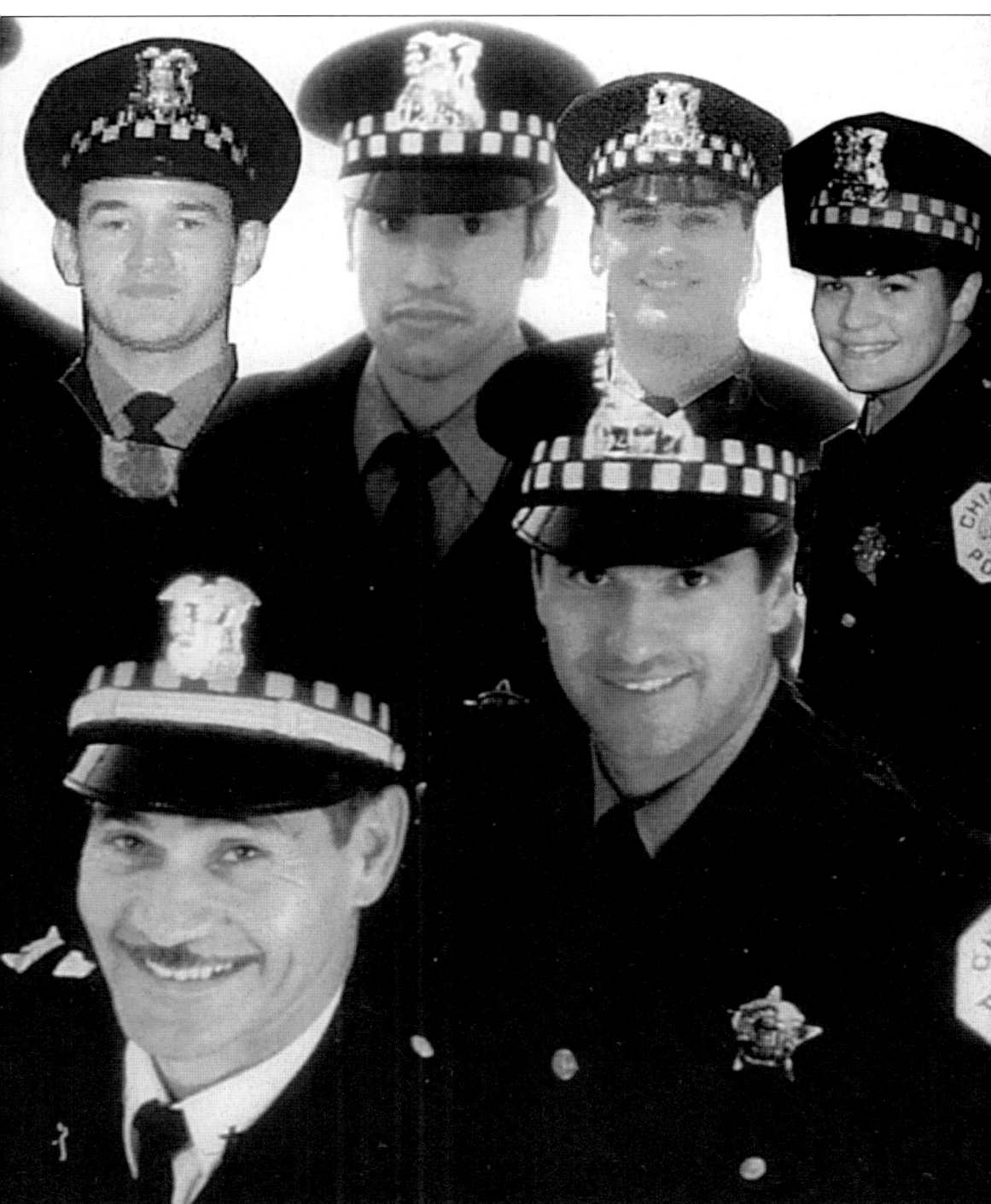

López, and Hector Silva; (back row) Concepcion López, Paul López, Nelson Gonzalez, Harry López, Antonio Valentine, Orlando Rodriguez, unidentified, and Irma López. The four brothers are Richard, Adolfo, Harry, and Efrain López. Irma is the daughter of Efrain. (Courtesy Efrain López.)

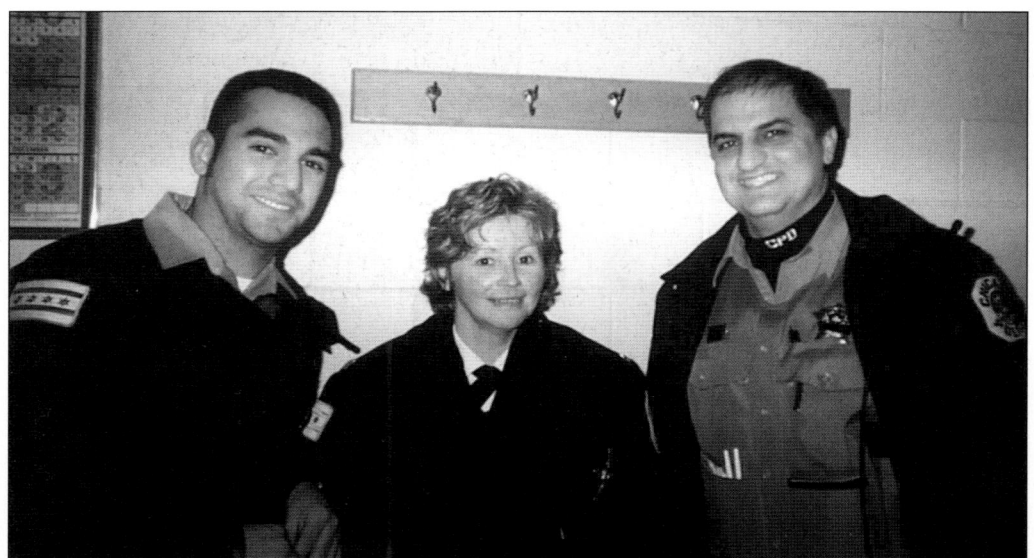

Maria Magdalena Soto Maher (center) has been a police officer with the Chicago Police Department for over 22 years. She has worked herself up in the ranks of the department. She is currently the second highest ranked Puerto Rican in the department. As Deputy Chief of the Area Five patrol division, Maher is in charge of six police districts, with over 2, 000 police officers total. She is pictured with two of her officers, (left) Mario Limon and (right) Atour Bethishoa. (Courtesy Maria Magdalena Soto Maher.)

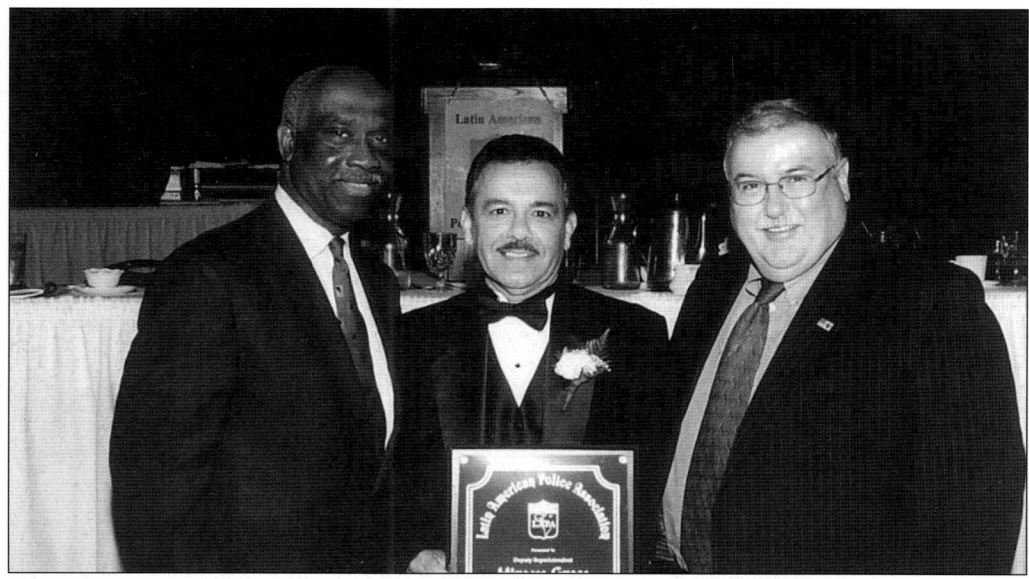

Hiram Grau (center) has been a police officer with the Chicago Police Department for over 23 years. He is the highest ranked Puerto Rican in the department. As Deputy Superintendent Grau directs the detective, organized crime, vice-control, and homicide divisions of the department. He is pictured receiving the 2004 person of the year award from the Latin American Police Association. On his right is former police Superintendent Terry Hillard and on his left is current police Superintendent Philip Cline. (Courtesy Hiram Grau.)

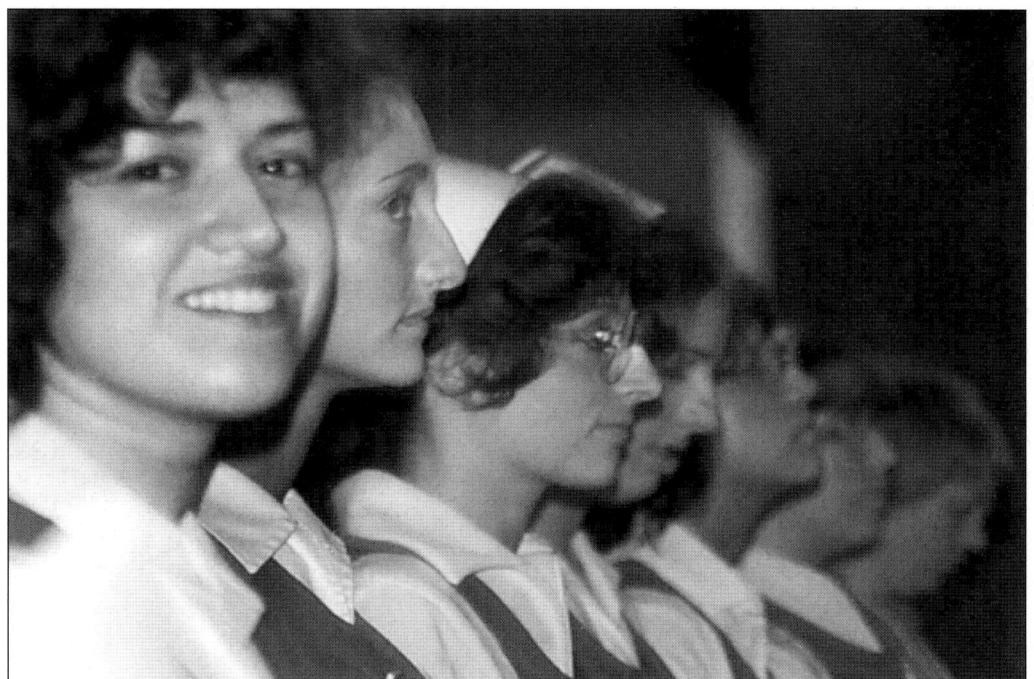

Maria Villalobos (at far left) graduated as a nurse in 1982 from Loyola University. Her sister, Susanna also graduated as a nurse in 1990 from Loyola University. (Courtesy Antonio Villalobos.)

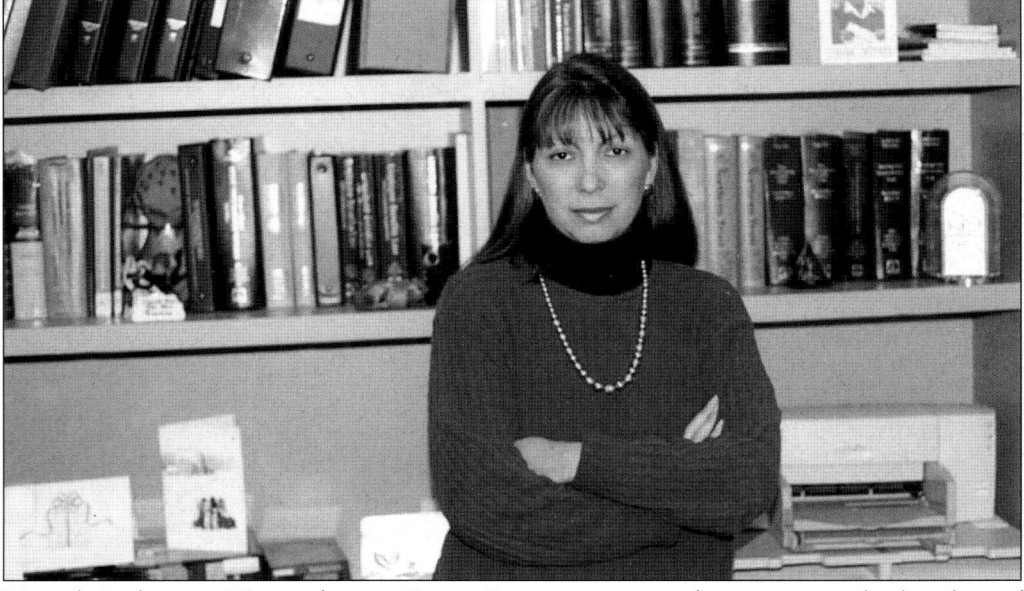

Marisel Ayabarreno Hernandez is a Puerto Rican attorney and a partner in the law firm of Jacobs, Burns, Orlove, Stanton and Hernandez. Hernandez specializes in labor law, and represents individuals in employment discrimination cases. Her parents worked in factories in New York. She was raised in New York and relocated to Chicago in 1985. She is shown here in her office in 1998. (Photo Wilfredo Cruz.)

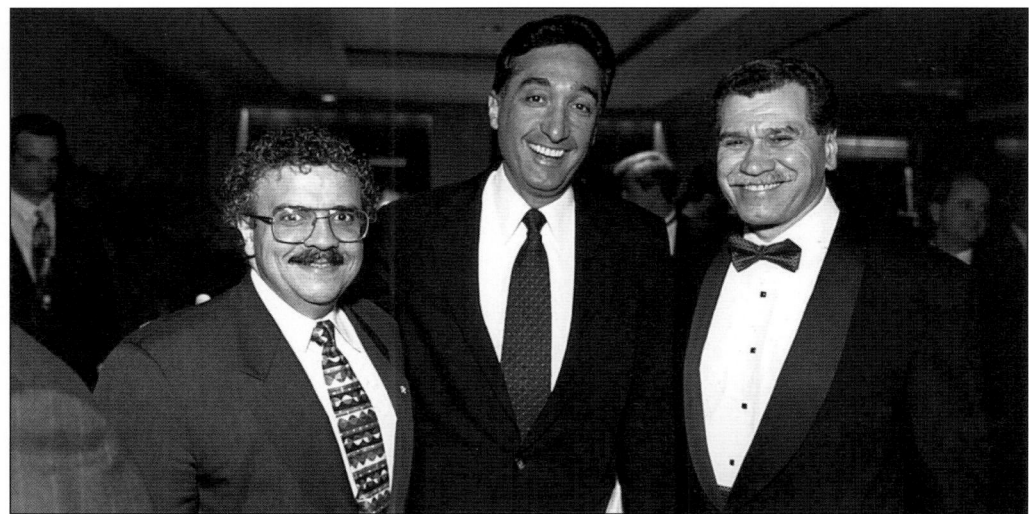

Hipolito (Paul) Roldan (right) has been executive director of the Hispanic Housing Development Corporation (HHDC) for over 28 years. HHDC is a non-profit agency that has developed over 1,900 affordable apartments and townhomes for Latino families. In 1988, Roldan was awarded a $250,000 "genius grant" by the MacArthur Foundation. He used $100,000 of his grant to establish a scholarship to attract Latinos into the community development field. He is shown here in 1996 with (left) Manny Mirabel and (center) Henry Cisneros. They celebrated HHDC's 20th anniversary at the Westin Hotel. (Courtesy Hispanic Housing Development Corporation.)

LET OUR FAMILY

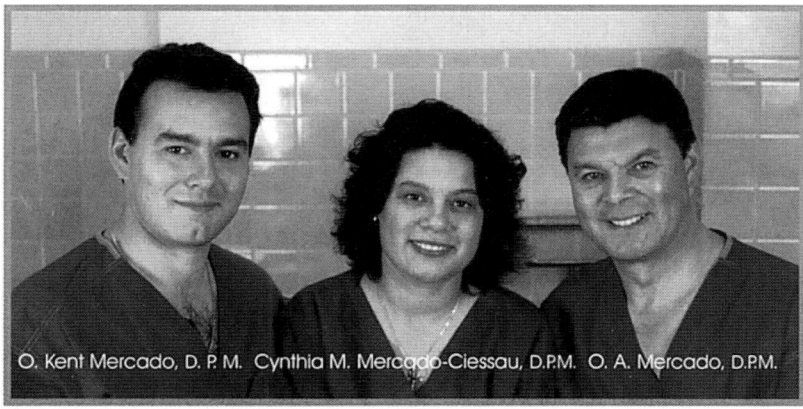

O. Kent Mercado, D. P. M. Cynthia M. Mercado-Ciessau, D.P.M. O. A. Mercado, D.P.M.

CARE FOR YOUR FAMILY

O.A. Mercado (right) is a nationally known Puerto Rican doctor in the field of podiatric medicine. He was professor of surgery at the School College of Podiatric Medicine. He has written six books in his field of expertise. His daughter Cynthia M. Mercado Ciessau (center) and his son, Kent Mercado (left) are also doctors in podiatric medicine. Together they run four Mercado Foot and Ankle clinics in the nearby suburbs of Chicago. (Courtesy O. A. Mercado.)

Six

POLITICAL ACTIVISM

For decades, Puerto Ricans in Chicago lacked political power. Despite their growing numbers over the years, there were no Puerto Ricans in the city council, none in the state legislature, and none in Congress. As loyal Democrats, Puerto Ricans regularly voted for Chicago's longtime mayor, Richard J. Daley. They also voted for the white aldermen who represented wards that were heavily Puerto Rican. Puerto Ricans hoped that the mayor, along with aldermen, would give them some of the thousands of high-paying city jobs they controlled. And they wanted to be invited to sit at the table of political power. But the mayor and many white politicians from Chicago's Regular Democratic Machine took Puerto Ricans and their vote for granted: they gave symbolic attention to Puerto Ricans by donning Puerto Rican hats at Puerto Rican parade celebrations, but very little truly meaningful attention was paid to Puerto Ricans . . . . and few Puerto Ricans held city jobs.

However, Puerto Ricans lacked the political muscle to force concessions from Chicago's strong political machine. Through the years, various Puerto Ricans ran as independents in aldermanic races against candidates from the Regular Democratic Machine. The Puerto Rican candidates all lost by wide margins. They lost because they lacked money, experience, workers, and a strong organization.

In 1981, Chicago's Mayor Jane Bryne handpicked Joseph Martinez to work as alderman of the 31st ward. Martinez was the first Puerto Rican alderman. But the appointment only angered Puerto Ricans, who claimed that white politicians now wanted to handpick the community officials who were supposed to be elected.

The election of Harold Washington, the first African American mayor of Chicago, in 1983, was crucial for Puerto Rican political empowerment. The mayor won the election with strong backing from Puerto Ricans and other Latinos. In return, Washington backed Puerto Rican candidates running for alderman and state senator. This time around, Puerto Ricans won the elections. Washington also appointed numerous Puerto Ricans to high level city jobs. Under Washington, Puerto Ricans were no longer invisible in the halls of power. Sadly, Washington unexpectedly died in office in 1987.

Richard M. Daley is now mayor of Chicago, and has been in office since 1989. With the mayor's backing, more Puerto Ricans have been elected to the city council, and one was even elected to become the first Puerto Rican Congressman of Illinois. "Mayor Richard Daley has been very good for Latinos," says Billy Ocasio, Puerto Rican alderman of the 26th ward. "He has given Latinos more jobs and city contracts than at any other time in the history of Chicago."

But other Puerto Ricans wonder whether the mayor's political support, jobs, and city contracts do not come with a steep price: complete political obedience and loyalty. "There are politicians who feel that if you're not part of their political operation, they can't trust you," says Illinois State Senator Miguel del Valle. "Therefore, they want to put someone in political office who is totally reliable. My definition of reliability is being true to the community. Their definition is doing what they tell you to do . . . Mayor Daley is looking for uniformity in Latino elected officials. In a democracy, that is not healthy."

Miguel del Valle hopes future Latino politicians will be independent thinkers, and not beholden to special interests or to other politicians.

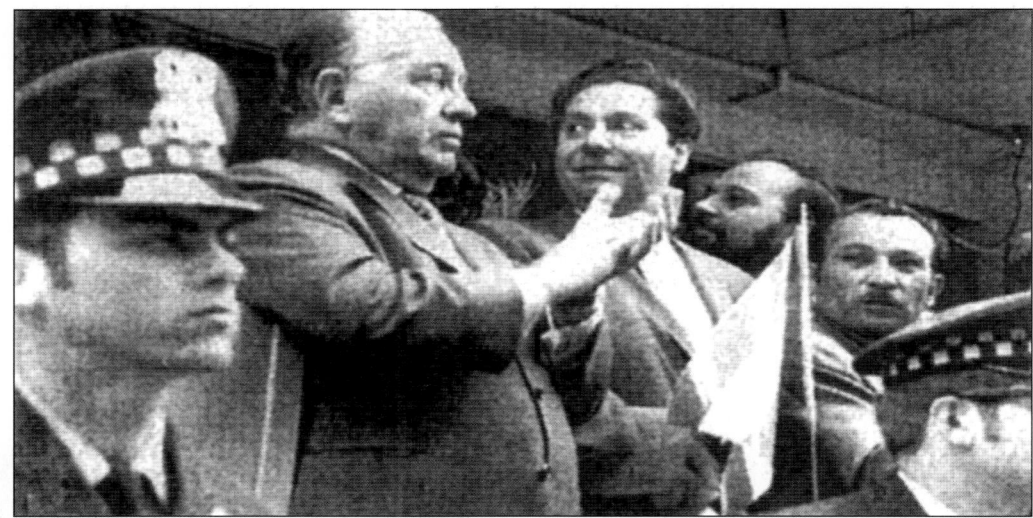

Chicago Mayor Richard J. Daley is pictured in the reviewing stand during the Puerto Rican parade festivities in downtown Chicago in the 1970s. The mayor is clapping for the participants and floats in the parade. Second from the mayor's left is Carlos Caribe Ruiz, president of the Puerto Rican Parade Committee. (Courtesy Joseph A. Ruiz.)

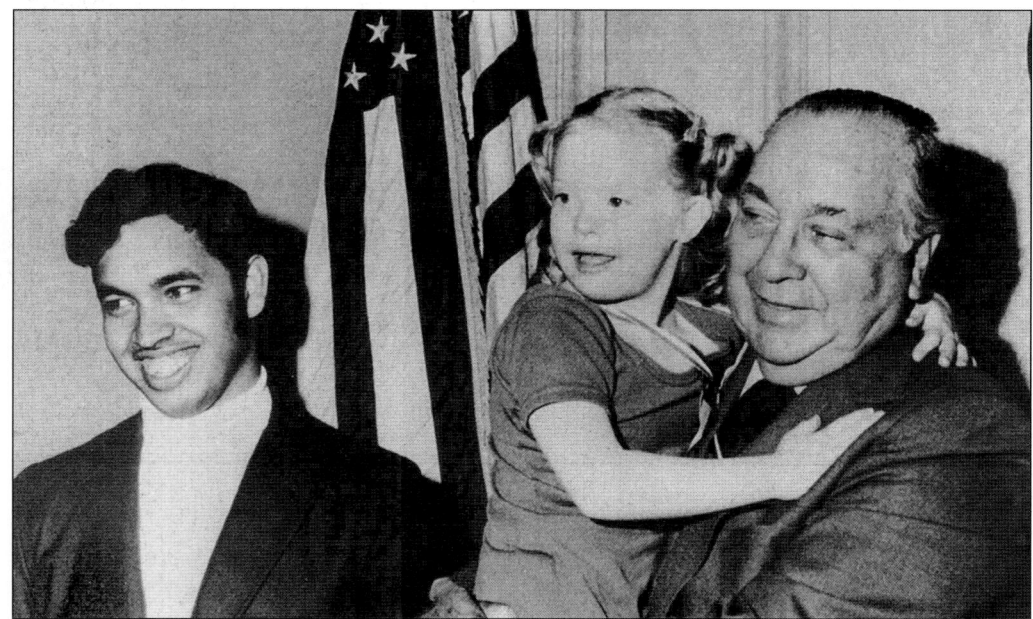

Orlando Rivera (left) was an outstanding Puerto Rican performer in the 1973 Special Olympics. He was awarded a gold and silver medal in swimming. Nine-year-old Joan Wolhaupter won gold medals in the 1974 Special Olympics. They both hear words of praise from Chicago Mayor Richard J. Daley in city hall in 1974. The Chicago Park District and others sponsored the Special Olympics. (Courtesy Anna Rivera.)

82

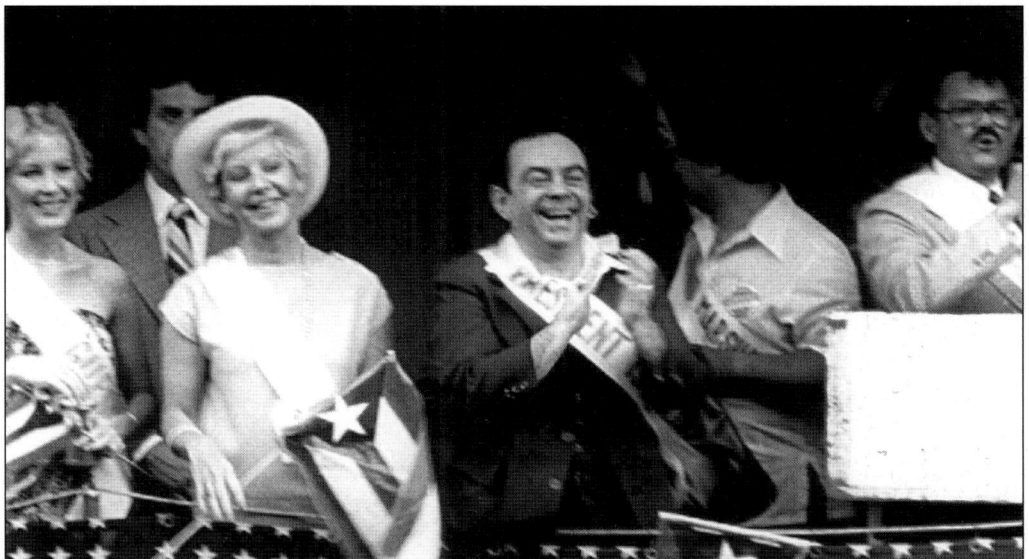

Chicago Mayor Jane Byrne and her daughter (left) hold the Puerto Rican flag in the reviewing stand during the 1979 Puerto Rican parade down Michigan Avenue in 1979. Standing with the mayor are Jose Perez and Juan Cruz, officials of the Puerto Rican Parade Committee. (Courtesy Tomas V. Sanabria.)

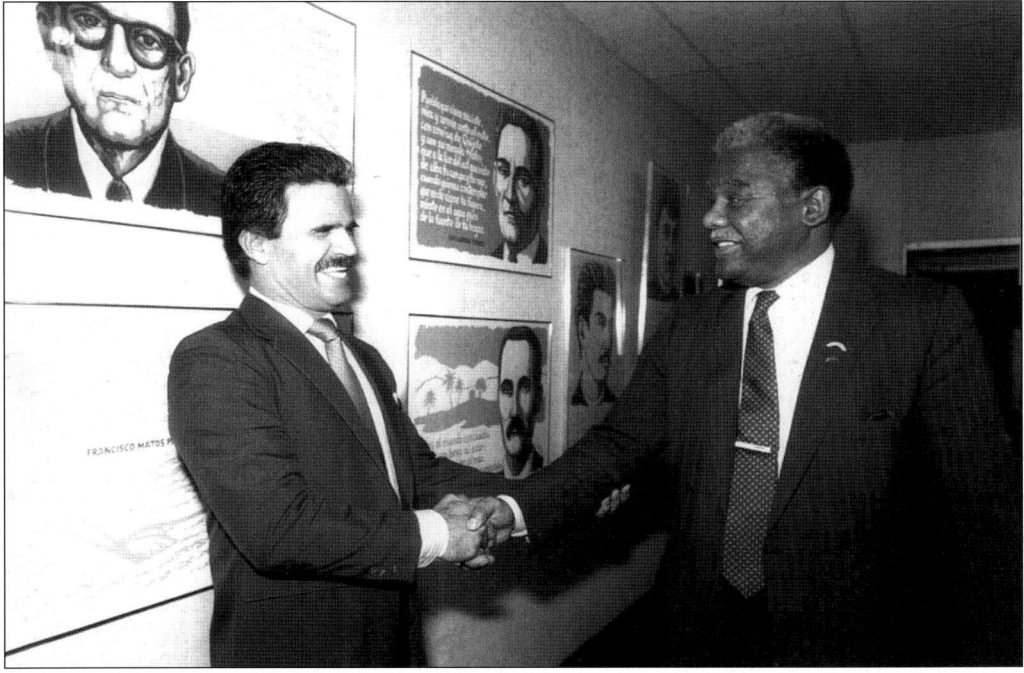

Chicago Mayor Harold Washington meets Luis G. Cajiga, a noted painter from Puerto Rico. The meeting took place in 1986 at Los Caballeros de San Juan Credit Union. Cajiga stands in front of his works, exhibited in the office of Los Caballeros de San Juan Credit Union. (Courtesy Caballeros de San Juan Credit Union.)

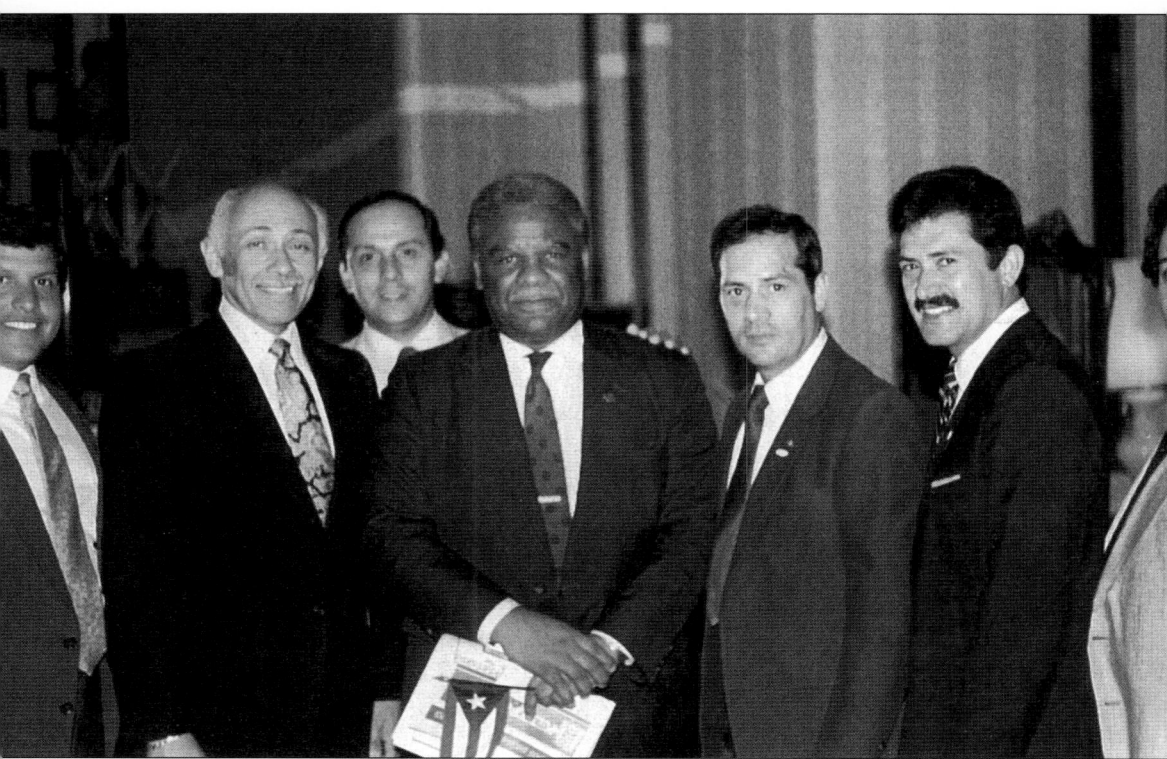

Chicago Mayor Harold Washington participated in the 1984 annual banquet of the Puerto Rican Parade Committee in the Palmer House in downtown Chicago. Joining the mayor, from left to right, are Jose Velgrara, Daniel Rivera, Julio Velgrara, Efrain López, Harry López, and an unidentified individual. (Courtesy Efrain López.)

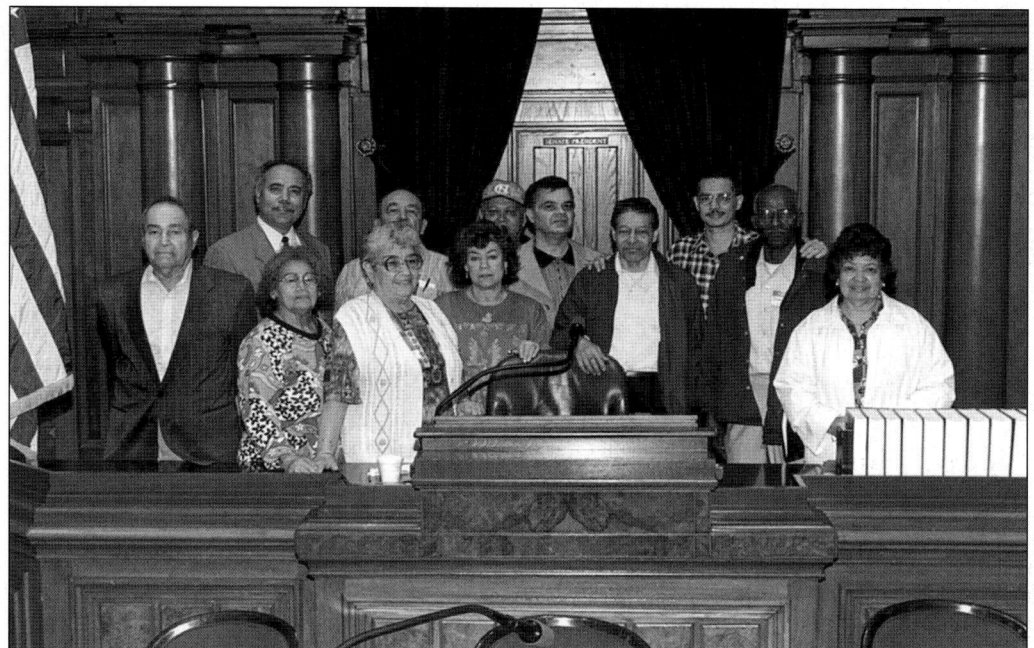

Illinois State Senator Miguel del Valle (with tie) met with Puerto Rican and Cuban seniors in the chambers of the Illinois General Assembly in Springfield, Illinois. The seniors were from Chicago's Casa Central agency. They visited the senator during a lobby day in 1997. Del Valle has been a state senator since 1987. (Courtesy Miguel del Valle.)

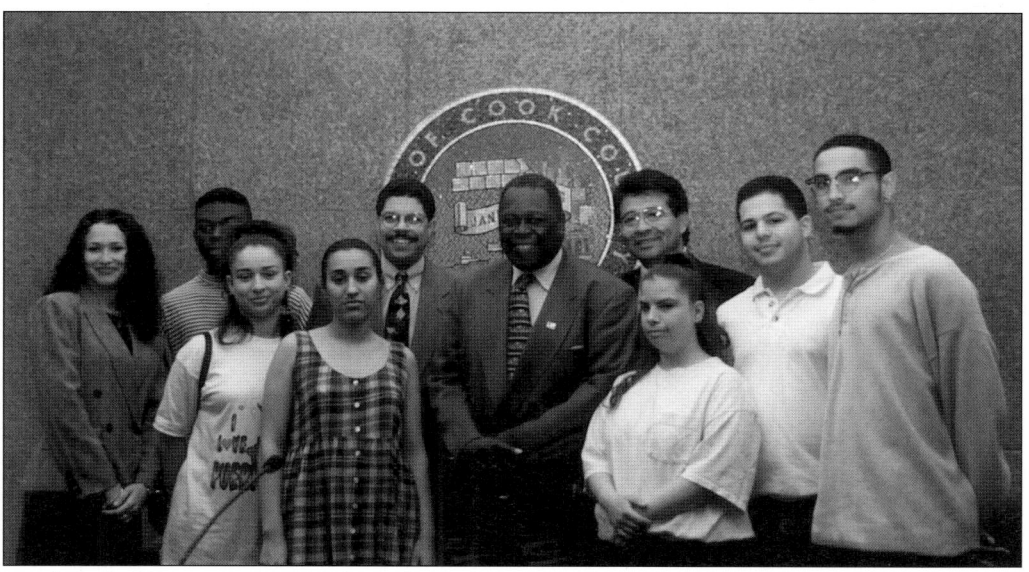

Unidentified Puerto Rican students from the Antonia Pantoja High School meet with three members of the Cook County Board of Commissioner in 1995. From left to right, they are: Roberto Maldonado, a Puerto Rican member of the Cook County Board; John Stroger, president of the Board; and Mario Moreno, a Mexican member of the board. (Courtesy Aspira Inc. of Illinois.)

Puerto Rican politicians are pictured gathered at the Chicago Cultural Center in 2004. They were joining the kick-off festivities for the 2004 Puerto Rican Parade. Pictured, from left to right, are: (front) unidentified person; Ariel E. Reboyras, alderman of the 30th ward; Manny Flores (Mexican), 1st ward alderman; and Roberto Maldonado, Cook County Board commissioner; and (back) Rey Colon, 35th ward alderman. (Puerto Rican Parade Committee.)

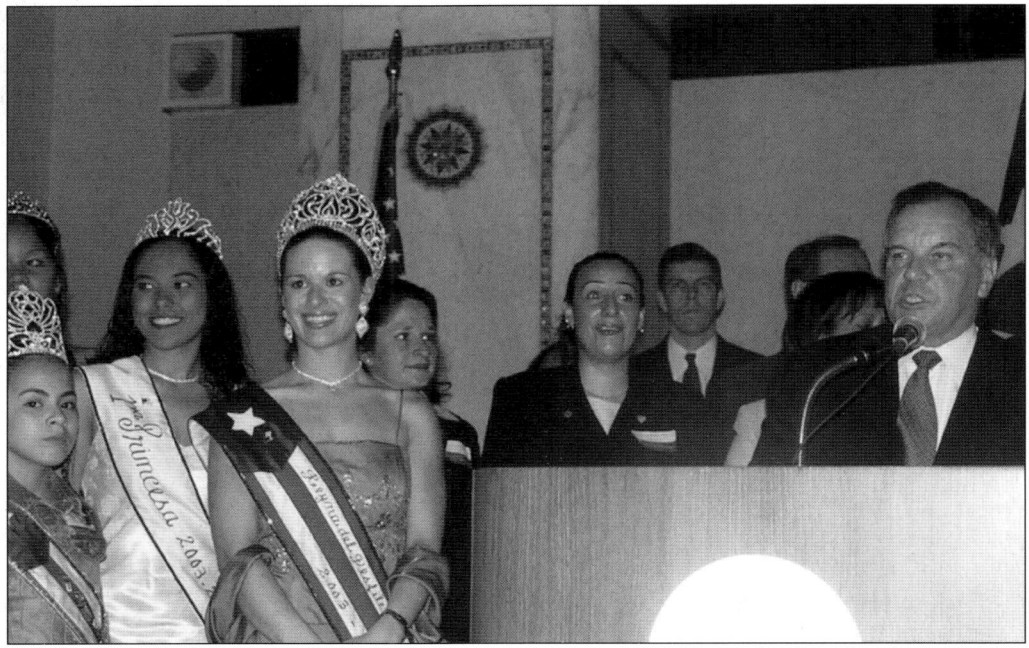

Chicago Mayor Richard M. Daley reads a mayoral proclamation declaring the commencement of Puerto Rican week in Chicago in June 2003. The event was held at the Chicago Cultural Center. To the mayor's right is Michel Ilas, the Puerto Rican queen of the 2003 Puerto Rican parade. She stands with members of her court. (Courtesy Puerto Rican Parade Committee.)

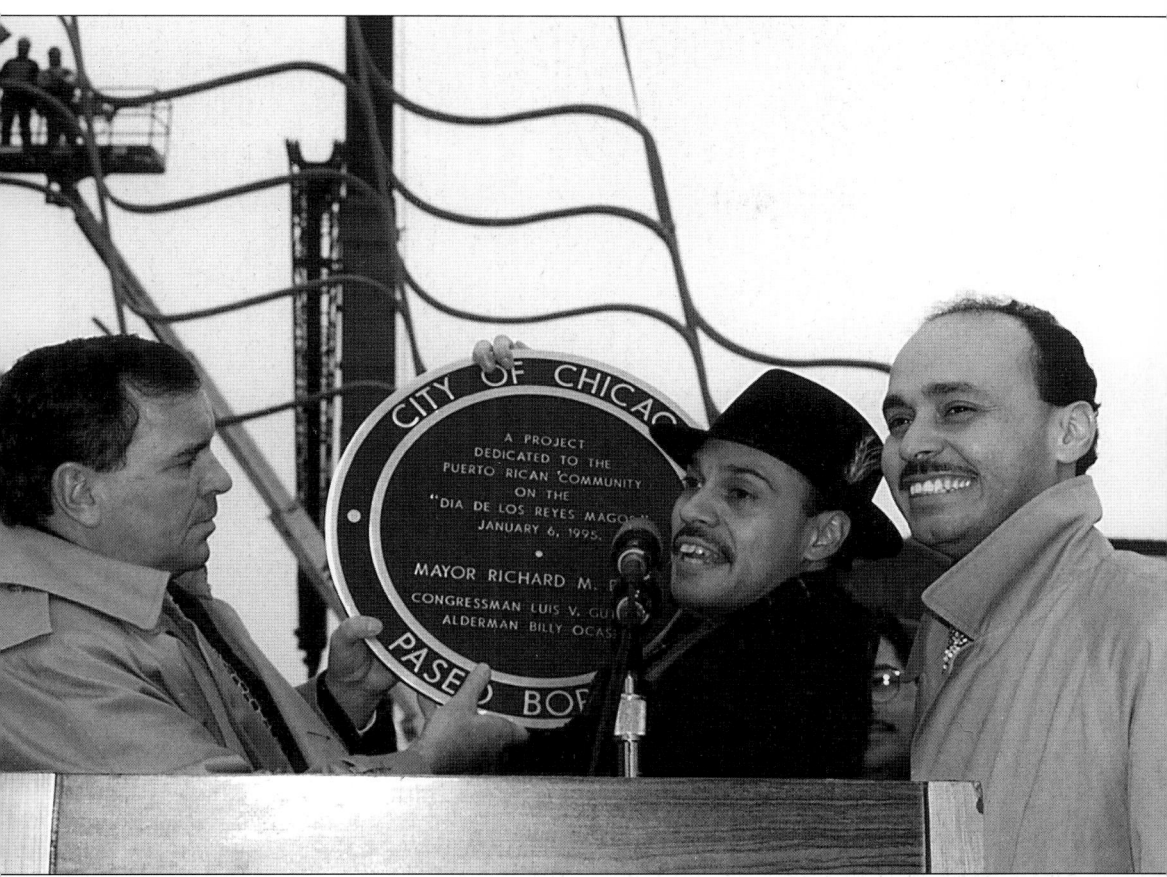

Chicago Mayor Richard M. Daley (left), Alderman Billy Ocasio (26th ward) (center), and U.S. Congressman Luis Gutierrez (D-Ill), inaugurate Paseo Boricua a commercial strip on Division Street. The inauguration included the installation of two large steel Puerto Rican flags on Western and California Avenues. The inauguration was held on January 6, 1995. January 6 is Dia de Los Reyes Mayos, when Puerto Ricans in Puerto Rico traditionally celebrate Christmas. (Courtesy *La Raza*.)

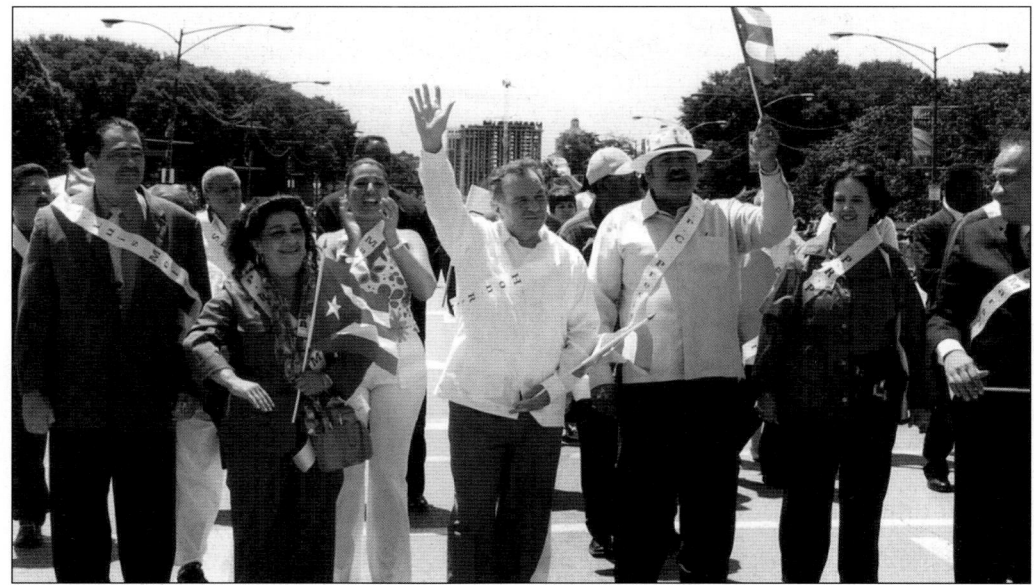

Chicago Mayor Richard M. Daley, wearing a guayabera (a light Puerto Rican shirt), leads the 2004 Puerto Rican Parade along Columbus Drive. Pictured with the mayor, from left to right, are an unidentified mayor from a town in Puerto Rico, Carmen Moreno, Efrain Malave, Ada Gonzales, and Samuel Betances, grand marshall of the parade. (Courtesy Puerto Rican Parade Committee.)

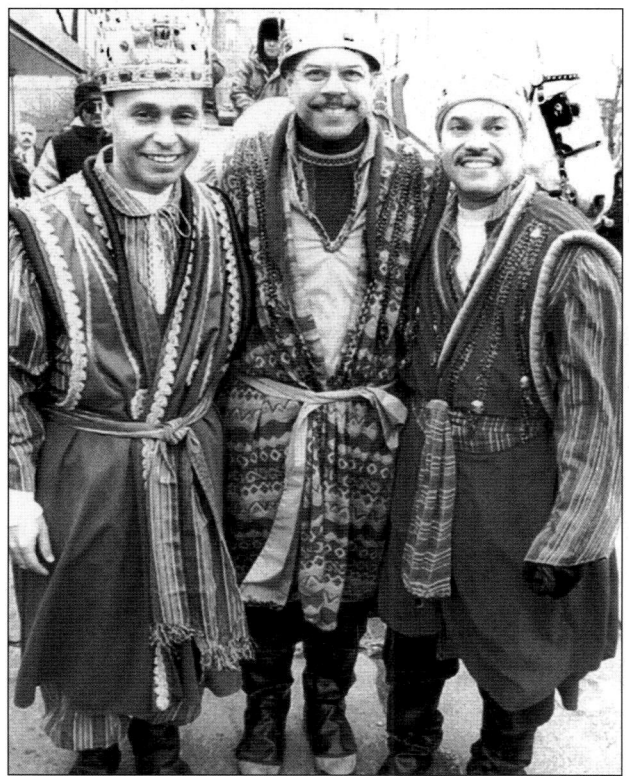

Pictured here, from left to right, are U.S. Congressman Luis Gutierrez (D-Ill), Roberto Maldonado, Cook County Board commissioner, and Alderman Billy Ocasio (26th ward). They are dressed as three kings on January 6, 2004. January 6 is Dia de Los Reyes Mayos. The three led a parade along Division Street. They later distributed about 6,000 gifts to neighborhood children. The event was sponsored by Ocasio's office, together with various community organizations. (Courtesy Puerto Rican Cultural Center.)

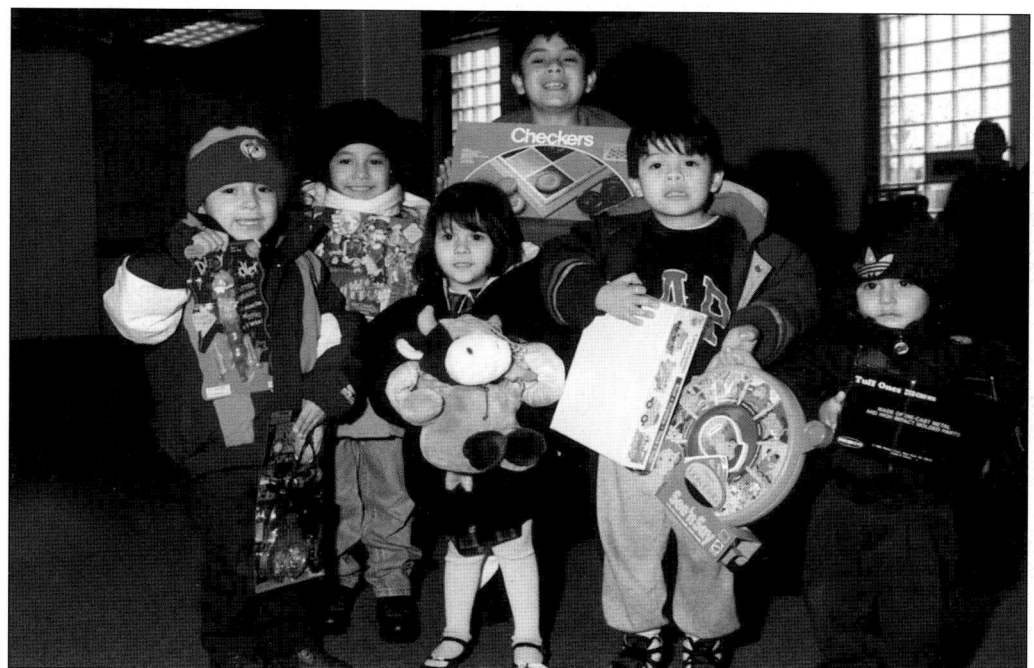

Children receiving gifts on January 6, Dia de Los Reyes Mayos (Three Kings Day) are seen here in the mid-1990s. The event was sponsored by the Puerto Rican Parade Committee. (Courtesy Puerto Rican Parade Committee.)

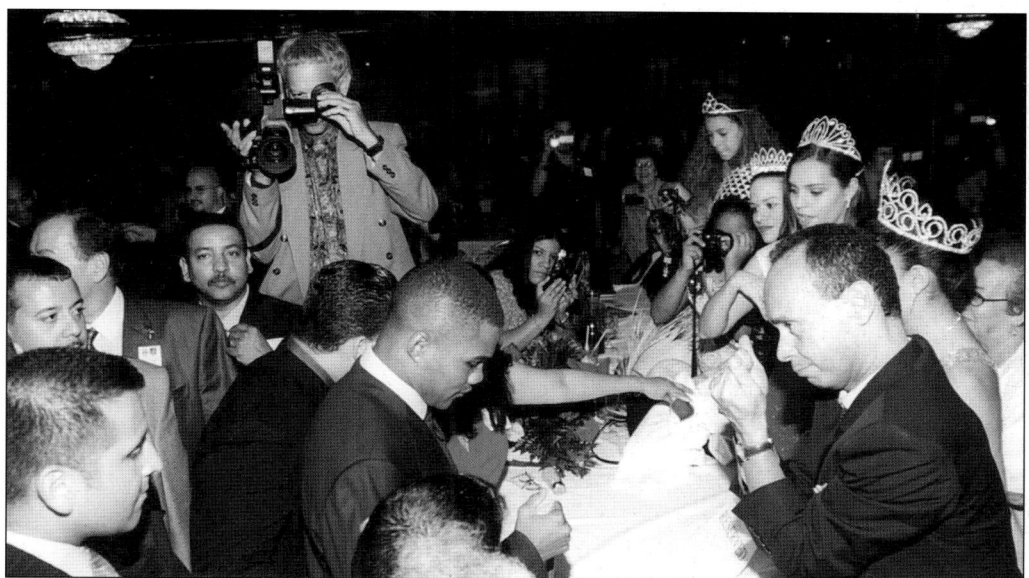

World famous professional boxing champion, Tito Trinidad (opening bottle), came from Puerto Rico to Chicago to be the grand marshal of the 2001 Puerto Rican parade. Trinidad is shown here at a banquet hall for dignitaries of the parade. Facing Trinidad is U.S. Congressman Luis Gutierrez (D-Ill), who joked with Trinidad by striking up a boxing stance. (Courtesy Puerto Rican Parade Committee.)

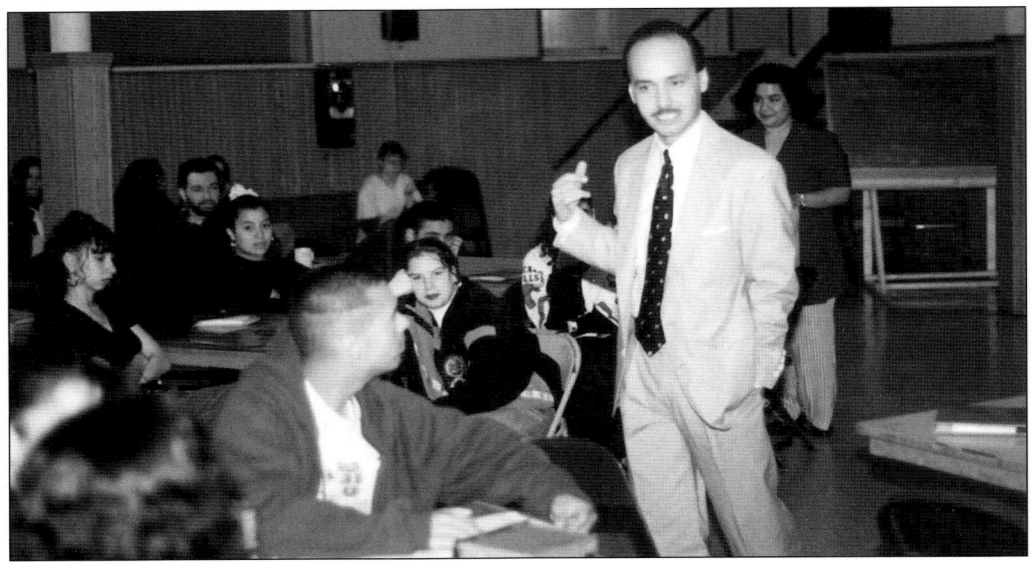

U.S. Congressman Luis Gutierrez (D-Ill) talks to students from the Antonia Pantoja High School of Aspira Inc. of Illinois in 1994. The students listen attentively as Gutierrez speaks about the importance of finishing high school and attending college. Congressman Gutierrez is the highest ranking Puerto Rican and Latino politician in Illinois. (Courtesy Aspira Inc. of Illinois.)

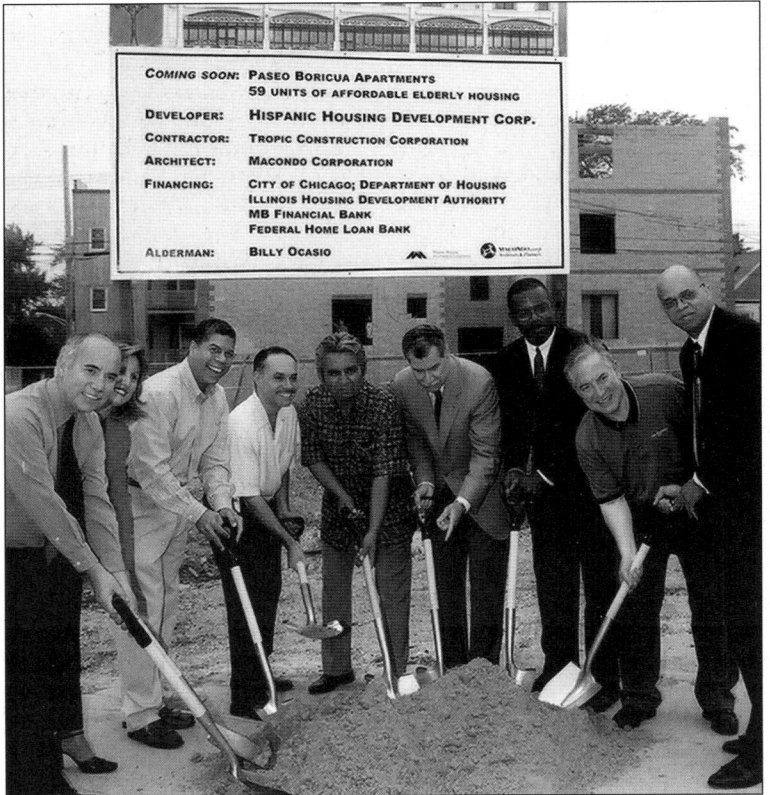

Seen here is a 2003 Hispanic Housing Development Corporation groundbreaking for 59 units of affordable elderly housing on Paseo Boricua. Pictured, from left to right, are Miguel del Valle, Cynthia Soto, Roberto Maldonado, Billy Ocasio, unidentified, Hipolito (Paul) Roldan, Eldridge Edgecombs, Tom FitzGibbon, and Terry Young. (Courtesy Hispanic Housing Development Corporation.)

Seven
SOCIAL ACTIVISM

By the 1960s and 1970s, second generation Puerto Ricans in West Town and Humboldt Park began to acquire a keen sense of political and ethnic consciousness. This was the era of black civil rights, the Vietnam War, and women's and ethnic social movements. A new generation of Puerto Rican community leaders was developing. Puerto Rican painters, muralists, poets, writers, college students, and community activists began to emerge. They began to assert and express their ethnic pride, nationalism, and militancy.

One pivotal event that awakened the political consciousness of Puerto Ricans was a riot that occurred in West Town and Humboldt Park on June 12, 1966. On that hot summer day, Puerto Ricans were celebrating after attending their first large ethnic parade in downtown Chicago. By evening things had gotten ugly. The police shot a 20-year-old Puerto Rican man in the leg. The young man was involved in a street fight and the police claimed he was armed. Witnesses claimed he was not. A large crowd gathered and more police were called in, including canine units. One police officer allowed his large German Shepherd to bite a Puerto Rican man on the leg.

For Puerto Ricans, the police dogs seemed to symbolize all their hurts, real and imaged. The crowd of over 4,000 celebrants attacked the police. They pelted the police with rocks, bottles, and cans, and set two police cars on fire. They overturned and smashed the windows of other police cars. More than a hundred officers, using tear gas and swinging night sticks, tried to disperse the crowd. Additional canine units were brought in but the dogs only further enraged the crowd. Puerto Ricans rioted for three days. Finally, peace was restored. All told, 16 people were injured, 49 arrested, and about 50 buildings destroyed.

City leaders were shocked that Puerto Ricans had rioted. The city held two days of public hearings to determine the cause of the riot. At the hearings, Puerto Ricans complained about police brutality, lack of jobs, lack of political power, bad housing, poor education, union discrimination, and poor city services.

The riot created a new spirit of militancy among Puerto Ricans. Community leaders marched to city hall demanding that Mayor Richard J. Daley seriously address the concerns of Puerto Ricans. The mayor appointed a few loyal Puerto Ricans to city boards. An Urban Progress Center office opened to serve Puerto Ricans. And public schools began teaching Spanish to some of their teachers. But overall, Puerto Ricans still found themselves outside the circle of power looking in.

Lacking political power, Puerto Ricans in the 1960s and 1970s voiced their concerns through protests, demonstrations, and confrontations. Community-based protest organizations like the Spanish Action Committee, the Young Lords, the West Town Concerned Citizens Coalition, and the Union for Puerto Rican Students were organized. These groups demanded that city and state officials, public schools, and colleges hire more Puerto Ricans and open their institutions to the Puerto Rican community. Much progress was made.

As Puerto Ricans slowly entered the halls of power in the 1980s and 1990s, the protests and demonstrations came less frequently. But as the photographs in this chapter illustrate, there has been a long history of social activism in Chicago's Puerto Rican community.

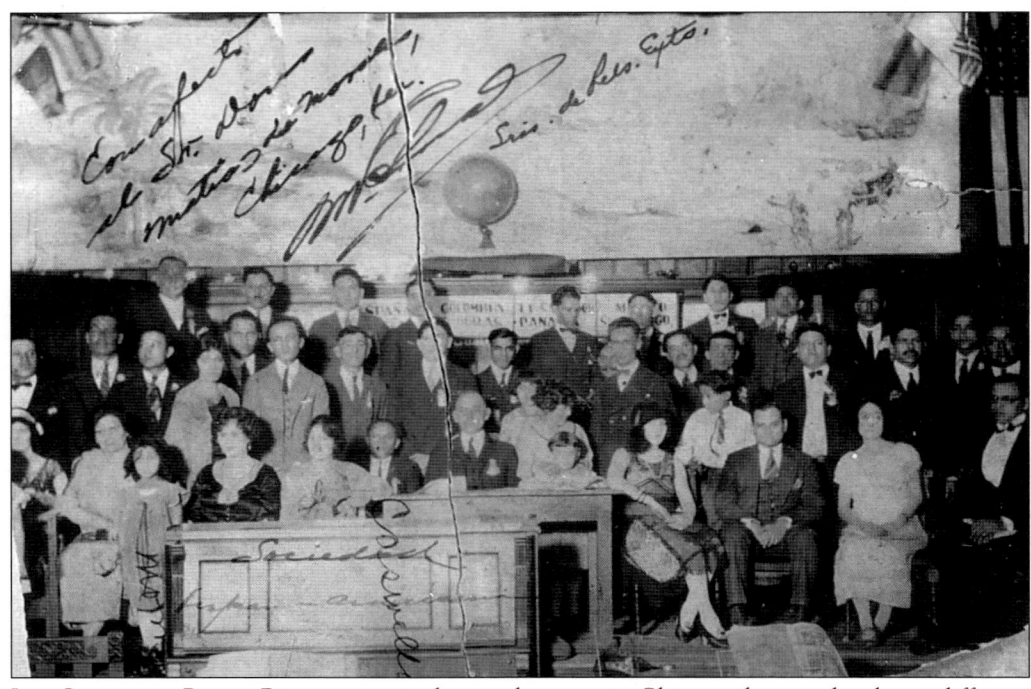

Jose Santana, a Puerto Rican, organized an early group in Chicago that tried to bring different Latino groups together. Founded in 1925, La Sociedad Hispanoamericana (Hispanic Association) met at Hull-House, the famous settlement house founded by Jane Addams. The group, shown here, worked for civic improvement and better cultural understanding among Latino groups. The group had fallen apart by 1933. (Courtesy Antonio Irizzary.)

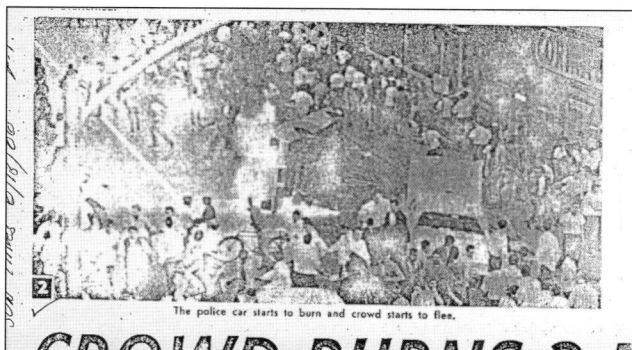

The police car starts to burn and crowd starts to flee.

CROWD BURNS 2 POLICE CARS

An angry crowd set two police cars afire and stoned others Sunday night in a Northwest Side neighborhood where a policeman had shot a man earlier in the day while breaking up a street fight.

Thirty-three persons were arrested and at least five were treated in hospitals before an "enforced peace" was restored to the area around Damen and Division four hours later. Officials said at least a dozen policemen were hit by thrown objects.

A total of 81 policemen with 58 squad cars, using tear gas and swinging night sticks, were used to quell the disturbance. Six canine units also were on hand.

Helmeted policemen charged into crowds several times, felling some demonstrators and routing others, only to have the crowds re-form at other locations.

Taunting area residents pelted policemen and firemen with rocks, bottles and cans.

After several sweeps through the Spanish-speaking area, police pushed the crowds back half a mile along Division from its intersection with Damen.

The disturbance began, according to Patrolman Thomas Munyon, when he and his partner, Patrolman Raymond Howard, broke up a gang fight among eight to 10 youths in an alley just north of the busy intersection.

Munyon said they chased the youths to the 2100 block of Crystal, a half-block north of Division, where he saw a man pulling a gun from under his belt. Munyon said he drew his revolver and fired intentionally low four times, hitting the man in the leg.

The shooting victim was identified as Cruz Arcelis, 20, of 1265 N. Wolcott. He was treated at St. Mary of Nazareth Hospital, 1120 N. Leavitt, for a gunshot wound and a broken left leg, then transferred to the House of Correction hospital. He was reported in good condition.

Treated at County Hospital for a gunshot wound in the right shoulder was Dan Montezuma, 16, of 1207

Turn to Page

A *Chicago Sun-Times* newspaper article reported on the riot that occurred in Chicago's Puerto Rican community on Division Street on June 12, 1966. The shooting of a young Puerto Rican man by police triggered a three-day riot. It was the first time Puerto Ricans rioted in any major American city. (Reprinted with Special Permission by the *Chicago Sun-Times*.)

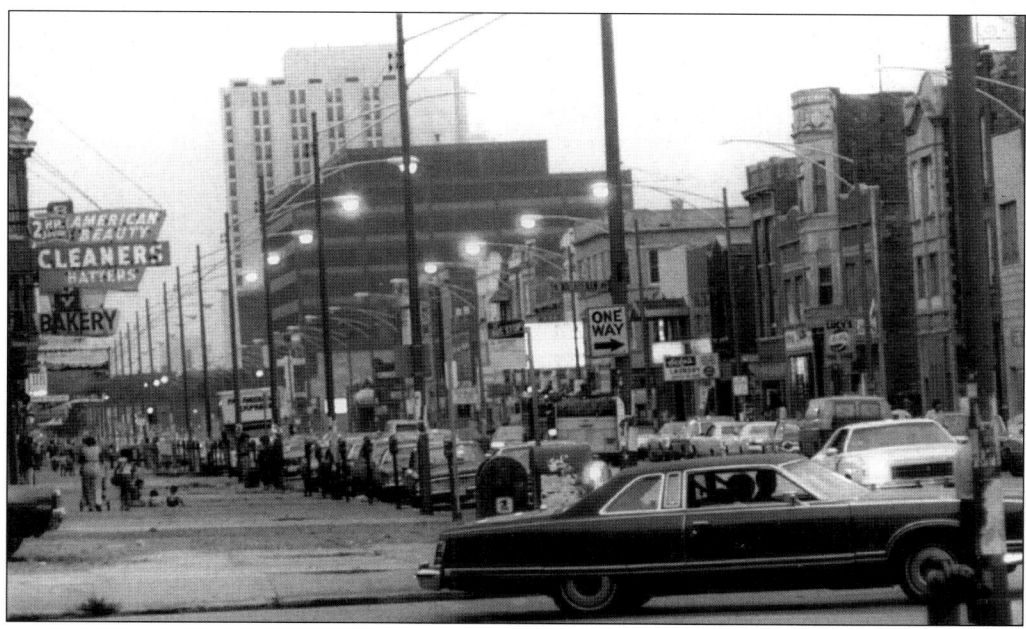

This is a view of Division Street at dusk in 1978. This is the street where Puerto Ricans rioted for three-days in June 1966. For many years, Division Street was the heart of Chicago's Puerto Rican community. Since 1995, the street has undergone major renovations and is now a thriving Puerto Rican business district. Gentrification in the area, however, is slowly forcing many Puerto Ricans to move to neighborhoods further west. (Courtesy Tomas V. Sanabria.)

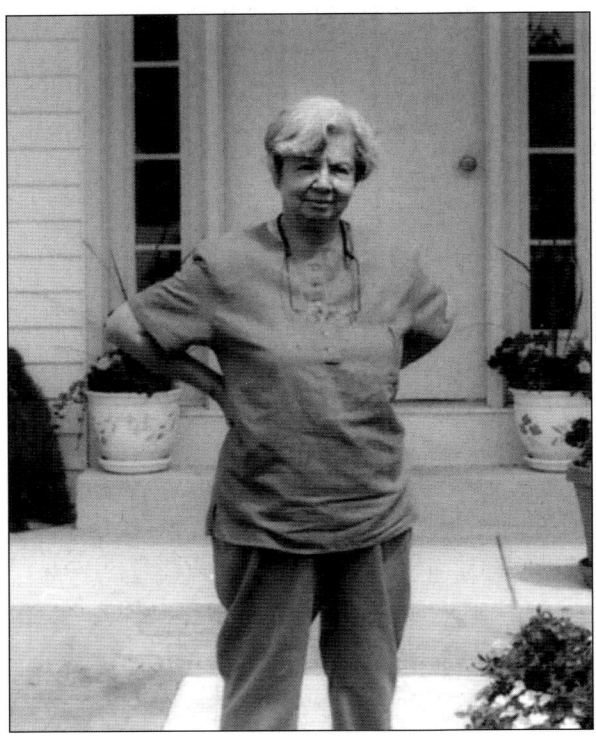

Mirta Ramirez is a well-known Puerto Rican community activist. After the June 1966 riot, she and other community leaders marched to city hall demanding that Mayor Richard J. Daley address the social concerns of Puerto Ricans. In 1968, she founded Aspira Inc. of Illinois, an educational agency that has helped thousands of Puerto Ricans finish high school and enter college. Ramirez stands in front of her home in Batavia, Illinois in 1998. (Photo Wilfredo Cruz.)

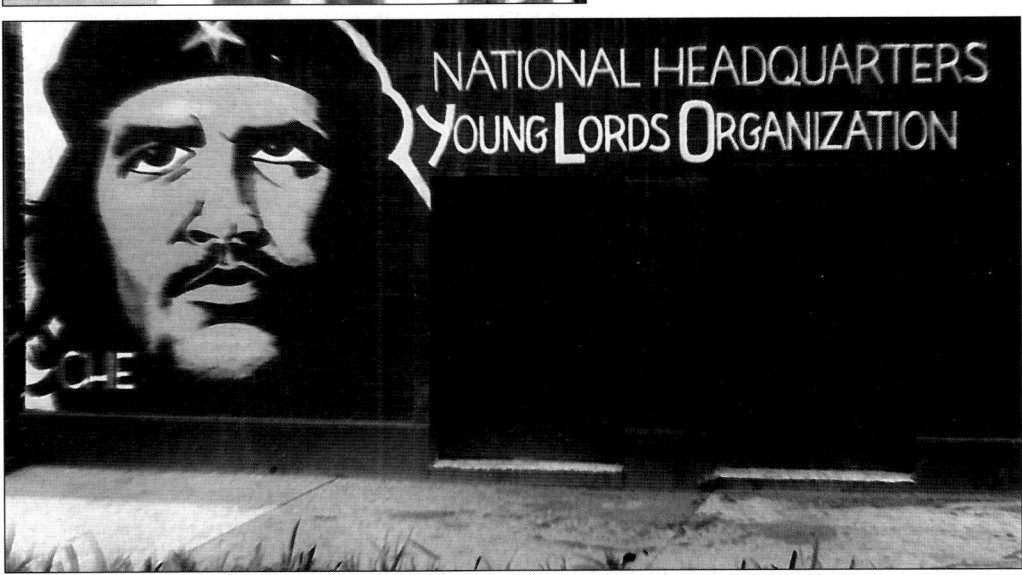

In 1969, the Young Lords were formed. The group was a former street gang that acquired political consciousness. It used protests and sit-ins to bring better city services to Puerto Ricans. The group opened a day-care center and breakfast program in a church basement, and created a people's park on an empty city lot. The group's leaders were regularly arrested by police for minor infractions. The group had disappeare,d by the mid-1970s. This was national headquarters of the Young Lords Organization on Armitage Street in the Lincoln Park neighborhood. (Courtesy Carlos Flores.)

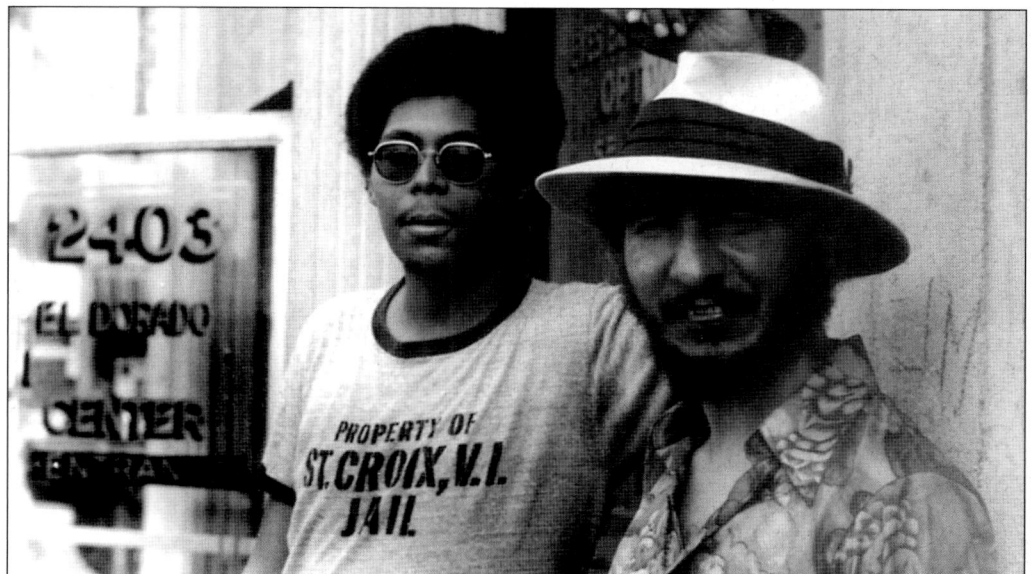

Miguel Rios (left) is seen here on Western Avenue in the mid-1970s with his friend, Aric Carrillo. Rios was a student activist and one of the founders of the Union for Puerto Rican Students at Northeastern Illinois University. The Union used protests and sit-ins to force university officials to increase the number of Puerto Rican faculty and students at the university. Rios passed away at age 33 from sickle cell anemia. (Courtesy Carlos Flores.)

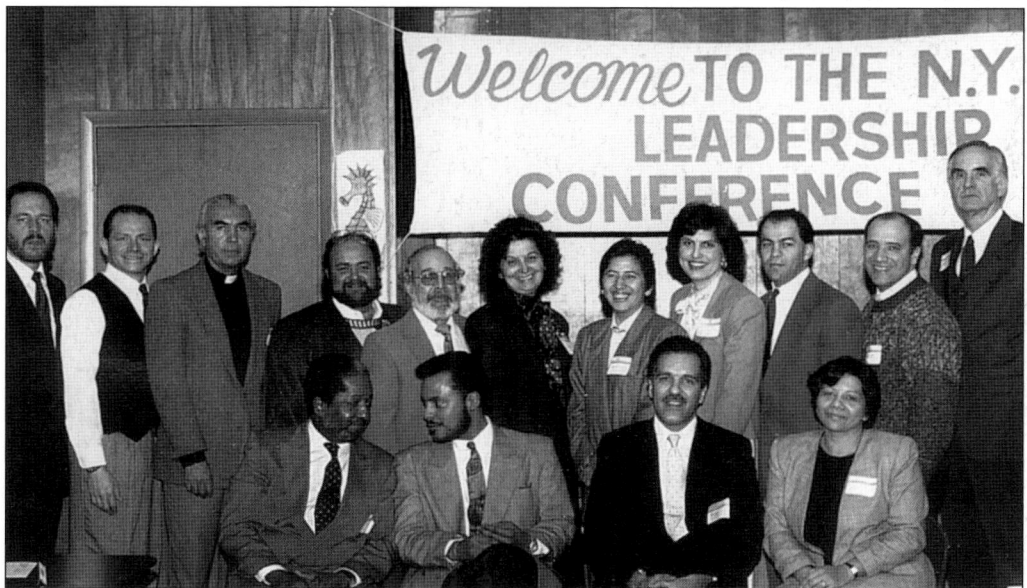

The directors of various social service agencies in Humboldt Park and Logan Square formed the Network for Youth Services in 1979. The Network attempted to use education, social services, and recreation to combat the gang problem in the Puerto Rican community. Some progress was made, but the group eventually disbanded. Pictured here in 1991, from left to right, are as follows: (bottom) unidentified, unidentified, Jamie Rivera, and Aida Sanchez; (top) Tomas V. Sanabria, Ray Vasquez, Carlos Plazas, and the rest are unidentified. (Courtesy Tomas V. Sanabria.)

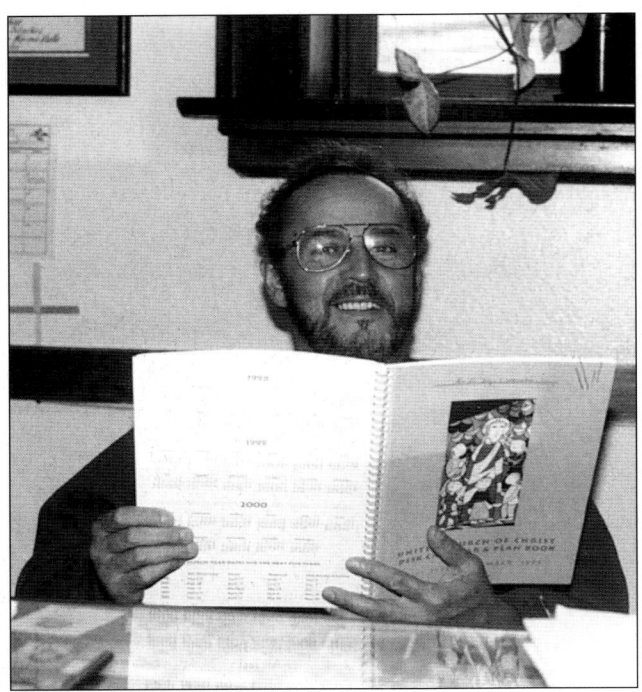

Rev. Jorge Morales, pastor of the First Congregation Church of Chicago in the Humboldt Park neighborhood is seen here in 1998. In 1976, Morales and others formed the West Town Concerned Citizens Coalition. The group used protests and demonstrations to force city officials to hire more Puerto Ricans, fix schools, clean neighborhoods, and provide more housing. The group held noisy demonstrations against the Chicago Post Office over the lack of Latino employees. (Photo Wilfredo Cruz.)

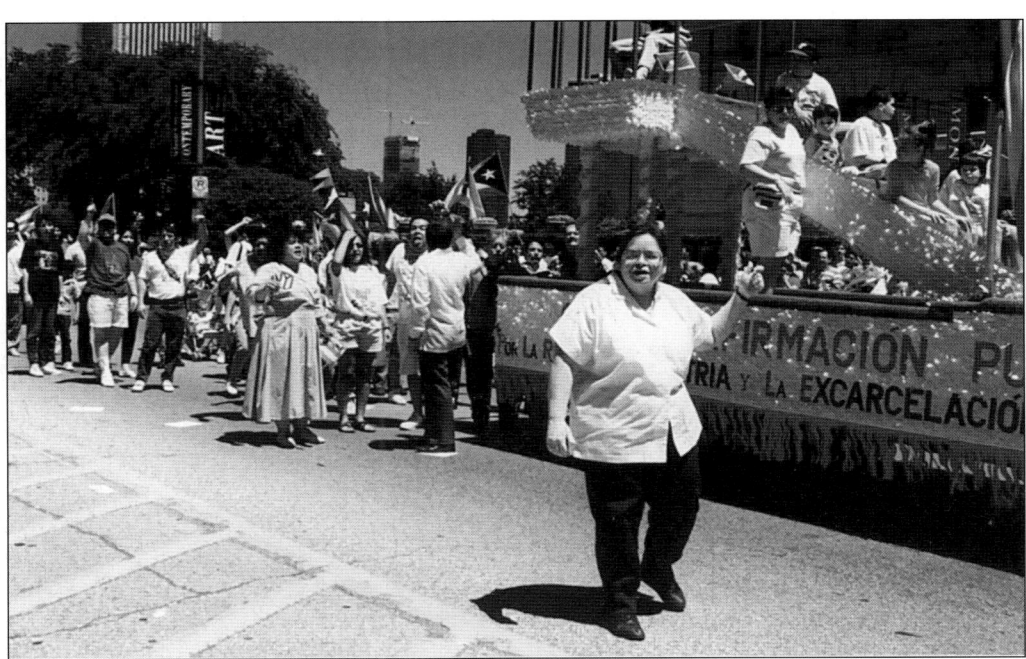

Meca Sorrentini is a community activist, and leader of the Puerto Rican independence movement in Chicago. She was instrumental in forming the Segundo Ruiz Belvis Cultural Center, which is dedicated to preserving and highlighting Puerto Rican culture. She is shown here in a late-1990s Puerto Rican parade in downtown Chicago. (Courtesy Puerto Rican Parade Committee.)

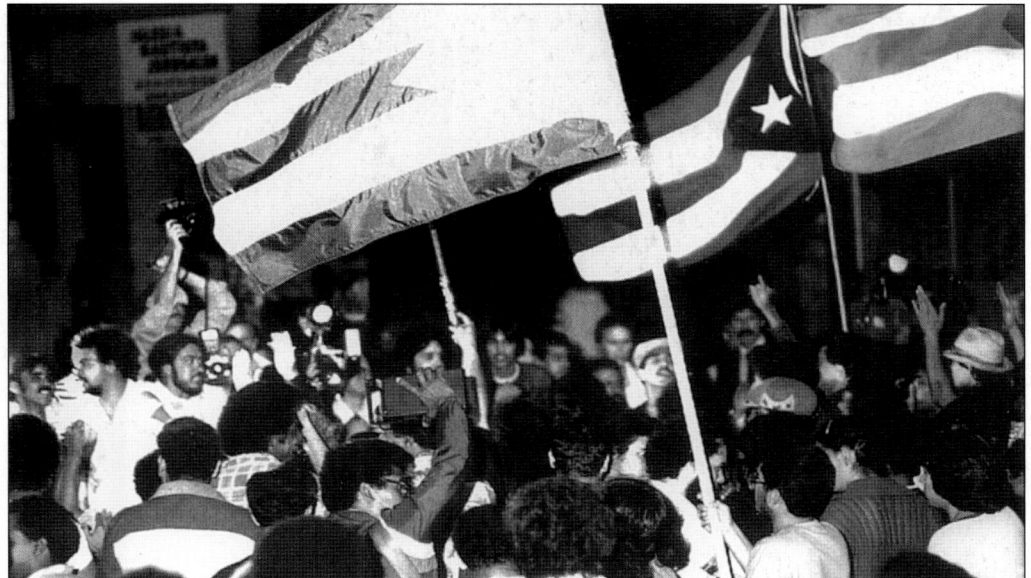

On Division Street, thousands of Puerto Ricans celebrate the release of five Puerto Rican Nationalists from U.S. prisons. The five were accused of shooting at representatives in the U.S. Congress in 1954. The Nationalists said they perpetrated the shooting to call world attention to the United States' colonial rule over Puerto Rico. The five were each given life sentences and served 25 years in prison. Through executive clemency, President Jimmy Carter released all five in September 1979. The five Nationalists, who are from Puerto Rico, visited Chicago. (Courtesy Tomas V. Sanabria.)

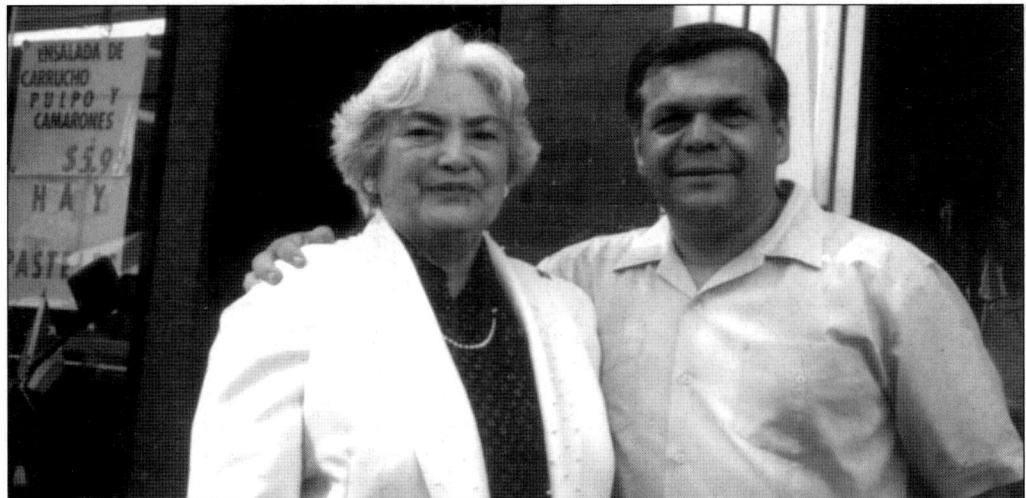

José López (right) is a popular leader in the Puerto Rican community. He is a professor of Puerto Rican history, and a leader of the Puerto Rican independence movement in Chicago. He was key in forming the Puerto Rican Cultural Center, Pedro Albizu Campos high school, Paseo Boricua, and various neighborhood agencies. He is shown here with Lolita Lebrón, a Puerto Rican Nationalist leader who commanded an attack and shooting on the U.S. Congress in 1954. The photo was taken on Paseo Boricua in 1996, while Lebrón was visiting Chicago from Puerto Rico. (Courtesy José López.)

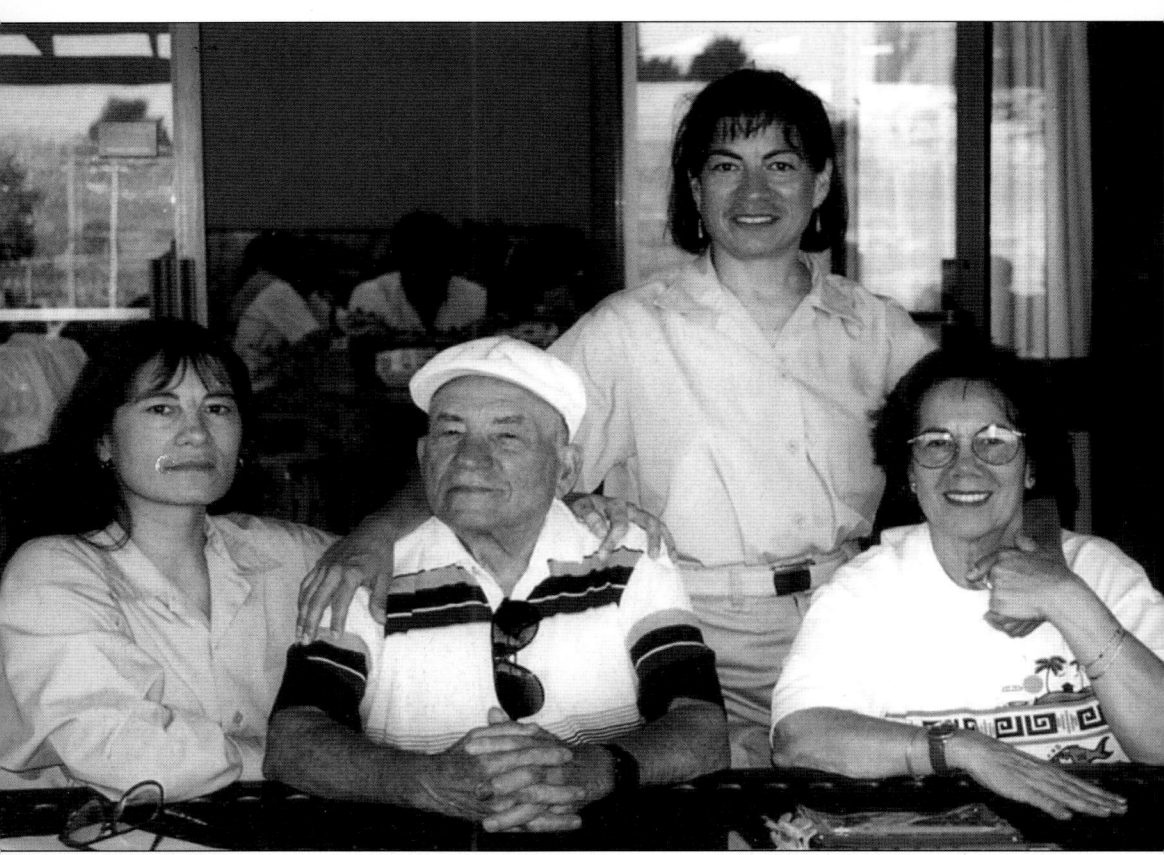

Josefina Rodriguez (seated, right) and her husband, Bernardo, visited their daughters, Ida Luz (seated, left) and Alicia, in 1997 at a federal prison in California. The sisters were accused of being members of the Armed Forces for National Liberation (FALN) a clandestine Chicago group advocating the independence of Puerto Rico from the United States. The group was accused of bombing dozens of banks and government buildings in Chicago and New York. In 1980, 11 FALN members were given life sentences. In September 1999, President Bill Clinton granted clemency to 11 FALN prisoners, including the Rodriguez sisters. They now live in Puerto Rico. (Courtesy Josefina Rodriquez.)

In 1993, the Chicago Park District refused to allow Puerto Ricans to permanently place a bronze statue of Pedro Albizu Campos (shown here) in Humboldt Park. Some public officials argued that Campos, as leader of the Nationalist Party in Puerto Rico during the 1950s, advocated the use of violence against the United States to try to gain Puerto Rico's independence. (Courtesy *La Raza*.)

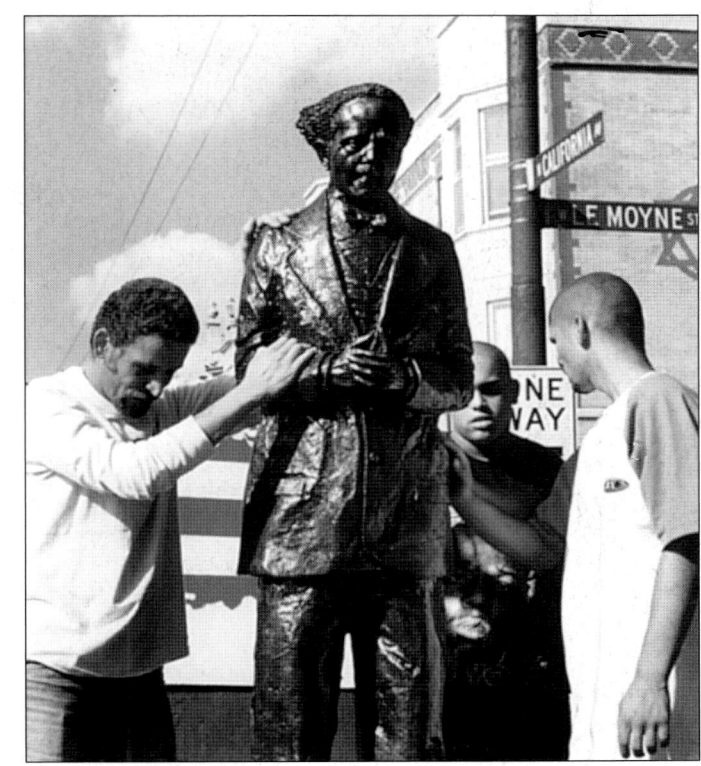

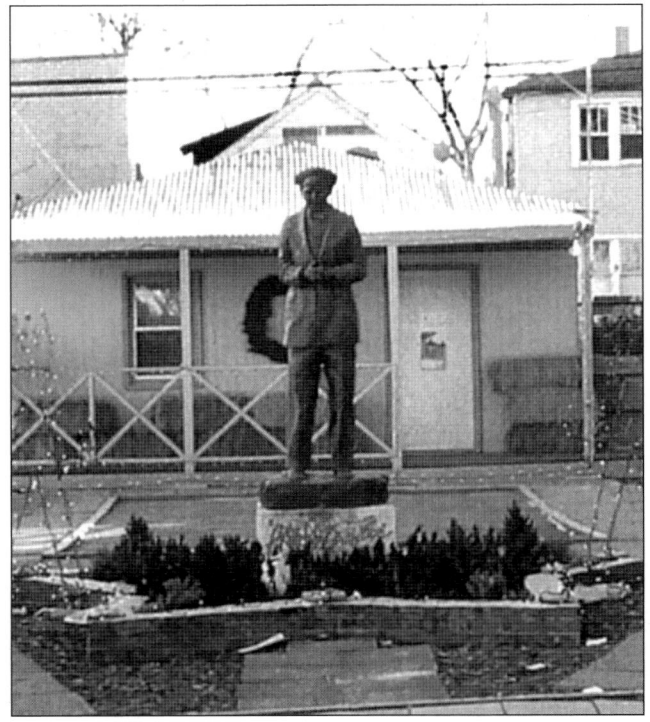

The statue of Pedro Albizu Campos, leader of the Nationalist Party in Puerto Rico during the 1950s, was placed at La Casita de Don Pedro on Paseo Boricua. This garden galley was created on an empty lot in 1997 by students and faculty of the Dr. Pedro Albizu Campos High School. As a public space, the Casita attempts to affirm the presence of Puerto Ricans in the city, and is a statement against the gentrification of the Humboldt Park community. (Courtesy Puerto Rican Cultural Center.)

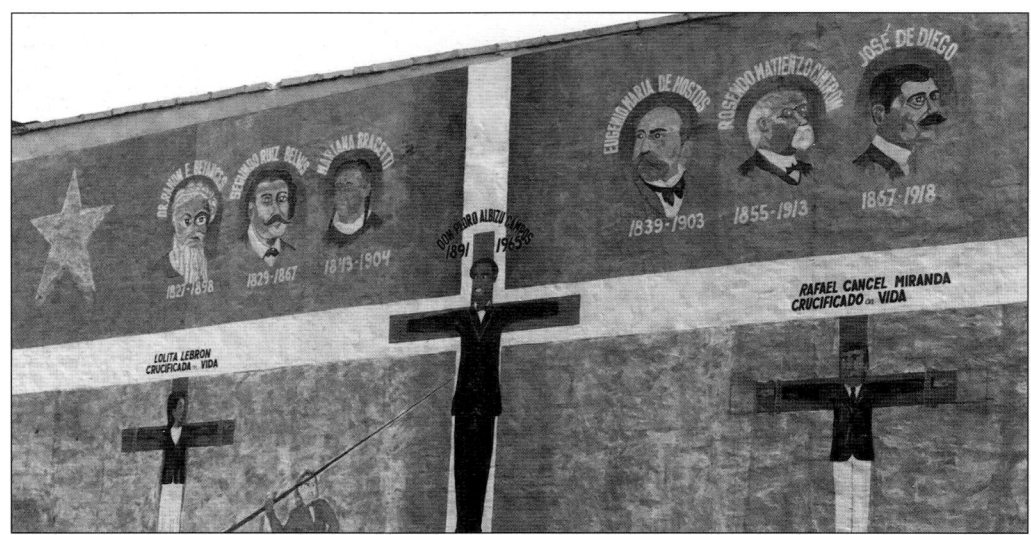

The Puerto Rican Arts Association originally painted this mural, titled "La Crucificción de Don Pedro Albizu Campos." This is the oldest exterior Puerto Rican mural in Chicago. It pictures Pedro Albizu Campos, leader of the Nationalist Party, hanging from a cross, and Luis Muñoz Marín, the firstPuerto Rican-elected governor of the island, poised to stab Albizu. Next to Albizu are Lolita Lebrón and Rafael Cancel Miranda, two Nationalist figures. The portraits at the top are of other Puerto Rican pro-independence patriots. (Courtesy Marixsa Alicea.)

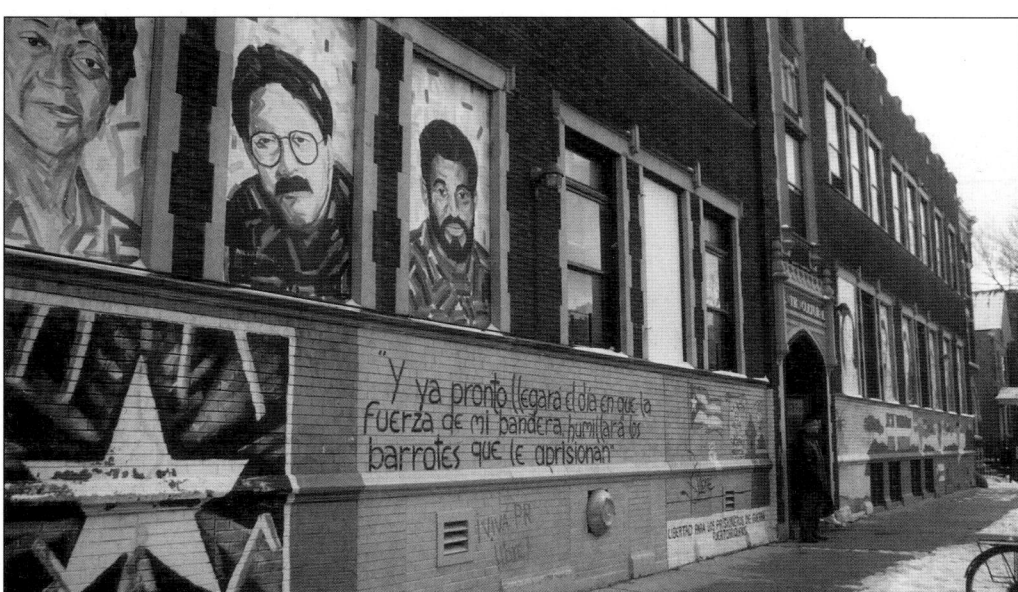

The Juan Antonio Corretjer Puerto Rican Cultural Center (shown here) was located at 1617 N. Claremont Avenue for about 30 years. The center was named after the national poet of Puerto Rico. The center housed the Pedro Albizu Campos High School, the Family Learning Center, and other programs. On the center's outside walls, Pablo Marcano Garcia painted 13 portraits of formerly imprisoned Puerto Ricans who advocated for Puerto Rico's independence from the United States. (Courtesy Marixsa Alicea.)

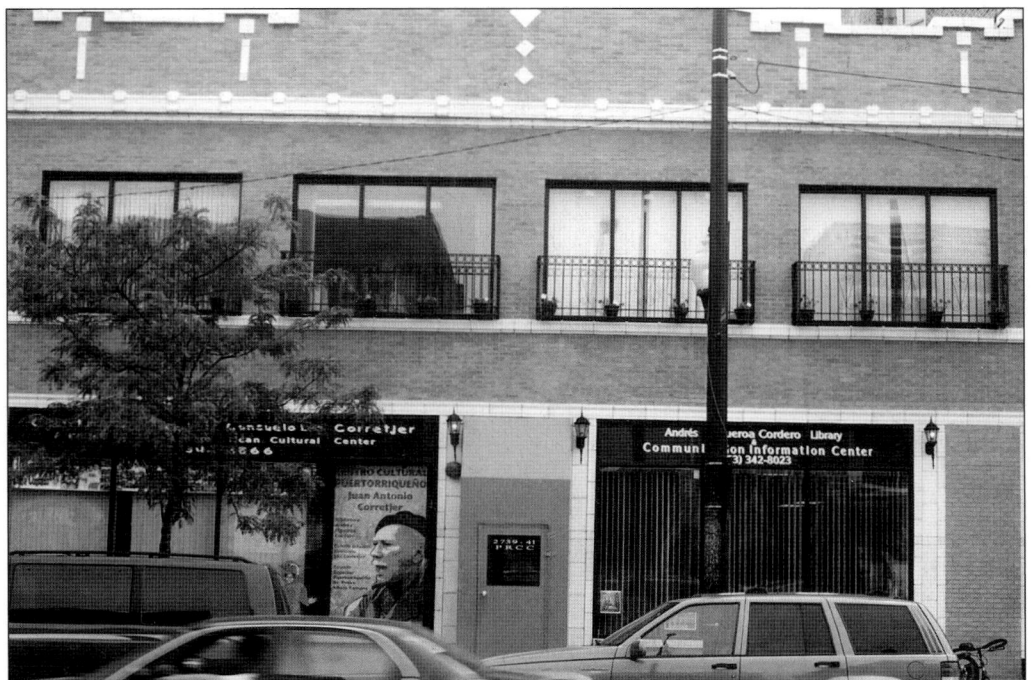

The Juan Antonio Corretjer Puerto Rican Cultural Center opened its doors in a newly constructed building in 2004. The center is now on Division Street on Paseo Boricua. José López is the executive director. (Photo Wilfredo Cruz.)

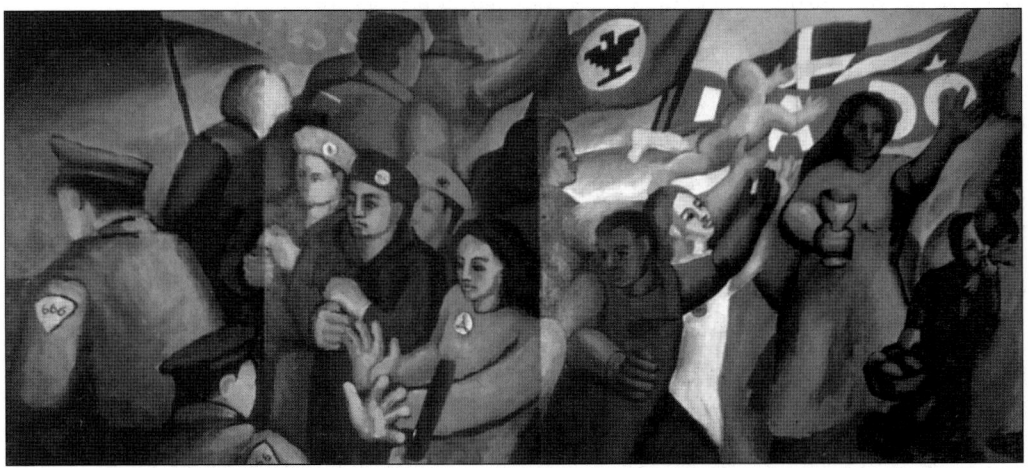

This mural, titled "Fuertes Somos Ya" (Strong We Are Now), was painted by John Pitman Weber in 1971, and is located in the Segundo Ruiz Belvis Cultural Center. The mural's themes are the end of violence and a call for unity to fight against injustice. One person wear's a United Farm Worker's Union beret, another a Young Lords beret, and another a Latin Kings beret. The Latin Kinds were a street gang the Young Lords tried to politicize. The woman wears a Latin American Defense Organization (LADO) symbol. LADO was a group that fought for racial justice, housing, and better living conditions. (Courtesy Marixsa Alicea.)

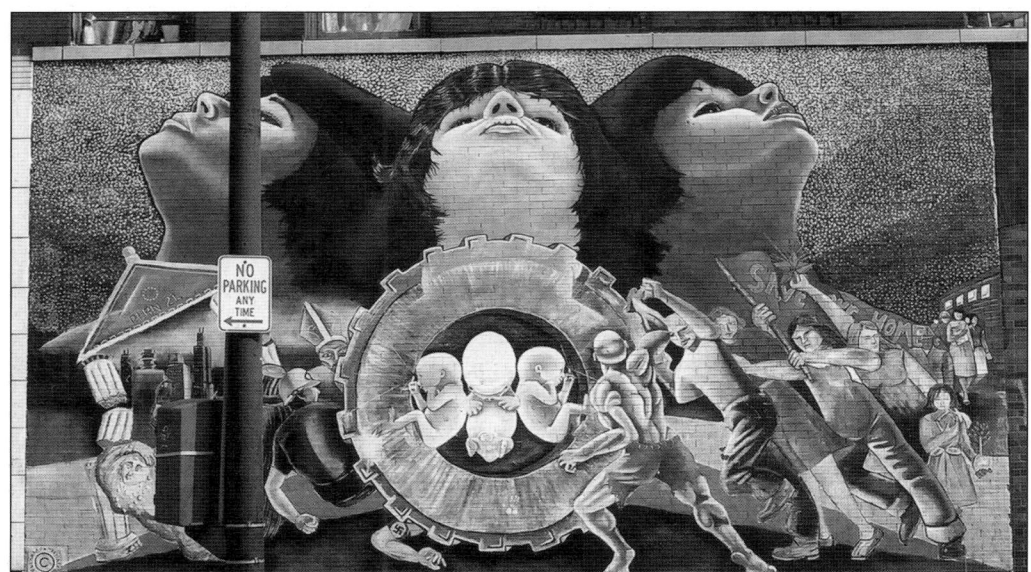

This mural, titled "Smash Plan 21," was painted by Oscar Martínez, José Guerrero, and Judith Motyka in 1978, on Spaulding and North Avenues. The mural protests Plan 21, an urban renewal plan the city developed in the 1970s. Plan 21, and others like it, set the groundwork for the gentrification of Puerto Rican neighborhoods like Lincoln Park, West Town, and Wicker Park. The mural was washed off the building in the late 1990s. (Courtesy Marixsa Alicea.)

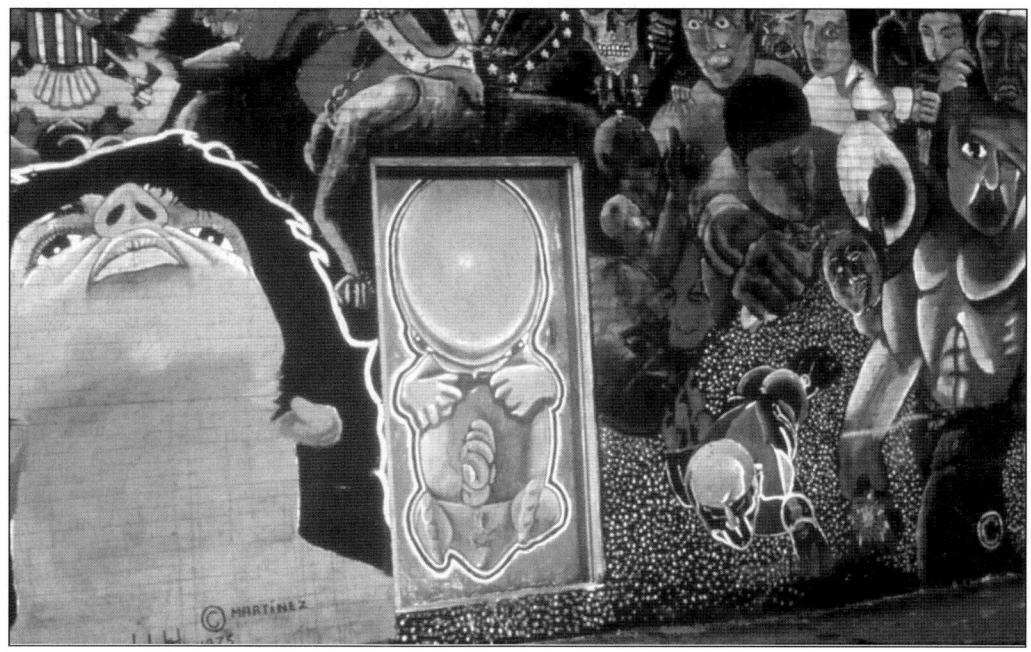

Oscar Martínez painted this untitled mural in 1975 in the Lakeview neighborhood. The mural protests America's Bicentennial celebration. The mural wonders how a country can celebrate freedom when its people of color still face discrimination and negative treatment. (Courtesy Marixsa Alicea.)

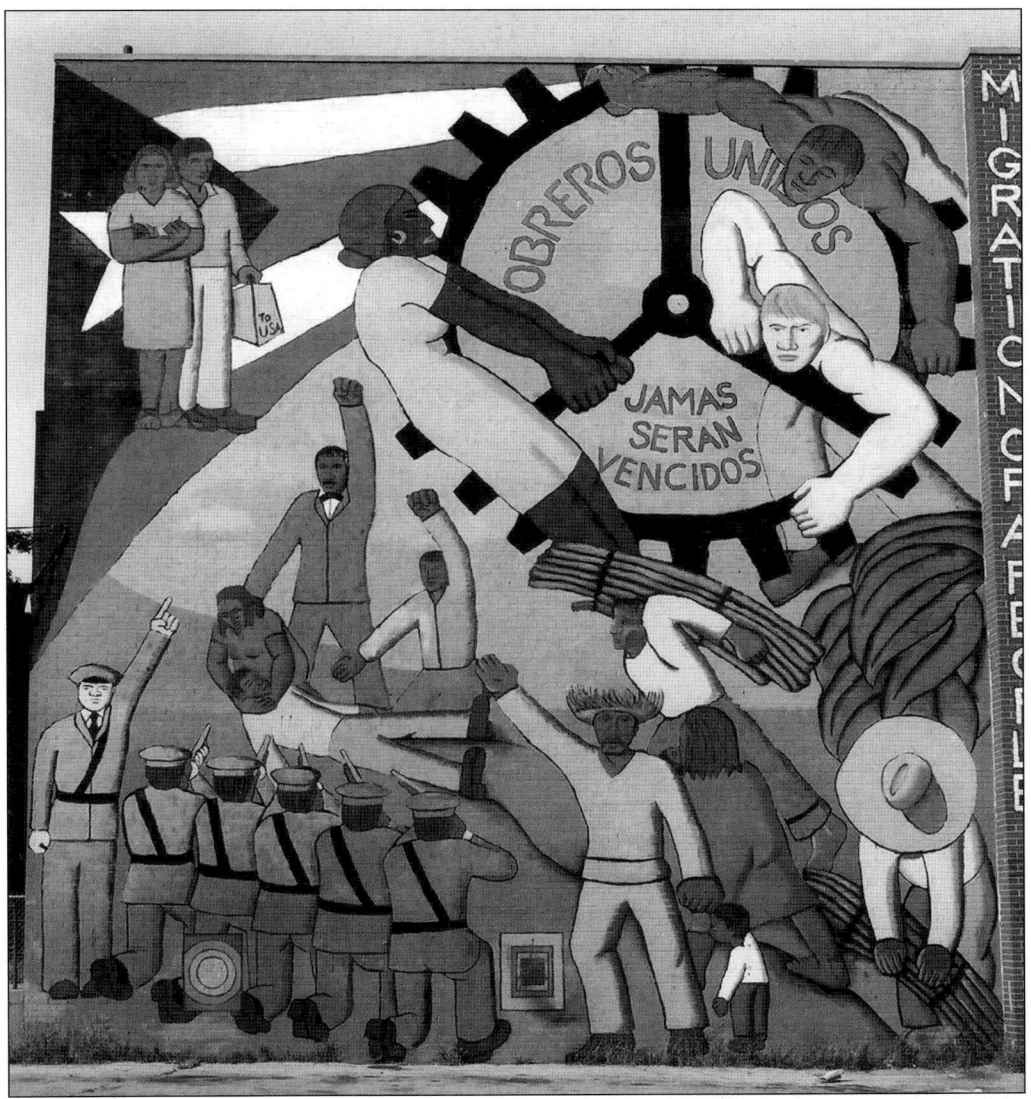

Ed Maldonado and Bo Solari painted this three-story mural, titled "Migration of a People," on a building in the West Town neighborhood in 1974. The mural shows the migration of Puerto Ricans to the U.S., the exploitation of workers, and police brutality. The Spanish words on the mural say "workers united will never be defeated." Few Puerto Ricans now live in the gentrified neighborhood of West Town. (Courtesy Marixsa Alicea.)

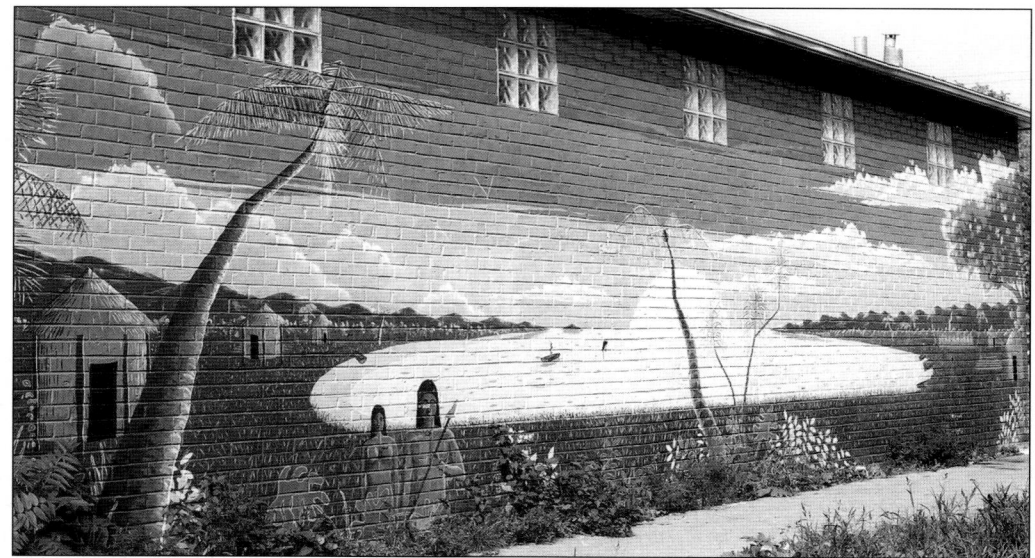

Noted Puerto Rican painter Gamaliel Ramírez painted this mural, titled "Taino Village," in 1977. The YMCA sponsored the mural which was painted on Bell Street and North Avenue. Tainos were the indigenous people of Puerto Rico, and part of the Arawak nation. The mural showed the lifestyle of Tainos, and attempted to instill cultural awareness among youth in the Puerto Rican community. The mural no longer exists. (Courtesy Marixsa Alicea.)

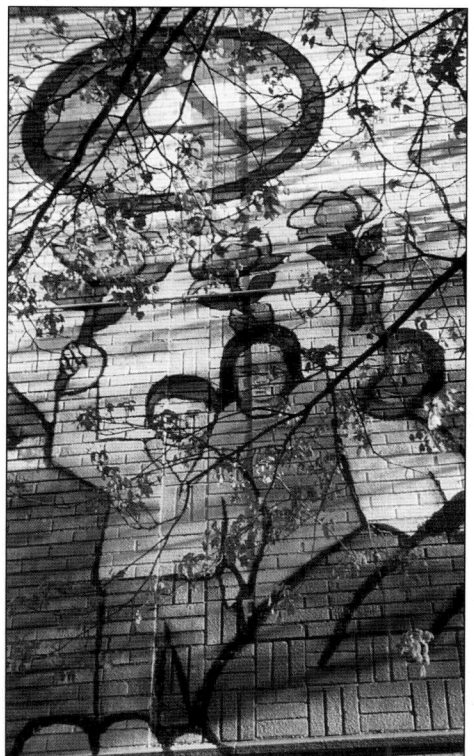

This mural, titled "Rompiendo Las Cadenas" (Breaking the Chains), was painted by John Pitman Weber in 1971 on a building in East Humboldt Park. The mural depicts black, brown, and white hands breaking chains with the words injustice, poverty, racism, war, and drugs written on the chains. A woman hanging out of a burning building represents the arson fires that were common in the neighborhood in the 1970s. The mural depicts a positive image of hope, with one of the hands holding up children, each with a rose in their hand. The Latin American Defense Organization (LADO) co-sponsored the mural. (Courtesy Marixsa Alicea.)

Eight
ARTS AND CULTURE

One aspect of Chicago's Puerto Rican community that is well organized is its varied expressions of cultural pride. Puerto Ricans acquire an important sense of self-affirmation and joy when they celebrate their heritage and culture. For years, the West Town Concerned Citizens Coalition organized the annual Fiesta Boricua. This popular, day-long, free event brought famous Puerto Rican salsa bands to town. Large crowds savored the Puerto Rican food sold by vendors while listening to the latest salsa singers. Puerto Rican painters, like Gamaliel Ramírez, painted commemorative posters for Fiesta Boricua. The colorful posters stressed themes of education, music, and culture.

Fiesta Boricua takes place on September 5. The one-day event is now sponsored by 26th ward alderman Billy Ocasio. Fiesta Boricua is held on Division Street between the two large Puerto Rican flags. Over 130,000 people attended this cultural event in 2003. On four stages, famous Puerto Rican singers from New York and Puerto Rico treat the crowds to the hot sounds of salsa.

Puerto Ricans love their salsa music. The music, probably more than any other art form, expresses their urban experiences. Some second generation Puerto Ricans born in Chicago may not speak Spanish fluently . . . . yet they understand Spanish, and take a deep liking to salsa. Salsa lyrics speak of love, urban pain, poverty, heroism, love of country, and endless human emotion.

About five years ago, a group of artists formed the Puerto Rican Arts Alliance, which promotes Puerto Rican culture. The group organizes photography exhibits and performances. They sponsor an annual, popular, one-day festival on the Puerto Rican cuarto. Excellent cuarto players from New York and Puerto Rico play at the festival. The cuarto is a guitar-type musical instrument native to Puerto Rico. The cuarto's music is associated with the jibaro, the rural people of Puerto Rico.

The highlight of the variety of cultural events in the Puerto Rican community is the annual Puerto Rican parade on Dearborn and Wacker on June 15. Thousands of on-lookers line up downtown to enjoy 80, or so, colorful floats, marching bands, bike clubs, salsa music, and Puerto Rican flags. The parade is sponsored by the Puerto Rican Parade Committee. After the downtown parade, the Puerto Rican Parade Committee sponsors Fiestas Puertorriqueñas, a week-long series of cultural activities that take place in Humboldt Park. Hundreds of thousands of Puerto Ricans and others enjoy the festivities. The park is filled with carnival rides for children and vendors selling Puerto Rican food and arts.

The annual election of the president of the Puerto Rican Parade Committee is a major event in the Humboldt Park community. Thousands of Puerto Ricans vote for their favorite candidate. Various candidates campaign heavily, promising to improve the finances of the committee and to better promote Puerto Rican culture. Some candidates hope to use the position as a springboard for future political office.

A new group, the Institute of Puerto Rican Arts and Culture, was recently formed. This group also showcases Puerto Rican culture, through performances, photography exhibits, lectures, and plays. As the photographs in this chapter demonstrate, Puerto Ricans are proud of their culture, and are busy sharing their culture with other Puerto Ricans and other Chicagoans.

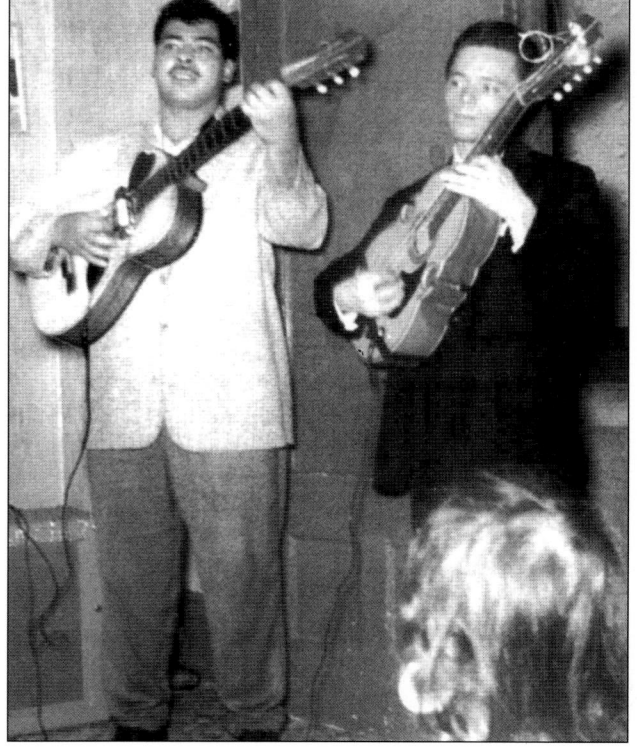

"Remembering The Man & His Music"

~Carlos Caribe Ruiz~

15th Anniversary Memorial Celebration

April 24, 2002

Carlos Caribe Ruiz established the Puerto Rican Congress on North Avenue in 1952. The organization sponsored baseball and basketball leagues for youth. The organization also taught generations of Puerto Rican youth how to dance, play, and appreciate traditional and modern Puerto Rican music. Several well-know local salsa bands were formed at the Congress. Ruiz, shown here, was a renowned musician and dancer. He passed away in 1987. (Courtesy Joseph A. Ruiz.)

Unidentified Puerto Rican musicians played traditional Puerto Rican music in a Puerto Rican home in 1960. Trios would sometimes play for free on special occasions like birthday parties, Christmas, and New Year's Day. By playing free, the musicians hoped the family would recommend them to friends and other families. The host family usually gave the musicians plenty of drink and food. (Courtesy Anna Rivera.)

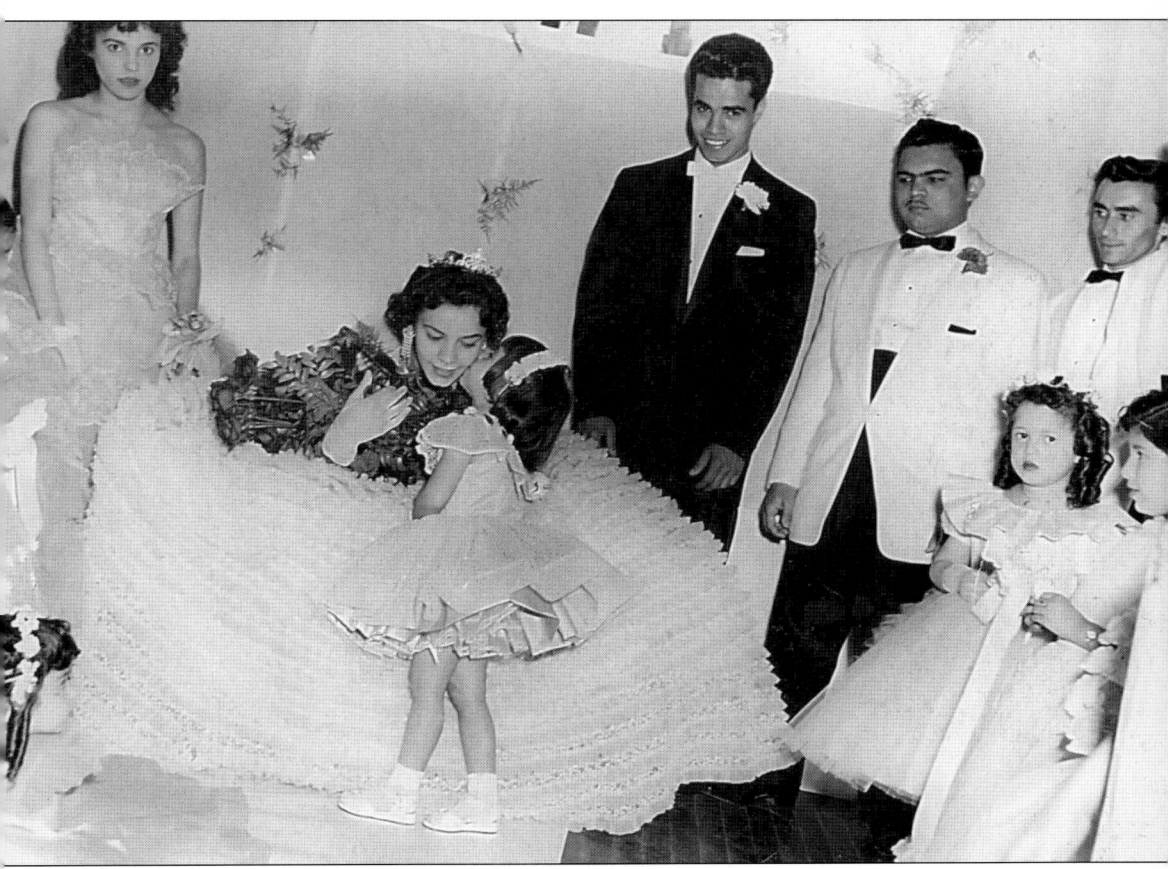

Young women from the different councils of Los Caballeros de San Juan (Knights of San Juan) would compete to see who would be selected as the year's Puerto Rican queen. In 1961, this unidentified young woman was crowned queen. The queen represented Los Caballeros de San Juan in their early, modest Puerto Rican parade along 63rd Street. (Courtesy Cesareo and Luz Maria Rivera).

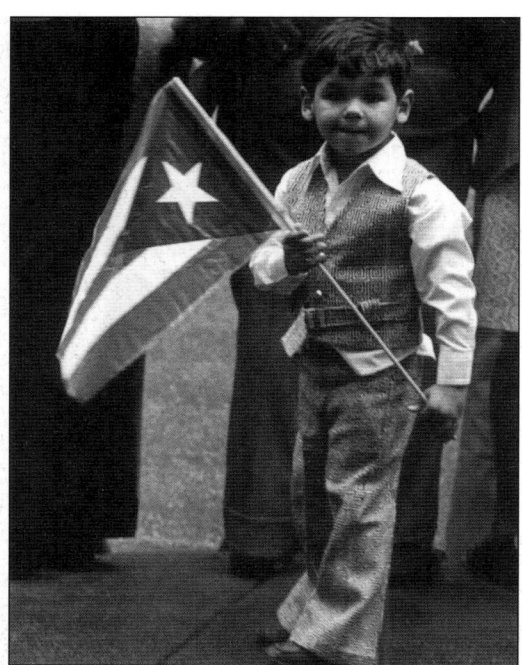

A boy waving the Puerto Rican flag as the 1971 Puerto Rican parade marches along State Street. (Courtesy Carlos Flores.)

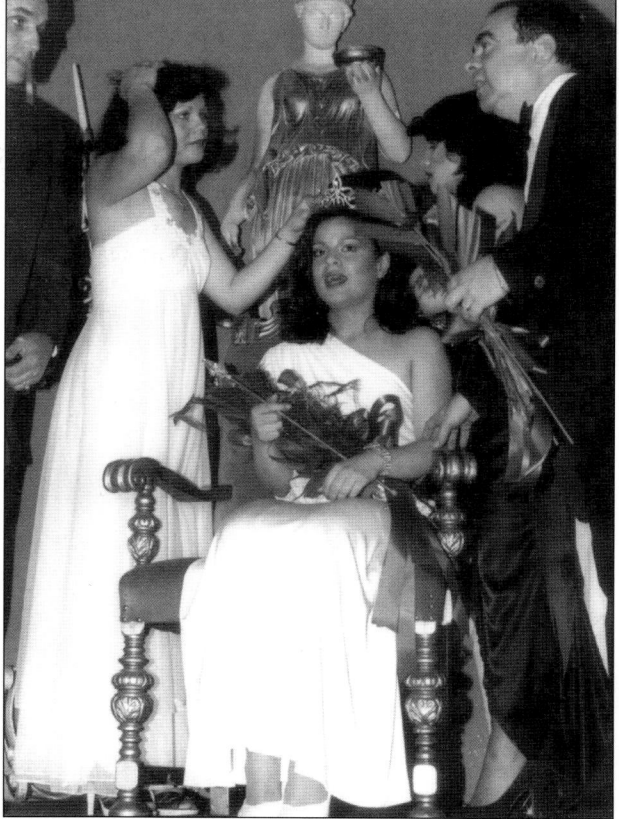

Citywide, young Puerto Rican women competed each year to see who would be selected as the Puerto Rican queen. The Puerto Rican Parade Committee selected the queen and sponsored the annual Puerto Rican parade in downtown Chicago. This unidentified young woman was crowned queen of 1980. Coronation of the queen took place in a fancy downtown hotel. (Courtesy Tomas V. Sanabria.)

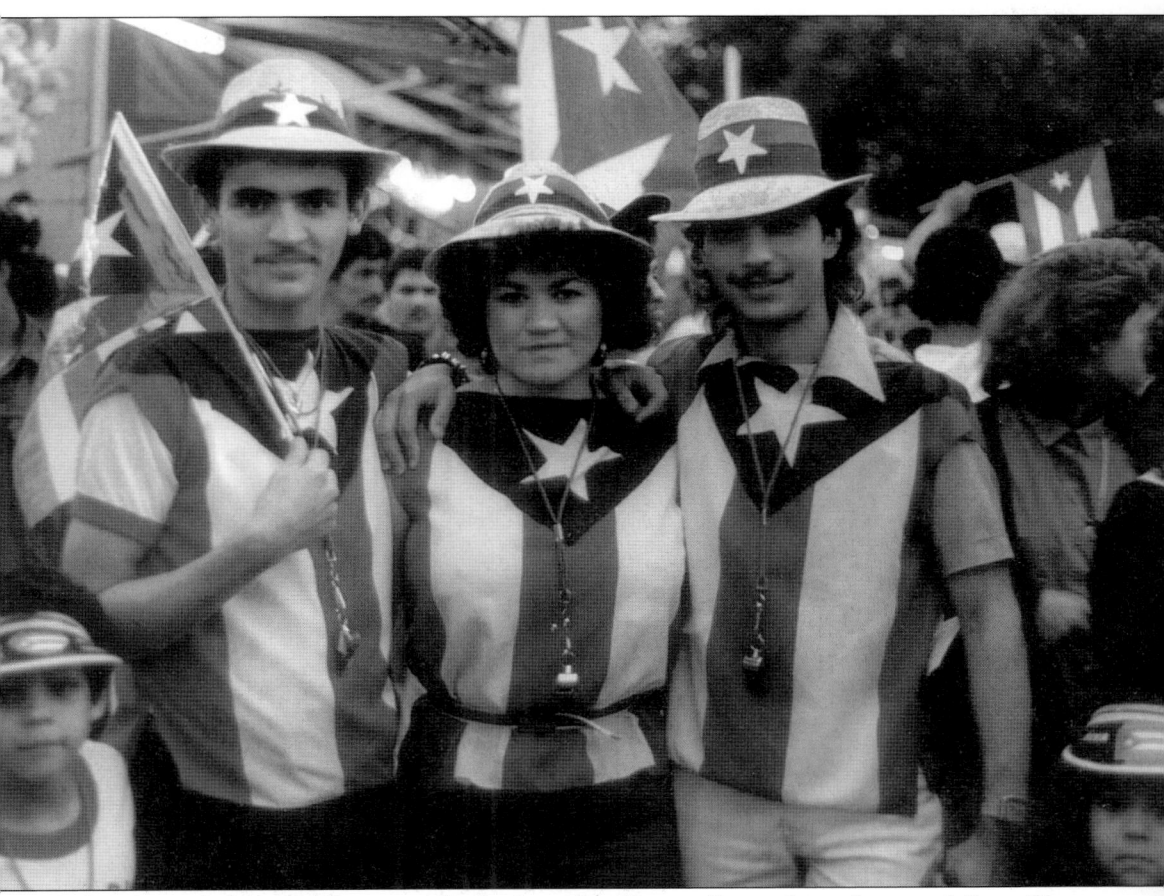

A family, including children, proudly displays their Puerto Rican shirts, hats, and flags. The family was enjoying the week-long Fiestas Puertorriqueñas in Humboldt Park in the early 1990s. (Courtesy Delma Serrano.)

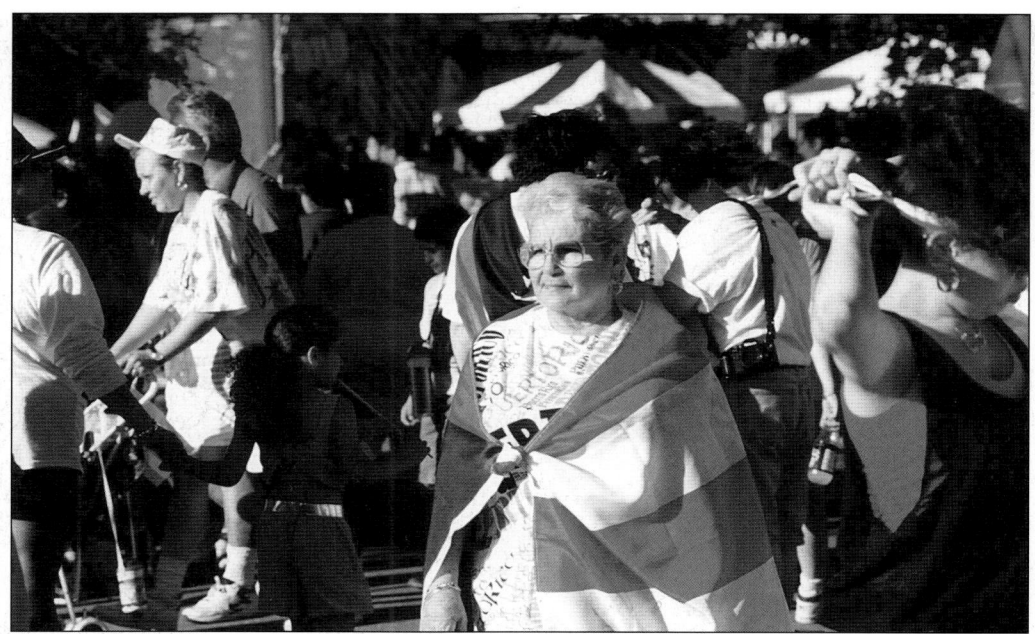

An unidentified Puerto Rican senior proudly wraps herself in the Puerto Rican flag during the Fiestas Puertorriqueñas in Humboldt Park in 2003. (Courtesy Puerto Rican Parade Committee.)

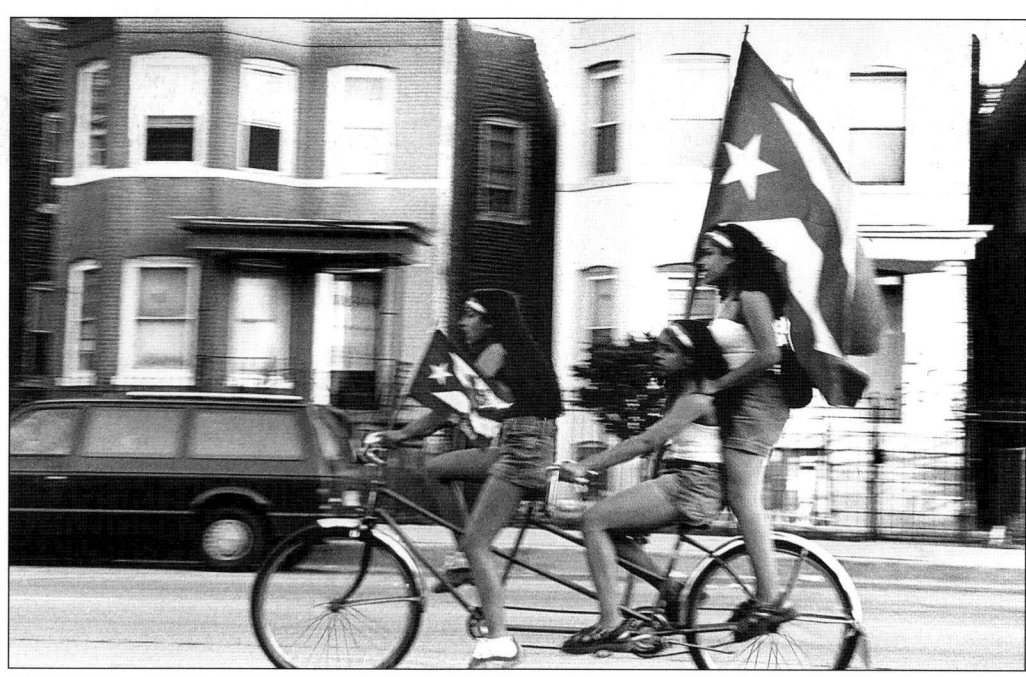

Three young Puerto Rican girls ride a tandem bike on Kedzie and Armitage in the Humboldt Park neighborhood. The girls were celebrating Puerto Rican week in June of 2001. Puerto Ricans love to display their flags on bikes and cars during the annual Puerto Rican week celebration. (Courtesy Alexandra Cruz.)

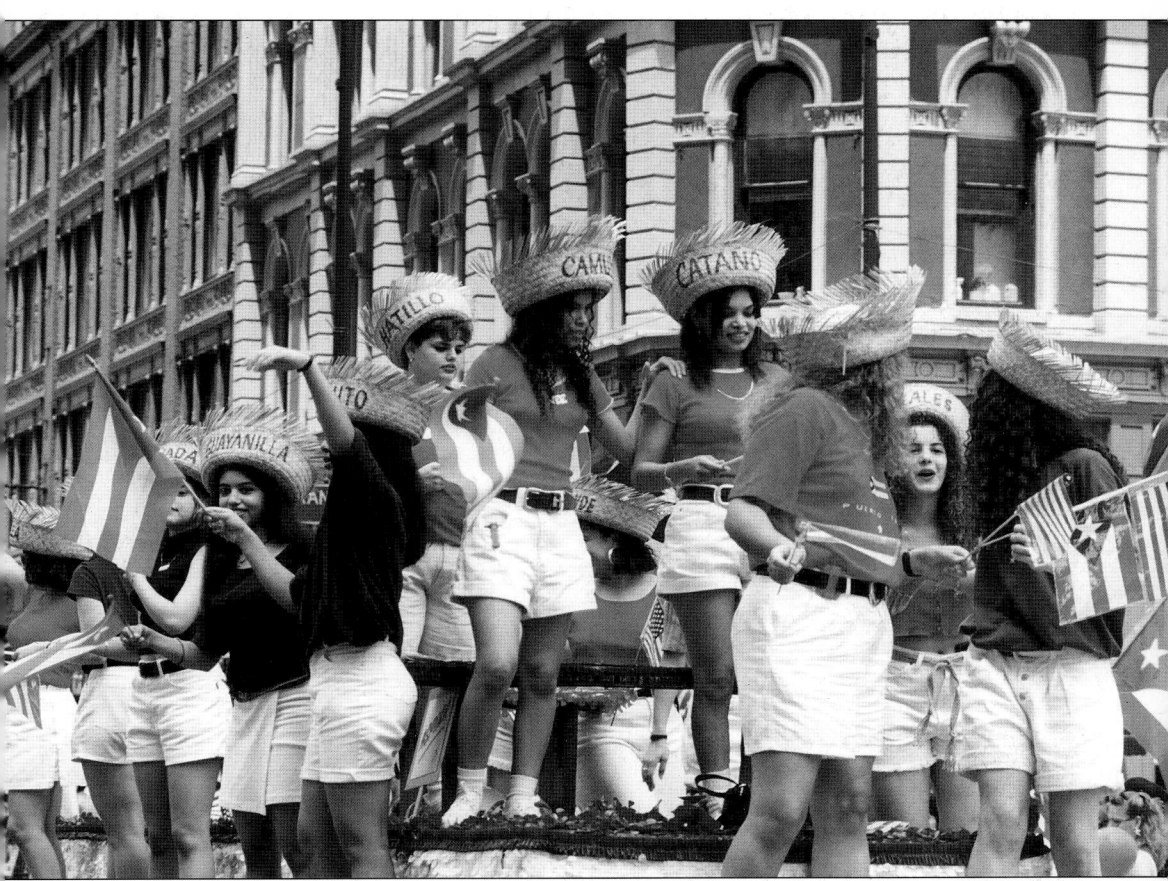

Young women on a float are seen here wearing traditional Puerto Rican hats with the names of the different towns in Puerto Rico. The young women were participating in the Puerto Rican parade on Dearborn Avenue in the mid-1990s. (Courtesy Puerto Rican Parade Committee.)

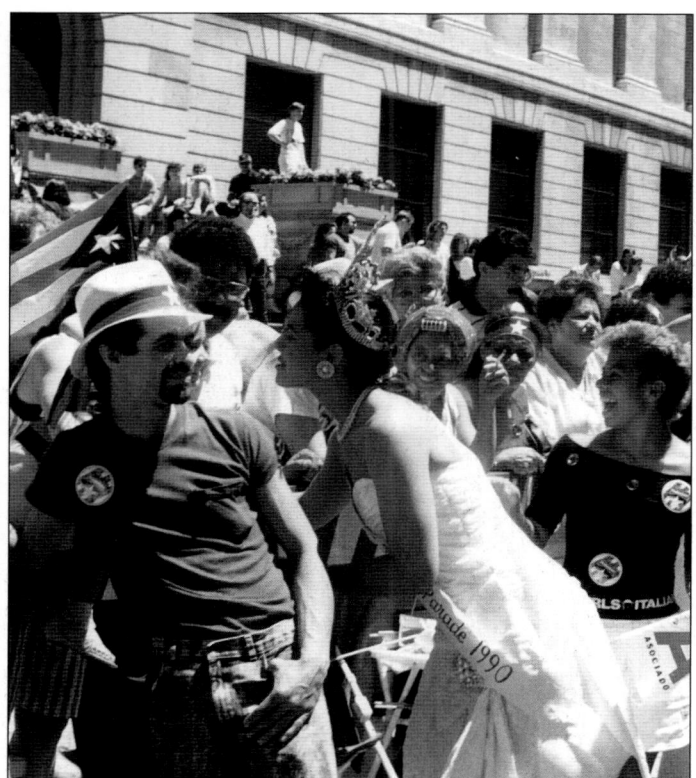

Thousands of spectators enjoyed the 1990 Puerto Rican parade along Michigan Avenue. An unidentified parade participant stopped to chat with a member of the audience. (Courtesy Puerto Rican Parade Committee.)

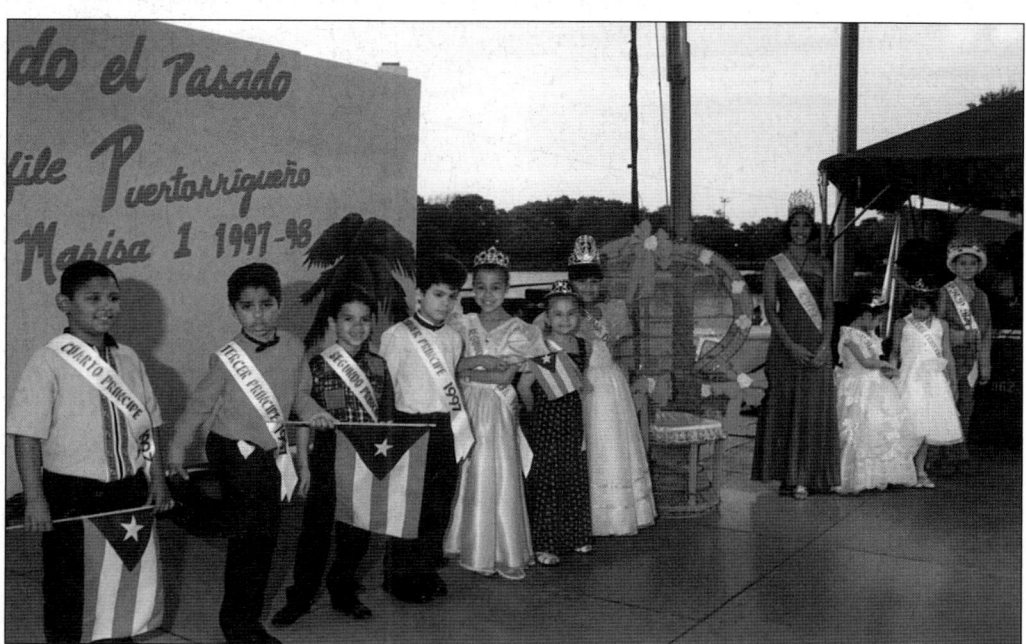

A juvenile king and queen and their courts were selected for the 1997 Puerto Rican parade. The Puerto Rican Parade Committee sponsored the event. (Courtesy Puerto Rican Parade Committee.)

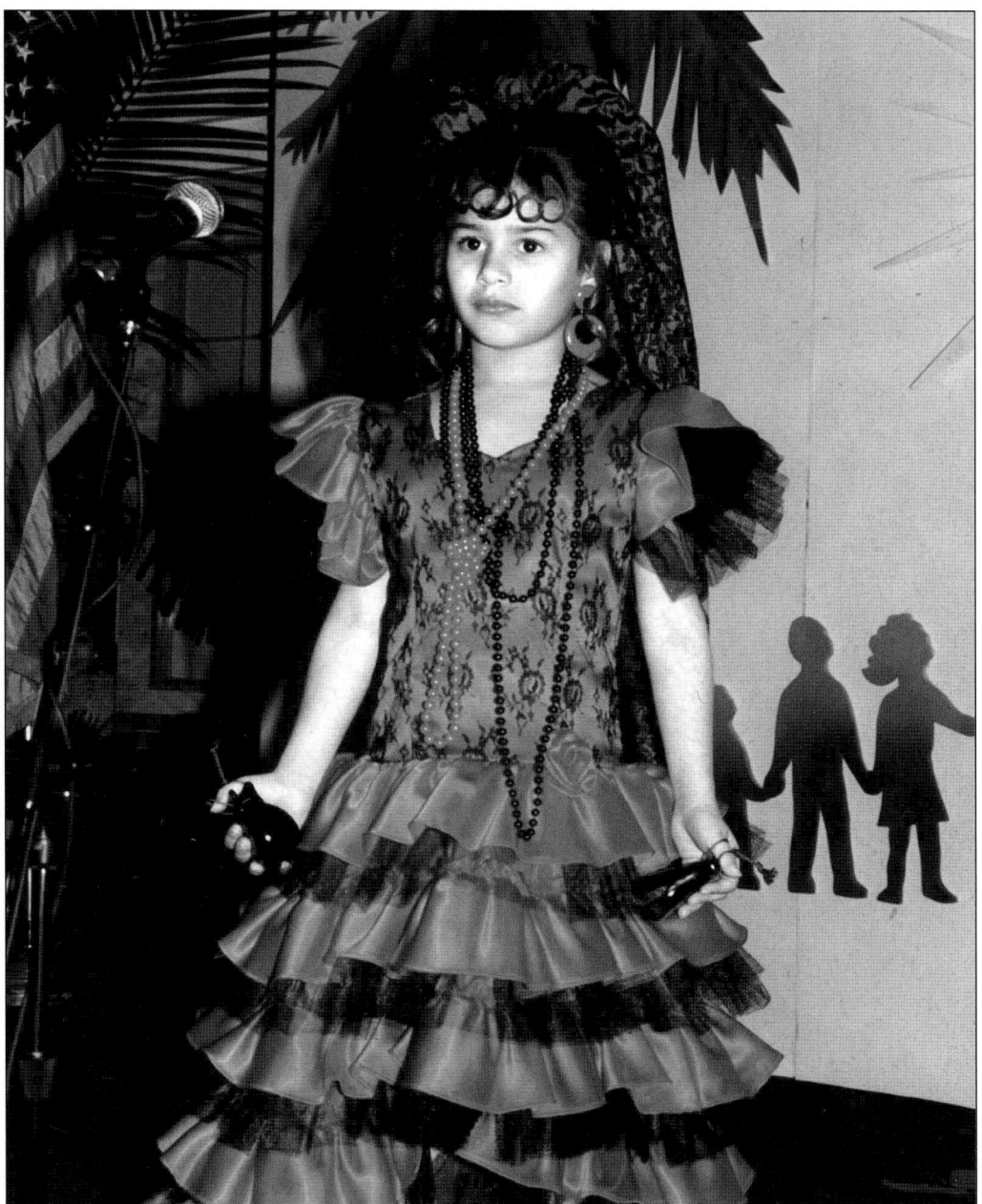

An unidentified participant in the juvenile queen pageant for the 1997 Puerto Rican parade impressed the audience with her Spanish costume and dance. Puerto Ricans are a mixture of Taino Indian, African, and Spanish. (Courtesy Puerto Rican Parade Committee.)

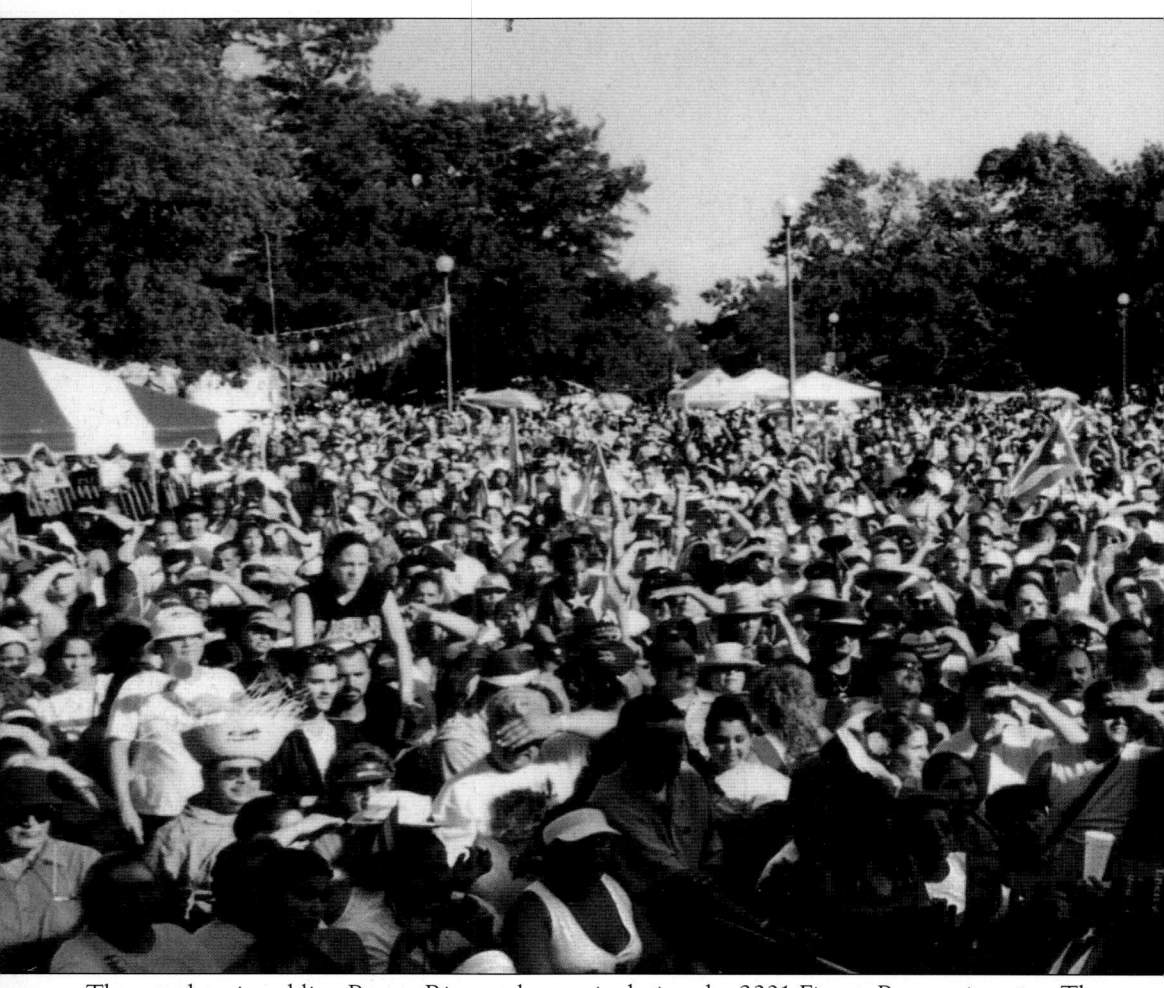

Thousands enjoyed live Puerto Rican salsa music during the 2001 Fiestas Puertorriqueñas. The Puerto Rican Parade Committee estimates that between 700,000 to a million people take part

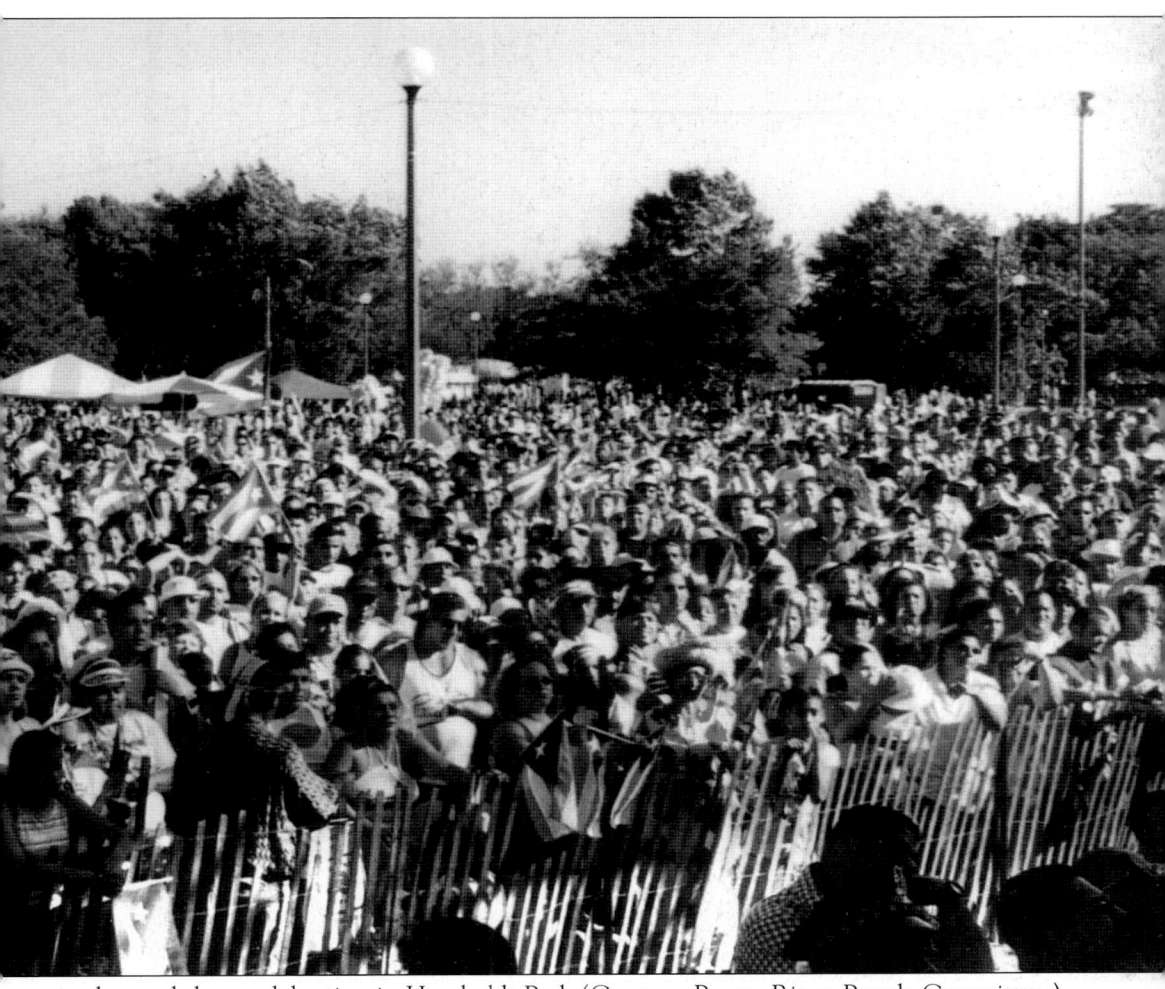

in the week-long celebration in Humboldt Park (Courtesy Puerto Rican Parade Committee.)

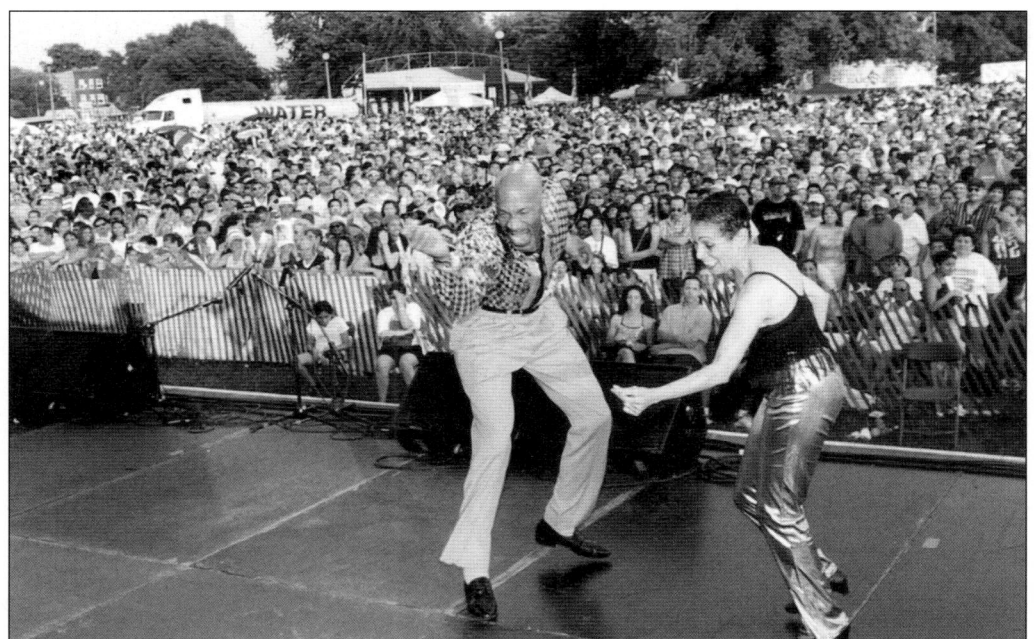

Two Puerto Rican salsa singers entertained large crowds during the 2002 Fiestas Puertorriqueñas. (Courtesy Puerto Rican Parade Committee.)

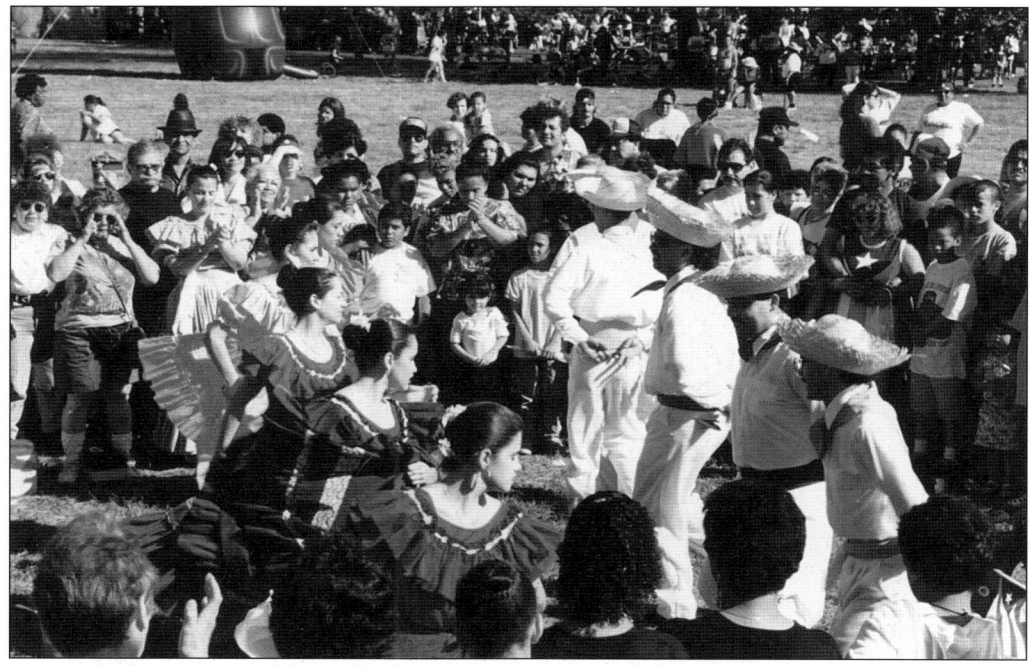

A dance group performed traditional Puerto Rican dances for the crowd during the 2002 Fiestas Puertorriqueñas. Tito Rodriquez (dancer on the right) is a teacher and promoter of Puerto Rican and African dances and culture. He has directed numerous Puerto Rican folkloric groups in Chicago. (Courtesy Puerto Rican Parade Committee.)

116

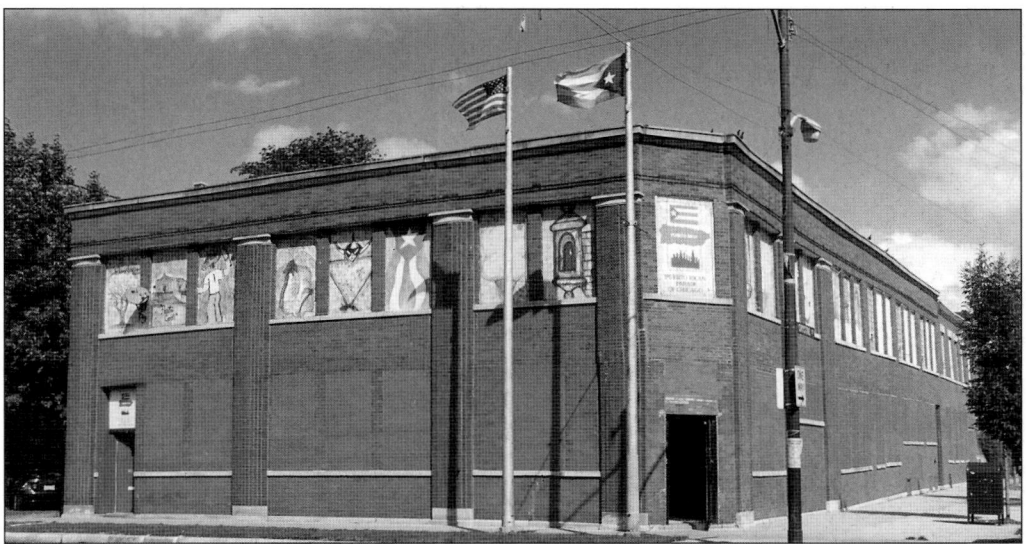

The building and offices of the Puerto Rican Parade Committee, at 1237 North California Avenue, are seen here. (Courtesy Puerto Rican Parade Committee.)

In addition to the annual Puerto Rican parade downtown, Puerto Ricans enjoy a smaller but lively neighborhood parade. This parade, the Puerto Rican People's Parade, takes place after the downtown parade. About 5,000 Puerto Ricans march from Western to California Avenue up to North Avenue and around Humboldt Park. This 2002 parade celebrated the 25th anniversary of the People's Parade. The parade featured floats, large puppets, and traditional music. (Courtesy Puerto Rican Cultural Center.)

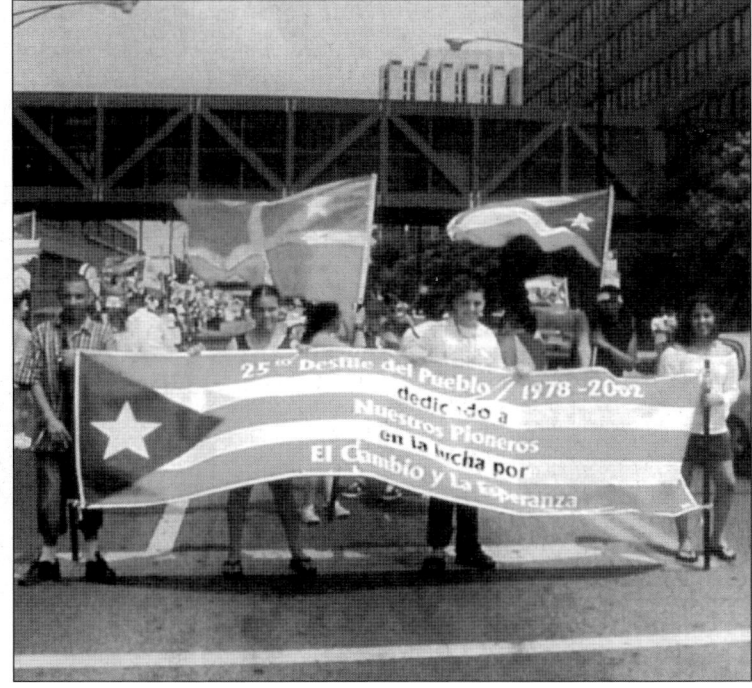

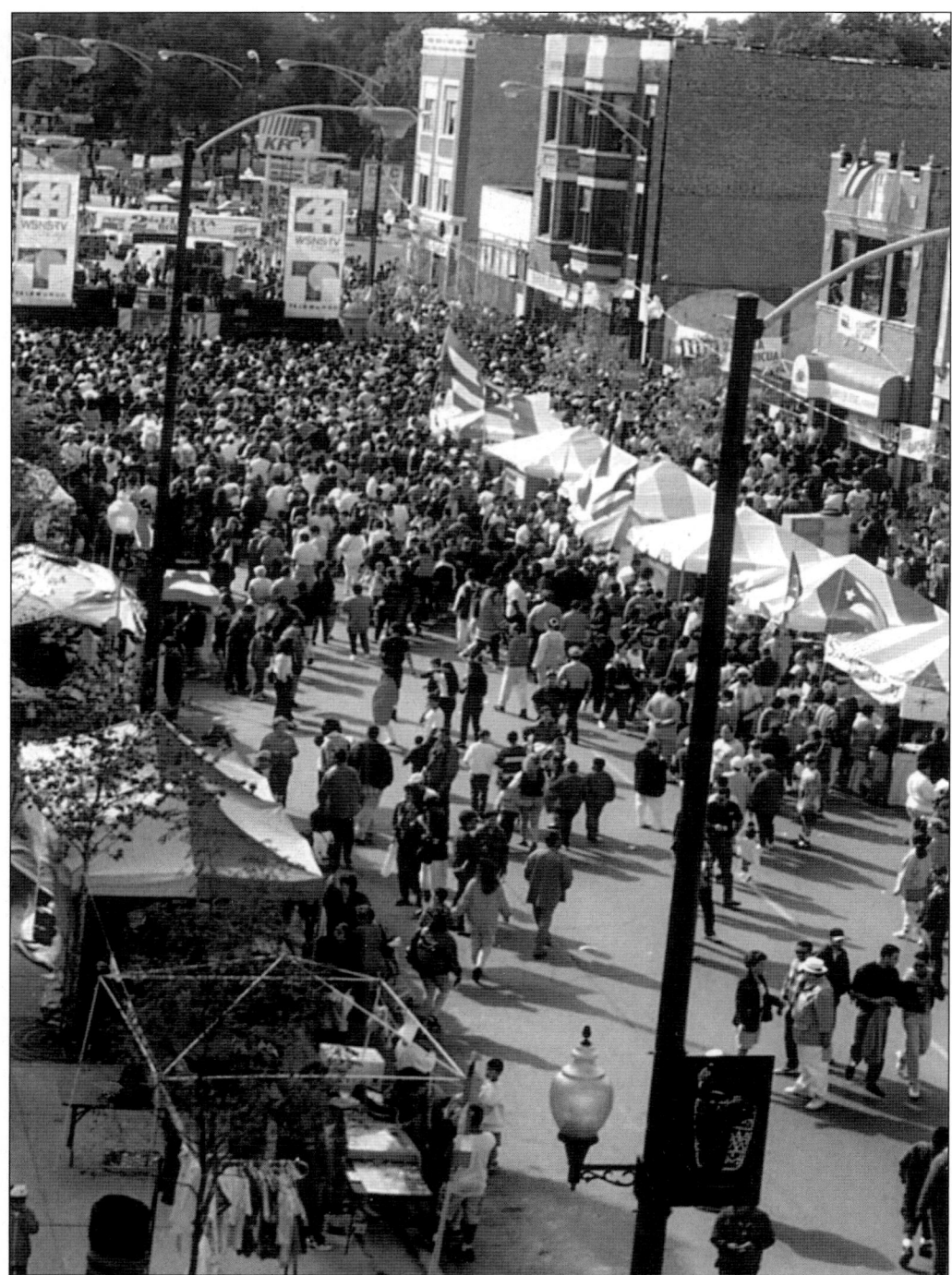

Over 80,000 people enjoyed salsa and other Puerto Rican music at the Fiesta Boricua in September 1995. The event took place on Division Street between California and Western Avenues. The large crowd is treated to music and vendors selling Puerto Rican food. (Courtesy John Colon.)

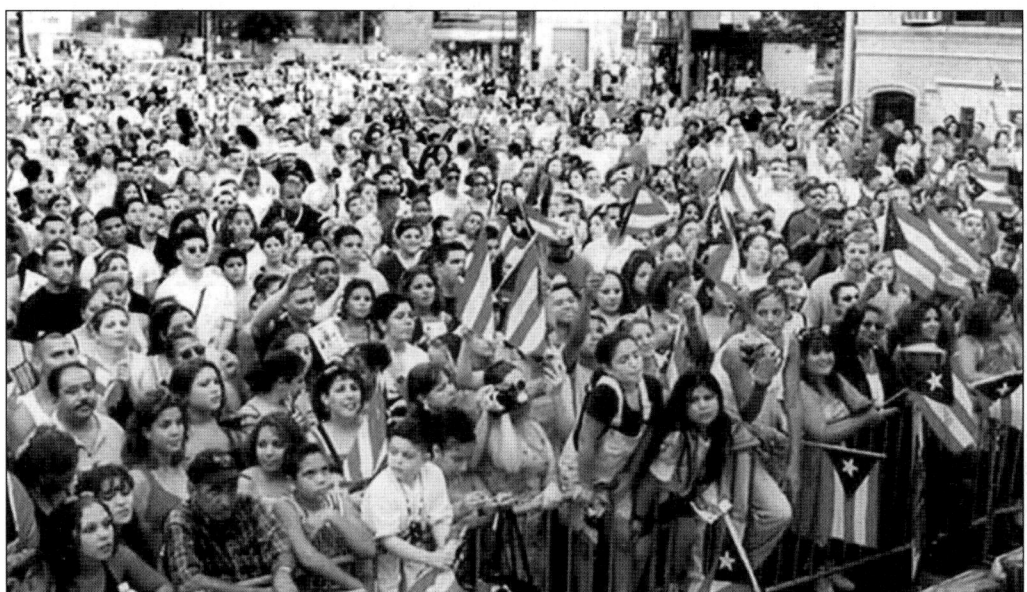

Large crowds enjoyed the live performances of Puerto Rican salsa singers during the 2002 Fiesta Boricua. Every year the crowds at Fiesta Boricua get bigger. It is estimated that over 130,000 people attended the event in 2003. The cultural event is hailed as the largest one-day cultural event in the Midwest. (Courtesy Puerto Rican Parade Committee.)

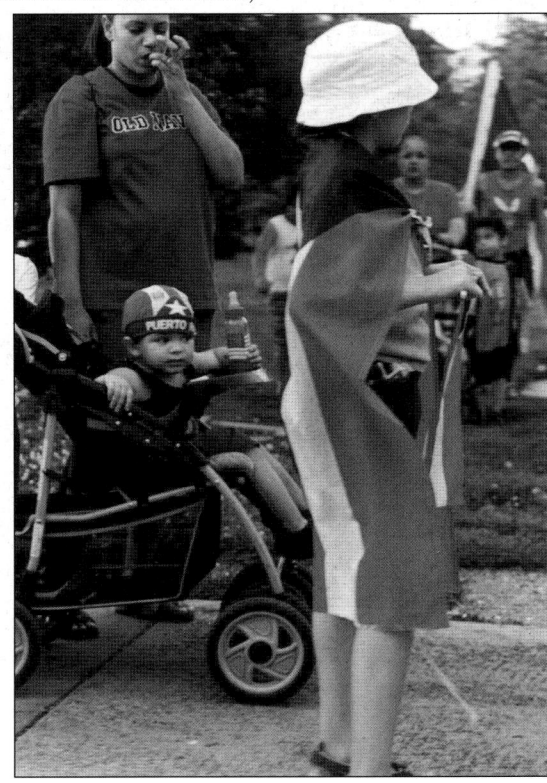

Children, even babies, wrapped themselves in the red, white, and blue colors of the Puerto Rican flag during the 2002 Fiesta Boricua. (Courtesy Alexandra Cruz.)

119

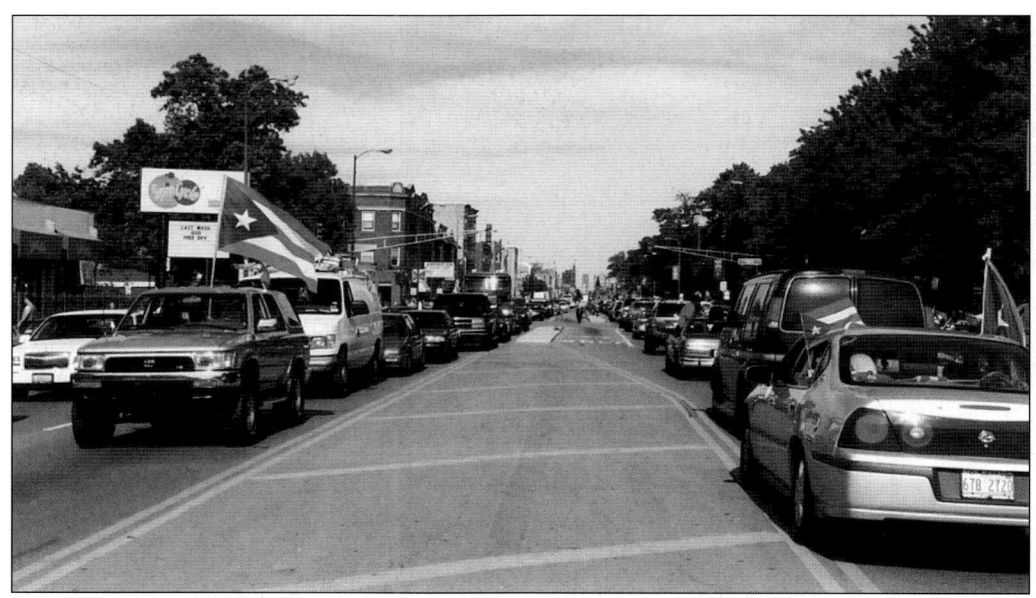

Puerto Ricans in Chicago have established their own tradition of hanging Puerto Rican flags out of cars during the Puerto Rican celebrations in June. Here, cars honk horns and occupants wave flags as they drive on North Avenue celebrating the 2004 Puerto Rican festivities in Humboldt Park. (Courtesy Alexandra Cruz.)

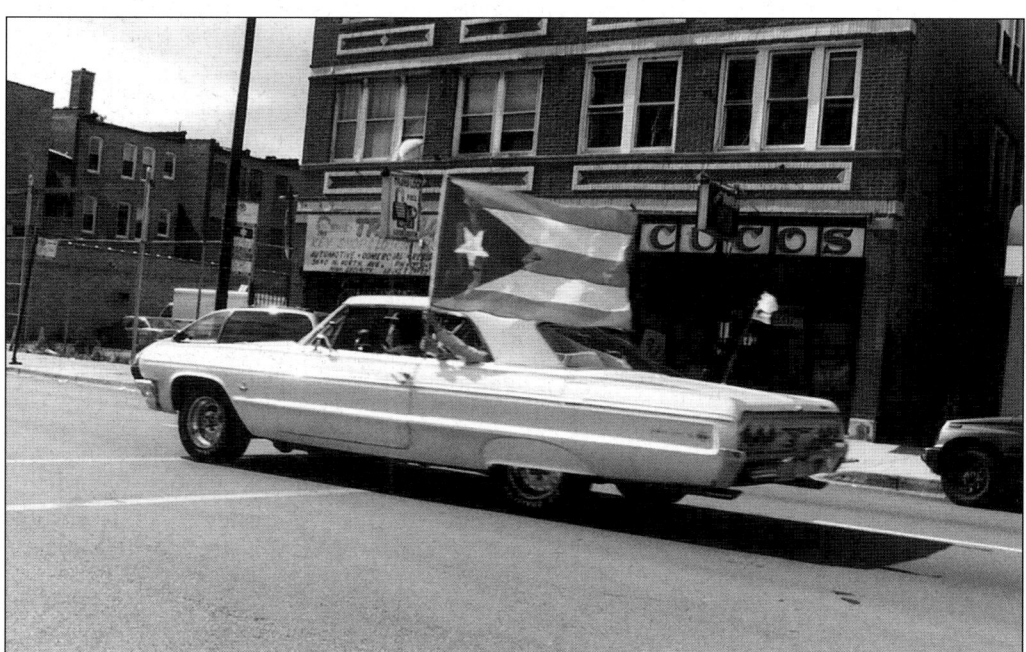

Occupants in a remodeled 1963 Chevrolet wave the Puerto Rican flag during the 2004 Puerto Rican festivities in Humboldt Park. In addition to waving flags out of the windows, some celebrants also place large flags on the hoods and trunks of their cars as they drive through the city honking their horns. (Courtesy Alexandra Cruz.)

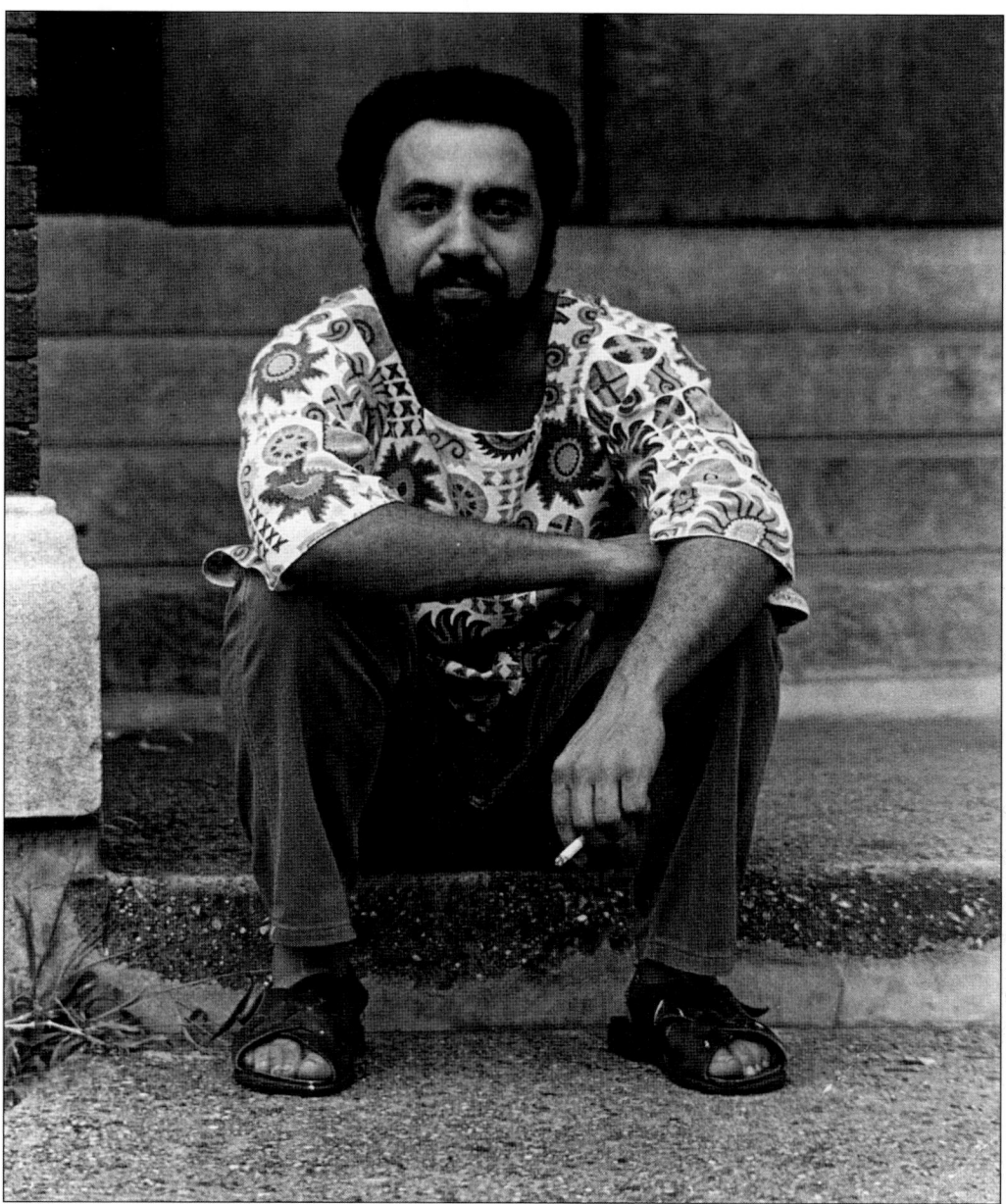

David Hernandez is a recognized poet, performer, and teacher of poetry. He has published four books of poetry. He calls himself a "street" poet. He is credited with sparking Chicago's poetry renaissance. Hernandez writes about drugs, gangs, bad schools, and hanging out on street corners. While he recites poetry, members of Street Sounds, a music performance ensemble, play music that compliments the poetry. He is shown here in the early 1970s in the Lakeview neighborhood. (Courtesy David Hernandez.)

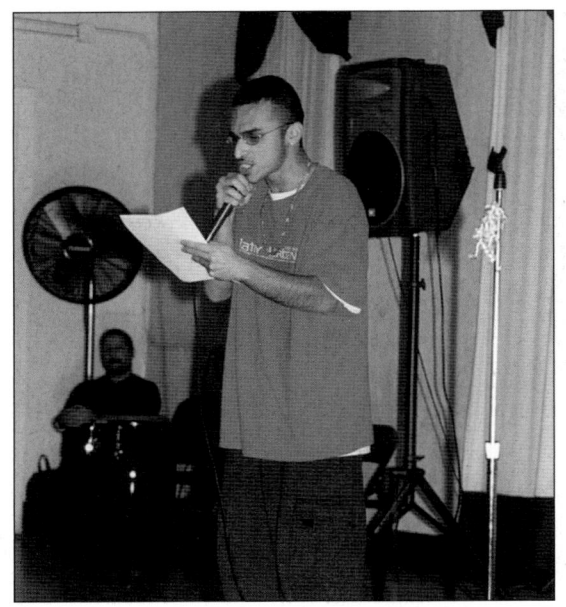

Jovannie Vargas, a Puerto Rican college student, recites his poetry during a 2002 poetry session at the Segundo Ruiz Belvis Cultural Center. The center runs an after school program where college students tutor high school students. Poetry is a way to get students more involved in their neighborhood. (Courtesy Segundo Ruiz Belvis Cultural Center.)

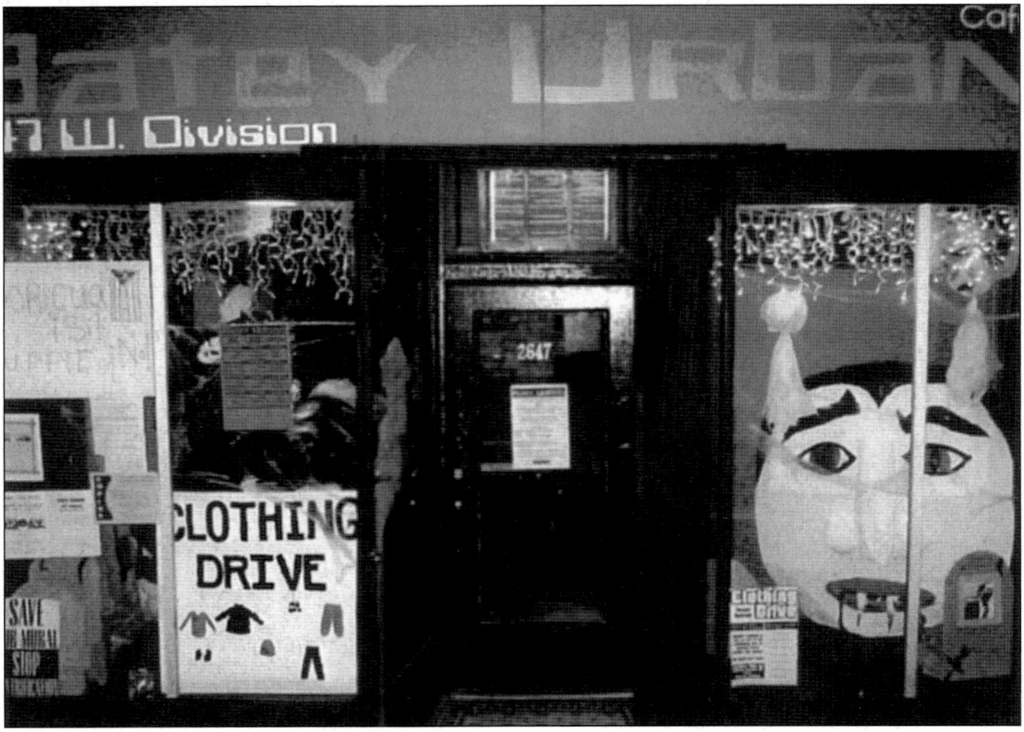

Batey Urbano on Division Street is a small place where Puerto Rican students from five area colleges meet regularly. The students play music and put on dances, performances, debates, and poetry sessions. The poetry of the students is very urban and talks about Puerto Rican issues, such as, crime, gangs, racism, and gentrification. Batey Urbano is supported by the Puerto Rican Cultural Center. (Courtesy Puerto Rican Cultural Center.)

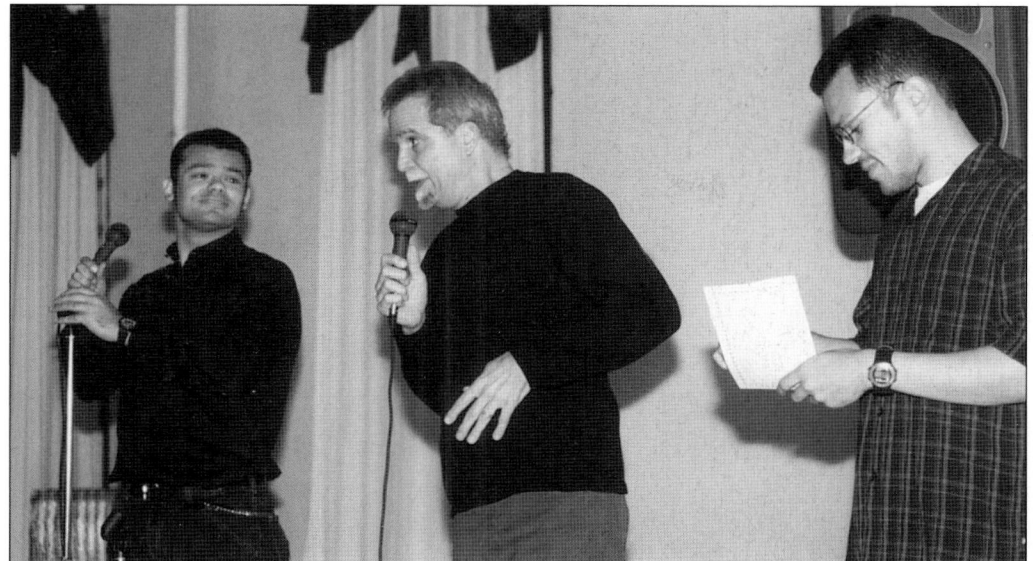

Gamaliel Ramírez (center) is a Puerto Rican painter known for murals and posters celebrating Puerto Rican culture. He also teaches high school students about painting. Here, he speaks about his art to a group at the Segundo Ruiz Belvis Cultural Center in 2003. On his right is Primitivo Cruz, and on his left is Jose Cruz. (Courtesy Segundo Ruiz Belvis Cultural Center.)

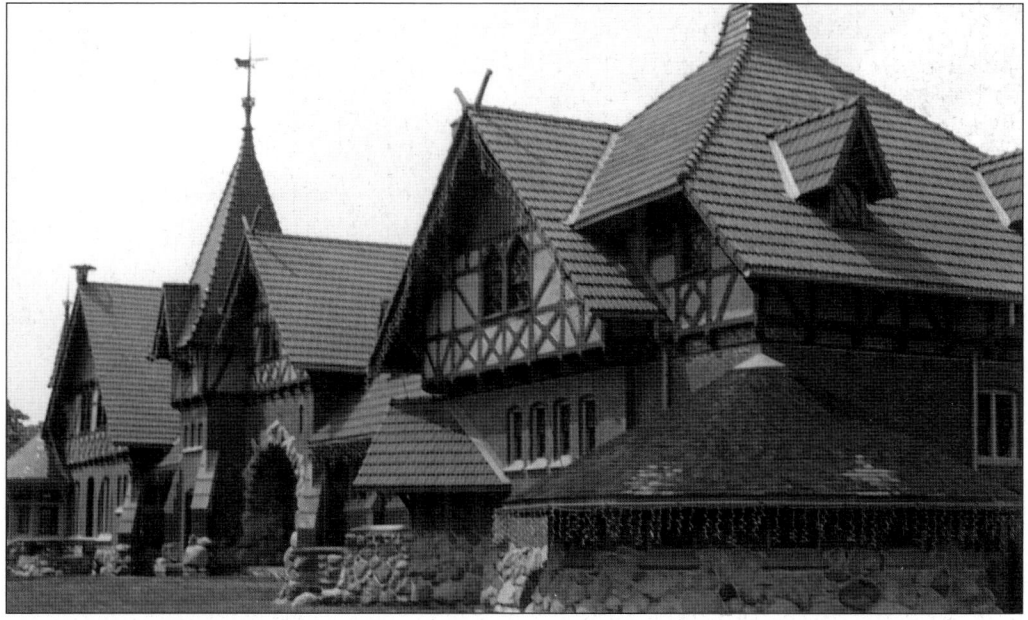

For almost 15 years, Puerto Ricans tried to convince Chicago Park District officials to give them this building in Humboldt Park for a Puerto Rican museum. But the talks went no where. Recently the Institute of Puerto Rican Arts and Culture signed a 15 year lease with park officials, gaining permission to use the building as a museum. The park district spent millions renovating the building's exterior, but several million dollars are still needed to complete interior renovations. (Photo Wilfredo Cruz.)

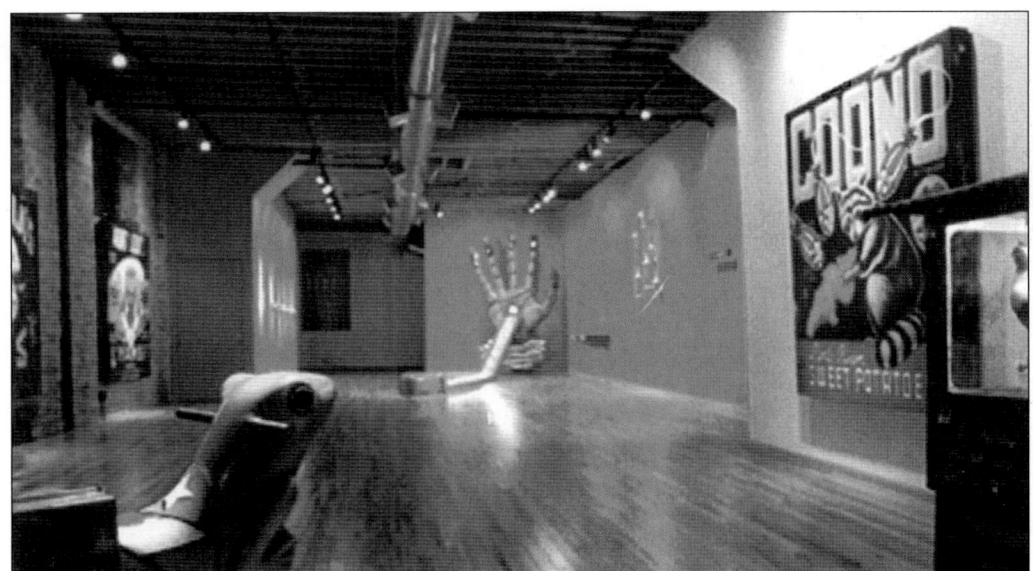

Galeria Tinta Roja is an art gallery on Division Street on Paseo Boricua. The gallery regularly exhibits photography and art of local and nationally known Puerto Rican artists. The gallery is owned by Jorge L. Ortega and Carmen Figueroa. (Courtesy Puerto Rican Cultural Center.)

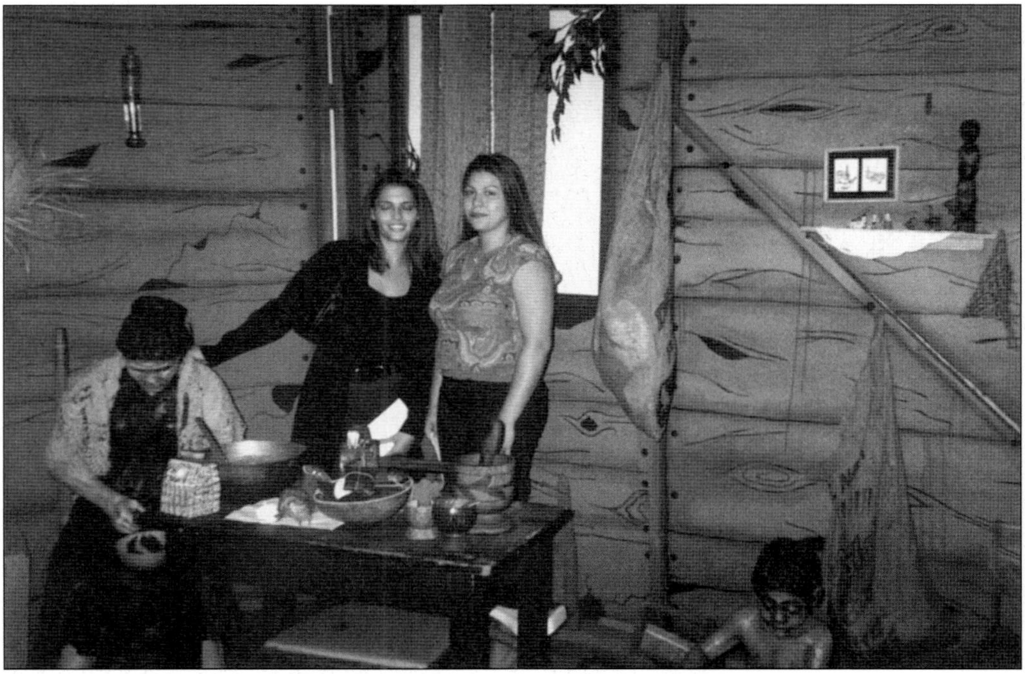

Two unidentified Kelvyn Park High School students each received $1,000 scholarships from the Segundo Ruiz Belvis Cultural Center in 2003. The center provides college scholarships yearly to promising Puerto Rican students. The students stand in a replica of a 1930s one-room home of the rural, or jibaro, people of Puerto Rico. The home is a permanent exhibition at the center. (Courtesy Segundo Ruiz Belvis Cultural Center.)

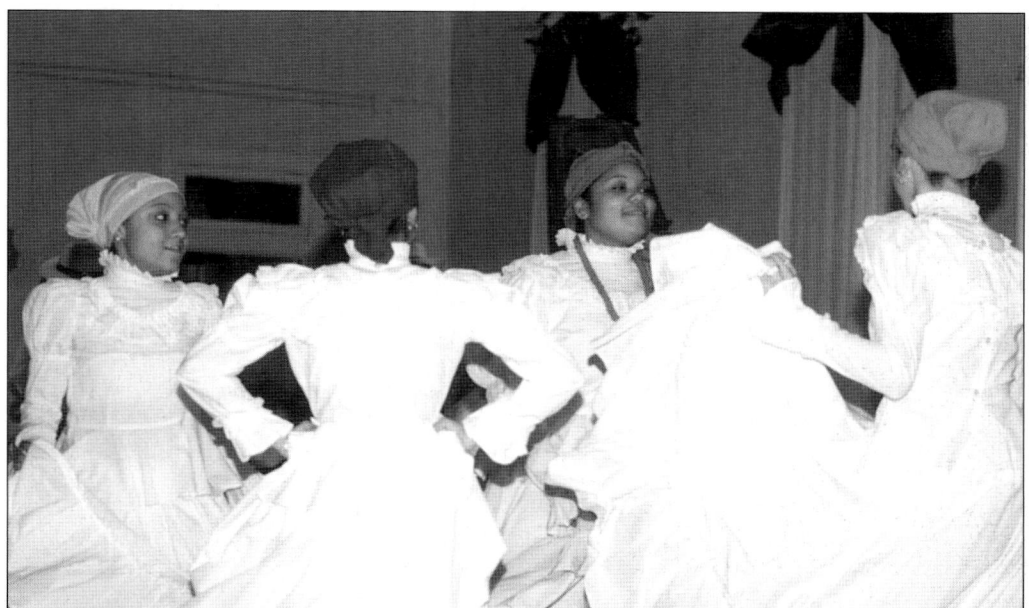

Grupo Yuba is an intergenerational group of Puerto Ricans who perform traditional Puerto Rican music and dances at many public events. Members of the group danced a bomba at a 2003 fundraiser at the Segundo Ruiz Belvis Cultural Center. The bomba is an Afro-Puerto Rican dance native to Puerto Rico. (Courtesy Segundo Ruiz Belvis Cultural Center.)

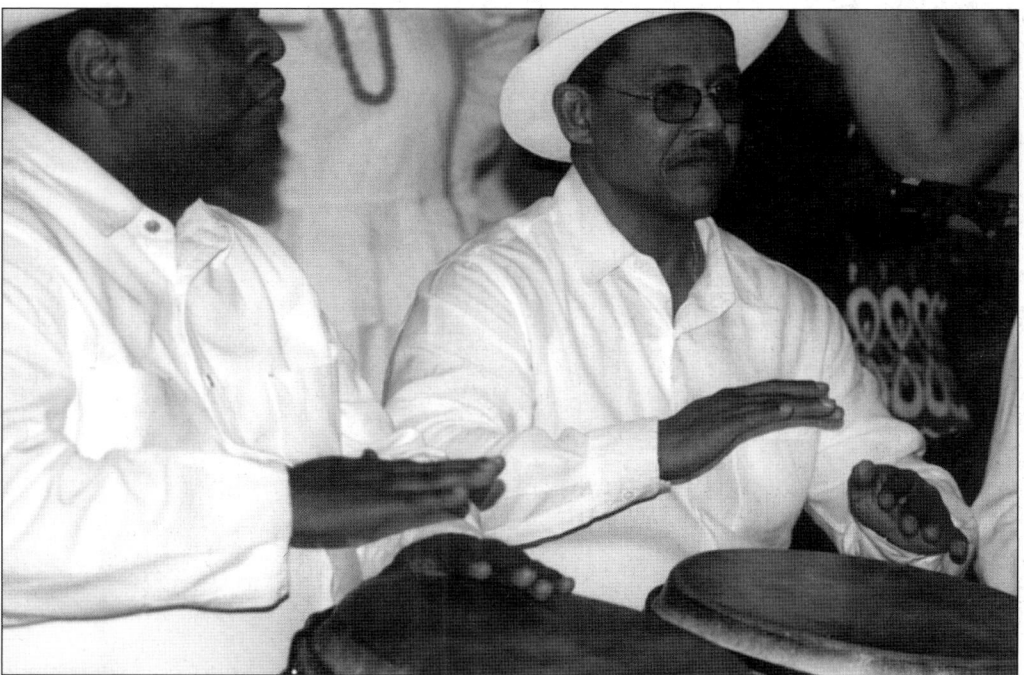

Members of Grupo Yuba participated in a mondongazo (a Puerto Rican stew of varied music) at a 2003 fundraiser at the Segundo Ruiz Belvis Cultural Center. (Courtesy Segundo Ruiz Belvis Cultural Center.)

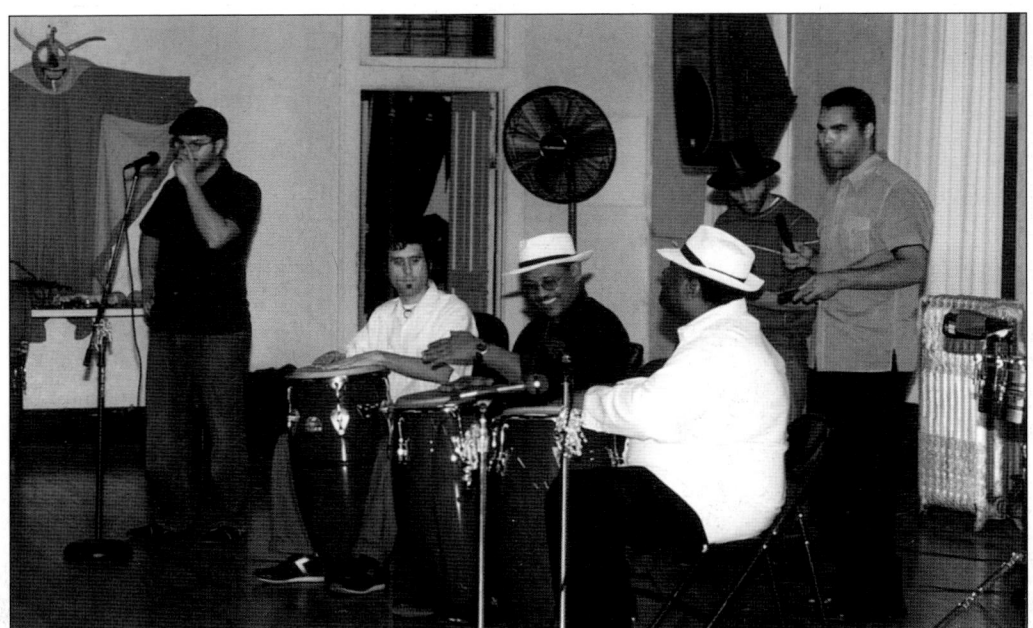

Puerto Rican college students formed the group Tumbao, which plays Afro-Puerto Rican music. Members of the group played at a 2003 event at the Segundo Ruiz Belvis Cultural Center. (Courtesy Segundo Ruiz Belvis Cultural Center.)

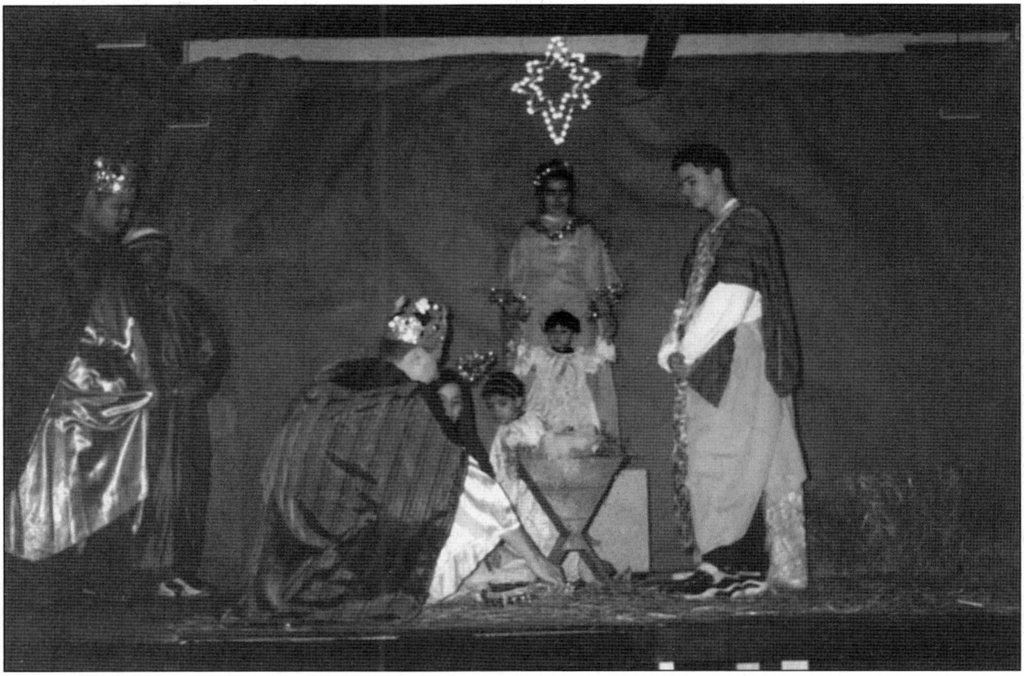

Students from the Antonia Pantoja High School put on a holiday play in 2002. The play was performed on January 6, Dia de Los Reyes Mayos (Three Kings Day) at Aspira Inc. of Illinois. (Courtesy Aspira Inc. of Illinois.)

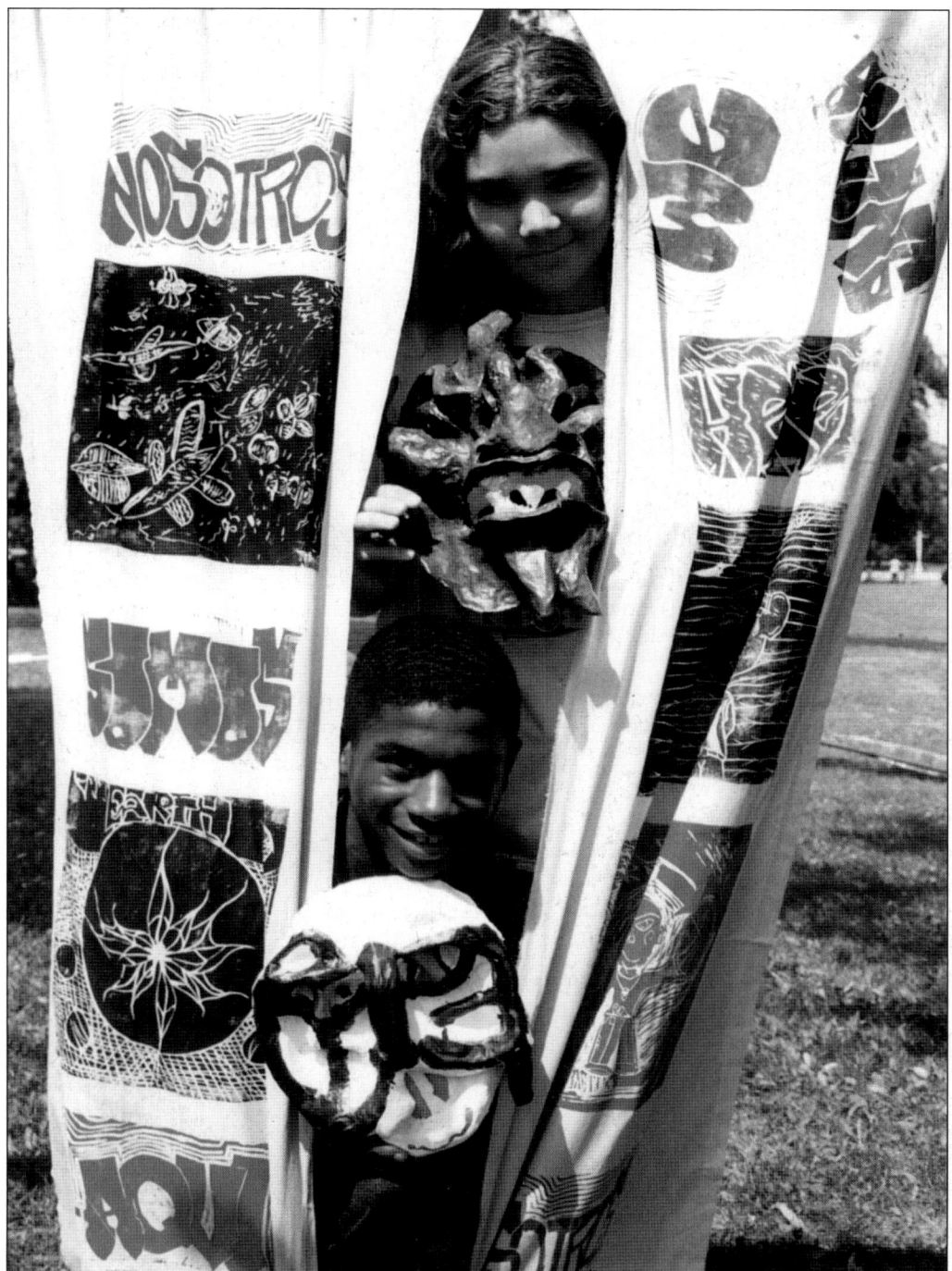

Unidentified youth showed off their artistic creation of masks during the 2003 summer arts program for youth at the Association House of Chicago. Association House is a social services agency in Wicker Park that is over a hundred years old. Since 1954, the agency has provided programs for Puerto Rican youth and families. (Courtesy Association House of Chicago.)

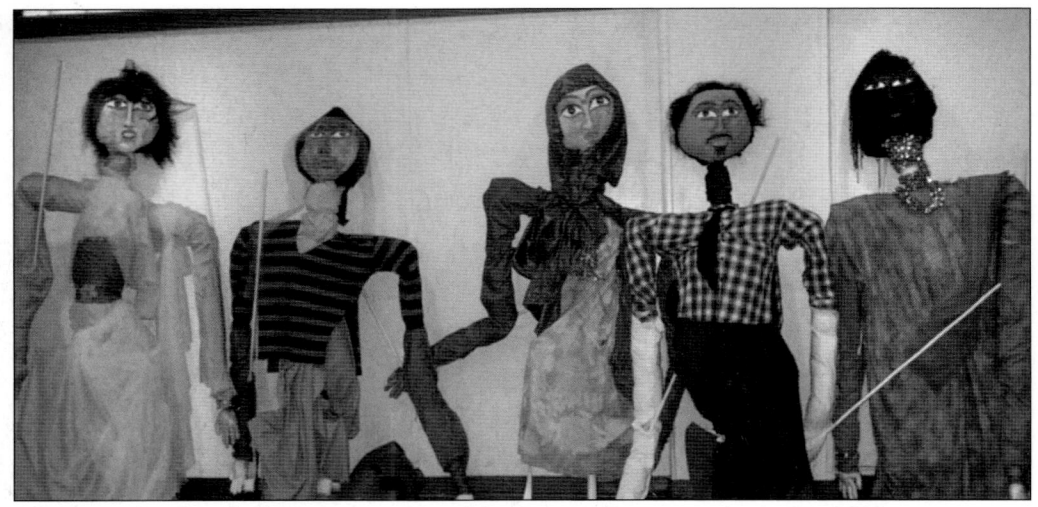

These are large, colorful puppets created by Puerto Rican youth at the 2003 summer arts program at the Association House of Chicago. Counselors in the summer arts programs teach youth different art forms. The puppets are used in an annual parade. (Courtesy Association House of Chicago.)

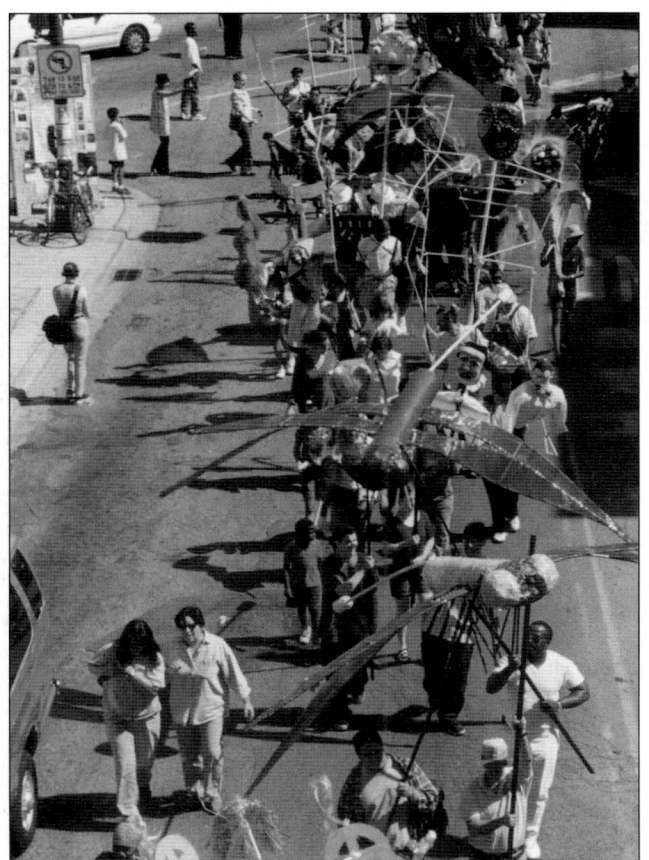

Students, parents, and community residents participated in the August 2003 Puppet Parade, sponsored annually by the Association House of Chicago. Students in the agency's summer arts program proudly carried the large puppets they created. The parade marched through the streets of the Wicker Park neighborhood. (Courtesy Association House of Chicago.)